PEASANT SOCIETY IN A CHANGING ECONOMY

WRITTEN UNDER THE AUSPICES OF
THE CENTER FOR INTERNATIONAL STUDIES,
NEW YORK UNIVERSITY

PEASANT SOCIETY IN A CHANGING ECONOMY

Comparative Development in

Southeast Asia and India

GEORGE ROSEN

UNIVERSITY OF ILLINOIS PRESS

URBANA : CHICAGO : LONDON

LIBRARY OF CONGRESS CATALOGING IN PUBLICATION DATA

Rosen, George, 1920–
  Peasant society in a changing economy.

  Includes bibliographical references and index.
    1.   Peasantry—Asia, Southeastern.   2.   Asia, South-
eastern—Rural conditions.   3.   Asia, Southeastern—
Economic policy.   I.   Title.
HD856.R67   301.44′43′0959   74–31041
ISBN 0–252–00464–7

In memory of my mother,
my aunt,
and my cousin Charlotte

One Chinese professor, American educated and very friendly to us, put it this way to me: "None of you Americans on either side of the Pacific have ever taken the trouble to find out why it is that the Chinese think like Chinese instead of like Texans, or for that matter, to take into account even the most elementary of all differences—the difference in attitude between poor people who have never had enough to eat and people to whom hunger has never really been more than an intellectual concept."

—John F. Melby, *The Mandate of Heaven*

Only an ambitious or a foolish man could, after seeing America, maintain that in the actual stage of the world, American institutions could be applied elsewhere but there. . . . When I speak of their institutions, I mean taken as a whole. There is no people but could usefully adopt some parts of them.

—A. De Tocqueville, *Journey to America*

Men still cling to the emotional basis of life that the feudal order gave them, while living and striving in a world whose every turn of wheel, throb of engine, and conquest of space deny its validity. This dual aspect of living is our riven consciousness, our tension, our anxiety.

—Richard Wright, Introduction to *Black Metropolis*

PREFACE

This book follows directly from my earlier book, *Democracy and Economic Change in India*, completed in 1965 and published in 1966 and 1967, in which I attempted to relate the processes of social and political change in India to that country's economic development. I then felt that the framework and method of analysis could be usefully applied to other countries to better understand their development. Since that book was published, I have spent over four years on the staff of the Asian Development Bank in Manila, working on economic problems of the Asian developing countries that are members of that institution. In the course of that stay my residence and my work led me to pay special attention to three Southeast Asian countries: the Philippines, Indonesia, and Thailand. I was struck by some of the similarities to India, and I felt that there was an opportunity to apply the interdisciplinary framework I had previously used for India to those countries.

It would be possible to write a lengthy book on any one of those three countries. This was not my intention; rather, I decided I would write an interpretative essay on each country, plus a shorter essay on India. In each I would attempt to relate the structures of rural society to political processes and economic policies. Since I found certain basic similarities in the social structures of the countries, I thought I could compare them and draw some common implications for policy in the final section.

This book is the result of that effort. One reader has commented, "The links that are forged [among these elements] often have the texture of string rather than steel. The work's importance lies more in the effort than the conclusiveness of the results." It should be viewed as a series of hypotheses and insights that may be useful in understanding the process of development in the countries concerned. I hope this book will encourage close examination of the social, political, and economic relationships in the three countries studied by their own social scientists, in the same way that my earlier book may have encouraged, directly or indirectly, the intense examination of the interrelationship among these elements that has been taking place in India over the past five years. It is also my opinion, expressed in the epilogue of my earlier book, that this approach can be useful in better understanding the process of change in other developing countries and continents.

As a final word, this manuscript was largely completed by July, 1972; most of the material and experience on which it is based is of even earlier date. While I have tried to incorporate mention of certain dramatic events since then, such as the introduction of martial law in the Philippines in late 1972, the serious crop failure in India in 1972–73, and the student uprising in Thailand in October, 1973, I have not been able to visit the countries since early 1972, and I can say little about those events. However, the book deals with long-term trends in those countries, and I do not believe that those recent events run counter to my general longer-term interpretation.

ACKNOWLEDGMENTS

This book would have been impossible without a joint grant from the New York University Center for International Studies and the Ford Foundation which made it possible for me to spend from September, 1971, to August, 1972, at the New York University Center writing this book. I thank Thomas Franck, Edward Weisband, Rochelle Fenchel, and Bert Lockwood, respectively director, associate director, and assistant directors of the Center, for their substantive and administrative support during this year; Bert Lockwood also edited the manuscript, in the midst of many other duties. At the Ford Foundation my thanks go to Eugene Staples, head of the Asia and Pacific division, and Edgar O. Edwards, program associate in that division, for their encouragement and interest. I also thank the Ford Foundation country representatives in India, Thailand, Indonesia, and the Philippines for their assistance during my visit to those countries in 1972, and for their interest in the study. David Szanton, in the Ford Foundation's Manila office, provided a continuous stimulus to this volume, both by his own interest in the subject matter as a professional anthropologist, and by his work in the Philippines. This work in fact convinced me that there were sufficient similarities among some of the countries to make a comparison possible.

I thank the many people who encouraged me to write this book, or made suggestions on all or part of it, or read early drafts of all or various parts of the manuscript. Among these especially are Cyrus Hui and Grace Obiogor, junior fellows at New York University's Center who worked closely with me on research related to this study, and by their questions and doubts certainly improved it. I also thank Milton Esman, Benjamin Higgins, and several anonymous readers for their comments on the entire manuscript, Lawrence Stifel for his comments on the Thailand chapter, and Wolf Ladejinsky on the India chapter. I hope it is clear that I have gained from these comments.

Many others were consulted during the course of this study. Where their help was relevant to specific points, I have acknowledged it in the footnotes. While I would like to thank the many others who helped in a more appropriate fashion, this is not possible. The list of persons to whom I am indebted includes, but is not limited to: S. Affif, E. Ayal, R. Bass, P. Bell, V. V. Bhatt, S. Chakravarty, M. L. Dantwala, S. D. Deshmukh, P. N. Dhar, J. Encarnacion, Scarlett Epstein, Ona Forrest, C. Geertz, W. Gilmartin, F. Golay, L. Gordon, A. D. Gorwala, M. Grossman, R. K. Hazari, A. Hirschman, S. C. Hsieh, Kyaw Htun, V. Jayme, N. Kagal, N. A. Khan, B. Kharmawan, K. S. Krishnaswamy, C. Leetavorn, L. Lefeber, Vanee Lertdurmrikarn, M. Lubis, B. Lusandanana, H. Matsumoto, M. Manohoran, L. Mears, P. Medhora, A. G. Menon, J. Mercado, T. Motooka, D. Mukherjee, O. McDiarmid, D. Narain, B. Onate, S. Okita, Liria Palafox, S. Roxas, V. Ruttan, S. Sabavala, A. Sametz, Ophelia Sta. Ana, N. Shah, W. Sycip, P. Tandon, S. Tolbert, Tun Thin, A. Vaidyanathan, B. Venkatappiah, A. Viravan, I. Walter, A. Weisblatt, and Suparb Yossundara.

I have had the opportunity to present some of my ideas at seminars at the N.Y.U. Center for International Studies; at two seminars at the University of Chicago; at a class of Professor P. R. Brahmananda at the University of Bombay; at a seminar of the Yale University Growth Center; at several of Professor Robert Hawkins's classes at N.Y.U. Graduate School of Business Administration; and at the Institute of Development Studies at Sussex University. All of these occasions provided opportunities for an exchange of ideas with the participants from which I have certainly gained, and from which I hope the listeners also gained. In addition, an earlier draft of the chapters on the Philippines, Indonesia, and Thailand appeared in various issues of *Solidarity*, published in Manila by Frank José.

Last, but far from least, this manuscript would never have appeared without the conscientious and intelligent typing and retyping (almost *ad infinitum* but I hope not *ad nauseam*) of Geraldine Bowman, helped at times by Linda Johnson, at New York University, and of Geri Kennedy and Pat Johnson at the University of Illinois Chicago Circle campus.

The year 1971–72, when much of this was written, would never have been such a stimulating and refreshing experience if it had not been for my relatives in Connecticut and New York, who proved to me the continuing importance of family ties in the United States, and my friends in New York City, who confirmed my earlier experiences of New York as one of the great and truly stimulating cities of the world. My wife and son bore the experience stoically. Unfortunately, my mother, my aunt, and my cousin, who contributed so much to the making of myself and of this book, will never be able to read it. I have dedicated the book to them.

Needless to say, there is no reason to believe that any one of those who have helped or commented agrees in whole or in part with anything I may have written. I alone am responsible for the assembly of the material, interpretations and conclusions drawn from it, and for any errors in the text.

CONTENTS

PART I A GENERAL
FRAMEWORK

CHAPTER 1   INTRODUCTION: THE PEASANT SOCIETY

A prerequisite of a theory of planning is an identification of the nature of the State and the Government. The planner . . . is part of a political machinery and is constrained by a complex structure within which he has to operate. . . . The limits of a planner's effective control depend on his position vis-à-vis the rest of the Government as well as on the nature of the political, social and economic forces operating in the economy.

—Amartya K. Sen, "Control Areas and Accounting Prices"

THEME

This book examines the relationship of ongoing social systems to the process of economic development in three countries of Southeast Asia (the Philippines, Indonesia, and Thailand) and compares this interrelationship with the experience in India, which has already been explored in my earlier book. It is assumed that various facets of the social systems of these individual countries are interrelated. I do not propose to examine the formal structure of these interrelationships; the characteristics of a social system, the nature of its equilibrium, and the interrelationship between change in any one of its facets—religious, social, political, and economic—and changes in other facets have been presented in a schema in that earlier volume.[1]

For purposes of convenience, the term used to describe the ongoing social system in each of these countries is "peasant society." This is used in preference to such other terms as "traditional society" or "feudal society." The term "traditional society" implies a more unchanging quality than is warranted—in all of these countries

---

1. See George Rosen, *Democracy and Economic Change in India* (Berkeley and Los Angeles: University of California Press, 1966), esp. Ch. 1 and Appendix A.

there have been major societal changes over the past centuries; the term "feudal system" implies a greater similarity to the so-named Western system than is accurate, in my opinion. In the next chapter I attempt to picture certain key characteristics of this peasant society. But the key point of this volume is that the characteristics of the peasant society influence the process and results of economic development in all the countries examined. In turn, the process of development itself changes the structure of the peasant society and the interrelationship among its various elements. Furthermore, I argue that unless the process of development satisfies some of the same goals satisfied by the peasant society, significant points of conflict will arise within the developing countries.

The broader questions to which this volume addresses itself, and which it tries to answer, are first, what is the relationship between the character of a peasant society and the character of a society undergoing rapid economic development; and second, how does the character of a peasant society change during the process of development?

More specifically on the economic level, the book asks how the characteristics of peasant society, as they function on both the local and national political levels, influence both the adoption of new technology in the agricultural area and the efforts to raise farm output; and how they influence the development of industry, including the effects on industry of the greater farm output, and vice versa.

The next section briefly identifies certain general characteristics of a hypothetical "peasant society" that seem to have important potential effects upon economic development. These characteristics are not logical constructs but are developed from historical and anthropological literature. However, they are meant to be general, rather than specific to a particular country. (Their existence in specific countries is examined in Part II.) This is followed by a chapter that discusses the meaning of economic development and the interrelationship between agricultural development and industrial development in the process of economic development. A set of loose hypotheses are presented concerning the effects of the structure of peasant society upon the process of economic development.

This introductory section is a preliminary to the country studies presented in Part II. These studies examine the relevance of my hypothetical structure of peasant societies to the Philippines, Indonesia, and Thailand, and they explore the extent to which the actual structures in those three countries have influenced the economic policies and achievements, more specifically in the area of agriculture and industry. These three country studies are followed by a brief review of India's social structure as presented in my earlier volume, and a summary of recent trends in India's economy, to provide a basis for comparing Indian experience with that of the three Southeast Asian countries.

In Part III the four countries are compared. Conclusions are also presented with respect to two major questions: the relationship between the characteristics of peasant societies in those countries and the requirements of economic development; and policy steps that may be useful in reconciling the values, structures, and needs of peasant society to a society in the process of rapid economic development.

THE PEASANT SOCIETY

In writing about peasant society one writes not only of a rural society but also of a social organization combining both rural and urban sectors. As Redfield points out in his distinction between primitive peoples and peasants, the peasant, unlike the primitive, is long used to the existence of the city; its ways are, in altered form, part of his ways. The peasant is a rural native whose long-established order of life takes important account of the city.

The account that the peasant takes of the city or town is economic, political, and moral. The peasant has some product which the city consumes and there are products of the city . . . which the peasant takes from the manufacturers of the city. . . . The economic interdependence of peasant villages and city finds political expression in institutions for control of the local community by power exerted from the city. . . . [And] the peasant knows himself as a part of a moral world in which the city man is also included. The city man expresses certain values . . . which he, the peasant, also cares about.[2]

This quotation illuminates a central fact: peasant society has never been self-sufficient. The peasant is in a complex mutual relationship with an urban superstructure, which governs him and which he supports by supplying food, through a system of interrelationships.[3]

The major economic activity of rural peasant society is the growing of agricultural products of which foodstuffs are a very large component. (In the Asian countries studied here, the major food crop is rice.) The basic unit of organization is the family-operated farm, using family labor with additional labor for seasonal and non-agricultural needs. Much farm output is either consumed directly by the family or used for the customary payments to the additional labor required. In turn, the family might provide such labor for other families in their times of need. But the peasant family is far more than an economic organization; it is the pivot around which the entire life of its members revolves. Often the constitution of the family is larger than the husband, wife, and their children; other relatives to the first degree and of several generations are included directly or in close proximity. Within the family there may be some specialization of activity, but this is normally crude, with functions based on sex or age rather than on training. The decision-making

2. Robert Redfield, *The Primitive World and Its Transformations* (London: Penguin Books, 1968), pp. 43–49.

3. This chapter has been strongly influenced by various general descriptions of peasant life. The following have been especially useful or provocative: Eric R. Wolf, *Peasants* (Englewood Cliffs, N.J.: Prentice-Hall, 1966); Guy Hunter, *Modernizing Peasant Societies* (London: Oxford University Press, 1969), Part I; George M. Foster, "Peasant Society and the Image of Limited Good," *American Anthropologist* 67, no. 2 (April, 1965): 293–315; Fred G. Bailey, "The Peasant View of the Bad Life," *Peasants and Peasant Society*, ed. Teodor Shanin (Harmondsworth, England: Penguin Books, 1971), pp. 299–321; J. Duncan Powell, "Peasant Society and Clientelist Politics," *The American Political Science Review* 64, no. 2 (June, 1970); James C. Scott, "Patron-Client Politics and Political Change," *American Political Science Review* 66, no. 1 (March 1972). The four articles specifically highlight certain characteristics of peasant society that influence its politics and the character of its economic behavior. For an interesting analysis of the influence of peasant social characteristics in Europe, see Hugh Seton-Watson, "The Intellectuals and Revolution: Social Forces in Eastern Europe since 1848," *Essays Presented to Sir Lewis Namier* (Freeport, N.Y.: Books for Libraries Press, 1971); for ancient Rome, see M. I. Finley, *The Ancient Economy* (Berkeley and Los Angeles: University of California Press, 1973), Chs. 2, 4. For a brief description of peasant society in pre-Communist China, see John K. Fairbank, *China Perceived* (New York: Alfred A. Knopf, 1974), pp. 63–73.

role is usually played by the eldest competent male, but it is not that of a dictator; rather, it approximates that of a chairman who seeks to achieve a family agreement by lengthy and, if need be, repeated discussion. In decision-making the preservation of status is a major goal and tradition an influential factor.

These characteristics carry over to the next-broader rural sphere, the village, which is the major nonfamilial unit of peasant society. At least one theory of the origin of the village suggests that it was an extension of the family, with nonfamily members introduced either by way of marriage (and thus absorbed into the family) or to perform a particular specialized task. To a large extent the village is the area of productive division of labor within the peasant society, insofar as that affects the individual producer. But this is a very minor specialization—all or almost all the inhabitants of the village are farmers, most of whom are landholders, and they all cooperate during hectic periods of planting and harvesting. In addition, there may be certain specialized tasks (of blacksmith, barber, priest, possibly merchant) which are performed by special families who may also operate farms.

At the top of the hierarchy there is a village leader, often from the family with the largest landholdings, perhaps by some traditional right of conquest or original settlement. The leader himself is usually a farmer, but he also serves as the village's contact with the outside world, perhaps in turn owing loyalty to a regional ruler or leader who rules over several villages, each of which pays him regular dues. These functions and the order in the hierarchy are largely hereditary. Similarly, the distribution of village output both internally and to the external ruler is on a customary basis. Shares are apportioned on the basis of hereditary status, which in turn is closely related to function.

The village is not just an economic unit; its members have other roles, both political and religious. The village leader plays a major role in arbitrating disputes within the village. As in the family, a premium is placed upon achieving consensus among the various leaders, taking whatever time is needed. The village leader with his near-peers, perhaps in an informal village council, is also responsible for translating the demands of the outside world into village actions or decisions, as well as for mobilizing the villagers in support of the area ruler, or protecting the village from excessive claims from external rulers and from the competition of other villages for land, power, and status. In exchange for this representational and protective role, the leader expects and is given loyalty from the villagers, and in turn gives loyalty to his ruler. This relationship has a strong element of quid pro quo, with exchange for services rendered. If the leader is ineffective, there may be a change; someone else from the leading hereditary family or from another peer family assumes the leadership.

While religious leadership is in the hands of the priest, all village families have specific roles to play in formal religious celebrations and feast days; in birth, marriage, and death ceremonies; and in the religious functions associated with economic and political activities—for example, with the blessing of tools, or the opening of a meeting. The various roles are closely interrelated; if a leader serves as godfather at a birth or sponsor at a wedding, this implies an exchange of loyalties in the political and economic areas. These religious and quasi-religious roles may be a function of one's status; even if ostensibly voluntary, they are in fact very much expected of a person of a particular status. Failure to fulfill them may result in loss of loyalty.

Bailey, among others, stresses this "multiplex" character as the major characteristic of the peasant society; i.e., relationships "are not specialized to deal with a single activity." Any relationship in any field (say, the economic) carries not only an economic strand, but also "political and ritual and possible familial strands." He contrasts this with a "modern society [whose hallmark] is the specialized role [of the individual] and the whole apparatus of its productive prosperity rests upon the division of labour between specialized roles."[4]

A substantial portion of the multiplex character of that society derives from the character of the farming within it. Life has little margin and is subject to numerous strains arising from the risks associated with subsistence farming. Droughts or floods can destroy

---

4. For the quotations see Bailey, "Peasant View," pp. 304–305. On this topic see also André Beteille, "The Social Framework of Agriculture," in Louis Lefeber and Mrinal Datta-Chaudhuri, *Regional Development Experiences and Prospects in South and Southeast Asia* (The Hague: Mouton, 1971), Ch. 7.

a crop for the whole area; the death of a draft animal or the birth of a disproportionately large number of female or male children, by creating a one-sided series of obligations for dowries or bride-payments, can seriously weaken a family. At the same time, increases in output over time appear to be largely beyond the control of a single family, since the effects of new technology can be overwhelmed by any of the above factors. Resources are limited and barely above the subsistence level; traditionally they are augmentable only by increasing family size, which again has been beyond the farmer's control. The patron-client system provides both minimum security and a means for integrating individual families into the larger village economy or society. The economic aim of the system is not to maximize output but to minimize losses or upset to the family in the event of random factors, and to the village in the event of an areawide decline in output. In effect the wealthier peasants, who are also the village leaders, assume a responsibility to protect their clients against upsets, and to provide the minimum consumption and capital needs of their clients through a system of sharing output, of providing credit, and of protecting the village from the exactions of higher patrons. In exchange they receive certain economic, political, and religious services which contribute to maintenance of their leading positions. The village economy operates close to subsistence with only small surpluses in any one year, with only that technological change which is consistent with patron-client relationships, and with roughly constant per capita output. Over time the economic system thus has the character of a zero-sum game, yielding a low level of output, with poverty shared in some relation to status.[5]

Above the village in the peasant society is the political and religious center usually found in a city. Between the capital city and the village the political and economic role of district or regional leaders might be large enough to support a smaller city, or the leaders in turn might simply be transmission belts from the village to the rulers in the capital. The capital is inhabited by the king or provincial ruler with his court, troops, associated priests, and others. A religious city contains temples, priests and their retinues, and

5. On this see G. M. Foster, "Peasant Society and Limited Good."

quarters for pilgrims. These cities are supported ultimately by the peasants, who, through the network of direct or intermediary relationships based upon status and exchange, provide dues to the rulers in the form of crops or labor. These cities also serve as centers of manufacture and trade from or through which goods move to the village. The function of collecting and transmitting dues in kind or in cash, or the labor at the village level, is normally the responsibility of the village leader. Trading of goods is normally handled by a special "outsider" merchant group with primary ties to the city, even if the merchant lives in the village. In the city too there would be a more complex division of labor, in part centering around the court, but in addition consisting of artisans and traders supplying goods to the court and the country; however, these merchants and artisans are clearly subordinate to the nobility and functionaries of the court.

In addition to this political and economic role, the city serves as the center of the Great Traditions of the peasant society. It was in the city that the religious system and theology was developed. Apart from its inherent religious virtues, this cosmological system often served to support the political structure by justifying to the rural peasant the exalted position and status of the urban ruler and his court. Between the worlds of court and country there was a sharp and unbridgeable line accepted by each.

The above discussion has been in terms of a static society, but even in its most traditional form peasant society was not static. In the more directly economic sphere the major inevitable element of change was population. Within a village, births and deaths had a major impact upon a family's economic and social position. More children both added to the family's labor supply and made possible a wider range of intermarriage; furthermore, more adult males increased a family's political support and potential force. But if a dowry system was associated with marriage, many female children could cause large expenses; and if inheritance was equal among male children, division could rapidly split inherited landholdings among the children as well as give rise to quarrels. Over a larger geographical area these elements would balance out, but within a village this would give rise to shifts in power among families. At the level of a royal family the conflict for power among male heirs, or the possible chaos from their absence, could greatly weaken a dynasty.

Apart from population change, the chances involved with weather and disease had a profound effect on the economic life of the peasant society. Weather was the main influence on crop production; disease was a major factor in the level of population. Years of good weather and little disease could build up surplus wealth and increase population. If the latter were large enough to surpass the village's capacity to support it, the existence of empty lands made it possible to set up new villages like the older ones, in the process strengthening the urban government. But these changes within the system were normally slow, often occurring over generations. They were expected and considered inevitable.

At the national level the strength of the country internally and vis-à-vis its neighbors depended partly on natural wealth, partly on government programs such as building irrigation works or encouraging certain types of production, and partly on trade with other countries. Here too the ruler's strength, his rivalries with competitors within his country, and his ability to resist attacks from without had a profound effect on the country's position. Nevertheless, until the colonial powers entered the scene the picture was a kaleidoscope of states rising or falling and borders changing; in fact, the colonial merchants took advantage of this rivalry to achieve power. In any case, for the individual peasant there would be little long-term economic change—his risks were high, and his own efforts to raise output were largely subsumed by factors beyond his control. He sought primarily to protect himself and his family in bad years, and to maintain, and where possible improve, his family's position in better years. Similarly, in the political field his role was passive—to follow rather than to lead, and by following to remain alive. He obeyed, delivered his dues and services in exchange for protection, accepted his share of output or gains according to his status, and had as little as possible to do with his city rulers. However, if they failed to protect his village, he shifted his loyalty to someone who could protect him.

With the entry of colonial powers, the circumstances of the peasant society changed greatly.[6] In almost all cases the original purpose of the entry of colonial powers was to make profits by trade. In order to control the trade, political power followed. Foreign traders and colonial powers set up trading enclaves and cities entirely different in character from the old cities. These new cities might serve initially as enclaves through which trade flowed between the peasant society and the colonial power; but as political power was established, these cities also became the centers of foreign government, of new religions, and gradually of industry and even more widespread commercial activities. In these enclave cities the laws, attitudes, and methods of work were those of the foreigners, not those of the peasant society. Schools were set up to teach foreign methods and languages and to train white-collar workers for specialized jobs in government, private offices, and factories. From these cities too would come the foreign officials, soldiers, and churchmen who lived in the provinces and represented the foreigners in the rural areas. They interpreted foreign laws or served as priests of foreign religions, or as heads of foreign-owned plantations or factories which were set up to process local raw materials and minerals on the spot. But these cities were enclaves, and while their effects on the peasant society were real, they took time. The foreign rulers quite frequently had no interest in consciously remaking or destroying the preexisting peasant society, except in certain specific areas: among these were always government and law, frequently religion, and possibly those aspects of peasant society where limited social reforms might eliminate some of the abuses of the pre-colonial system as seen by Westerners (e.g., suttee and thuggery in India). The new rulers were interested in exploiting the resources of the conquered country and not in disturbing its traditions, since such disturbances could lead to political unrest or rebellion. Therefore in the political field the foreign rulers often worked with and through local rulers and the former structure of peasant society, replacing stubborn rulers by more pliable figures and providing advisers if necessary. In the economic field the policy

6. In the following discussion of colonial influence it should be clearly understood that Thailand has always been politically independent. This qualification will not be repeated.

of importing manufactured goods from the colonial power in exchange for exports of raw material often led to the destruction of local industries. Equally important, foreign governments and merchants sought to monopolize trade; they forced native traders out of large-scale trade. At the middle level, by their encouragement of businessmen whom they trusted, who knew Western practices, and who had the capital to handle larger volumes of goods, they frequently encouraged the spread of Chinese or, as in India, communal merchants, at the expense of whatever local traders existed. (This entry of Chinese also took place in Thailand, but in a different fashion, reflecting that country's independence.)

The effects of colonial rule were profound. Within the country whose bounds were set by the extent of the colonial rule, there was more or less internal peace and exchange, construction of roads and irrigation systems, and some Western education. But even more significant was the inculcation of Western attitudes and methods of working among a small section of the population who wished to follow the new Western leaders, or who worked in the new cities and enterprises. Sometimes this strengthened existing gentry attitudes in favor of government work and against trade. The establishment of factories also encouraged the subsequent development of some local businessmen who invested resources in industry. In the rural areas the introduction of Western land laws permitted the sale and purchase of land by individuals; in almost all countries special steps, such as payment of taxes in money, were taken to encourage or force cultivation of export crops and their delivery to town. Peasants too could go to court to enforce sales or to settle disputes outside traditional channels. Commercialization of the supply of factors of production, especially land, became more important, and contract or market relationships modified or replaced the customary relationships between the peasant and his traditional rulers.

Perhaps most important, people of all types migrated to the new cities—some to be close to the new rulers or to take advantage of the "new" education, and, if educated, to work in the government and private offices; others to work as manual laborers in the factories and at the odd jobs of the cities. The better-off or higher-status rural families frequently sent sons to take advantage of the new education; poorer families, facing ever smaller land holdings and the pressure of growing families, sent sons to work in the mills and to be servants, peddlers, and haulers. But the structure of peasant society provided a vehicle of transition for the migrants. In many cases the migrant would move in with some relative; the people of a village or community often clustered together in a district of a large city, always with room for one more individual, and possibly for a family. The first settler from a particular family or village was expected to assist the later migrant, whether educated or not, to find and keep a job. Migrants in the factory or office would bring relatives in for other jobs in the same place; those from land-working families returned to their villages for the harvest, and for the major celebrations in which they played their traditional role. They also sent a high proportion of their urban earnings back to their families in the village; this contribution often provided the margin that permitted their village families to maintain their small rural land holdings.

At another level, in many countries local businessmen were often forced out and replaced by aliens. Business skills and habits of mutual cooperation and trust were lost and could not easily be rebuilt. Where there were local businessmen, the foreign rulers frequently looked down on them; this attitude strengthened the existing peasant distrust of trade and traders. In addition, many indigenous businessmen were strongly influenced in their operations by their rural backgrounds. The capital for a locally owned firm and the management of the firm were closely held, usually within the family or communal group. The businessmen often followed the traditional practices of the family; they distrusted outsiders, whether businessmen from different family and communal groups or the government, since both were regarded as sources of pressure and interference, and threatened potential loss of control. They frequently sought to use or bribe such outsiders. Some large families established their own affiliated banks and marketing organizations in order to be independent of outsiders. There was little social consciousness on the part of such businessmen, in the sense of loyalty to an agency or a set of values larger than those of one's own family or communal group. At the same time mutual distrust among these family groups limited the size and scope of the enterprise, since managerial and capital resources were confined to the resources available to a family or community, supplemented by such resources as could be acquired externally without loss of control.

In each country examined here, the period of colonial rule or influence was also one of slowly rising population, with growth accelerating after 1920. This was reflected in the opening of new lands and possibly the extension of roads and irrigation systems, so that output of crops rose significantly and the land could support more people. With the growth of population and the occupation of previously empty lands, existing land was subdivided, and the output derived from additional labor with the same technology declined to very low levels, possibly reaching zero. While land values were rising, many farmers were forced into debt and had to sell their lands. There was an increasing concentration of land ownership on one hand, combined with increasing tenancy, sale of land, and indebtedness on the other. However, some of the worst effects of these trends were mitigated by the continued influence of traditional relationships and responsibilities among peasants, and by the contempt for miserly behavior on the part of the wealthy.

Thus the "peasant society" was undermined by the intrusion of foreign pressures and commercial relationships; in the process new groups were formed with only tenuous connections with the village. By the time these countries approached independence, rather than having a single peasant society with a unified ethos, there was a fragmented society on the most obvious level, split laterally between the foreign rulers and the indigenous inhabitants. Among the latter too there were varying degrees of movement away from traditional patterns, depending largely on proximity to the centers of foreign power. Within the villages the social attitudes of peasant society continued to serve as a binding force, in spite of changes in the underlying economic structure and patterns of landholding. In the city the social structure changed more, with far greater instability of personal status and change in attitude; however, such characteristics of village life as loyalty to one's family and some reliance upon a patron remained strong. The split between villagers and urban inhabitants, whether foreign or local, became stronger as the urban inhabitants spoke an increasingly different language and assumed different customs. While respect continued, the suspicion which always existed became stronger as traditional ties broke down. The villager distrusted the urban inhabitant and the educated white-collar worker often employed by a foreign agency; the urban inhabitant, who had gradually lost his rural connections, frequently despised the villager as either stupid or obstructive. As this happened, a new role arose—that of broker between the village and the city. The broker was a person with a foot in both camps— and he was trusted by neither. To some extent the village merchant played such a role, since his connections were frequently outside the village. However, he was sharply distrusted by the villager because he derived benefit from increasing commercialization and was becoming increasingly wealthy in money and land at the expense of the peasant.[7]

With the advent of independence in these countries after World War II, the roles of these various groups changed. The foreign ruler lost his political control to local leaders. This resulted in a major shift in internal political and economic power. Foreign constitutional and bureaucratic forms were sometimes maintained or adopted, but the characteristics of the peasant society which underlay the social system changed the forms into a compatible political structure. All the governments now sought economic growth as a stated goal. In turn, the structure of the peasant society, functioning at either the village, state, or national level, influenced the village-level response by its effects on the peasant's reaction to new economic opportunities. Response at the national level was influenced by the effects of peasant society on the framework of policy within which economic development was to take place, and on the character of indigenous enterprise within the country.

The above discussion of the changing character of peasant society has permitted identification of some common and current

7. Beteille, "Social Framework," is especially good in his discussion of the interpenetration of the older characteristics of peasant societies by the characteristics of a commercial, urbanized society.

characteristics of peasant societies of Asian countries which might be expected to influence economic development. First, in all these countries the peasantry forms a large segment of the population. More than half the population is directly dependent on agriculture; income from agriculture is over one-third of the national income. (The proportions would be larger if figures were available for the entire rural sector.) Thus the rural population is a major political force within the country; the political structure, ways of working, and attitudes of that sector have a major effect on the functioning of the nation's polity.

Second, at the immediate level the family is the most important unit of social organization and demands the most loyalty. Outsiders are distrusted, depending on their distance from the family. For this reason weaker clients frequently attempt to coopt patrons into quasi-family relationships, which would reinforce patron-client responsibilities with family claims. Beyond the family, loyalty extends to others of the same village and then to those of similar caste or community groups.

Third, the dominant relationship patterning economic and political life within the village, and extending from the village to the city, is the patron-client relationship. This is a relationship between wielders of great power to those of less power; the former provide protection and favors for the latter in exchange for support. In the economic sphere at the village level this centers about the relationship between larger and smaller landowners, or between landowners and tenants or laborers, and is closely related to the labor requirements for production of the major food crop, which is distributed among village clients according to their status. Land ownership and growing of a food crop is not only a goal, but also an instrument; it is a major factor influencing the villager's social position and his ability to live up to social responsibilities, and it makes it possible for the villager to carry out his religious responsibilities.

When this patron-client relationship is extended to the national level, it implies a system of relationships between local patron-client groups and national figures, whether functioning through political parties or bureaucratic institutions. Through these the higher-level patrons provide protection, jobs, and opportunities for their local clients, who in turn provide votes or money for the patrons.

Fourth, the patron-client system of distribution insures that whatever food is produced within the village is distributed to all the villagers, in accordance with status and in exchange for contribution. Frequent village ceremonial functions provide an institutional means for redistributing output according to status; the patron has a responsibility to provide for such redistribution. On a national scale, elections perform a similar ceremonial role, with the election itself providing the occasion to redistribute government income to worthy potential supporters. As a distributive system it operates so that people will be provided with work and will share in output according to their position in society; they are protected to some extent from starvation, isolation, and unemployment.

Fifth, because most villagers are farmers, and because there is a close relationship between the status of the farmer and his duty to share output, those villagers who are not farmers or who do not share their gains are looked down upon. Miserliness and sharp dealing are frowned upon; trading, which requires such characteristics, is normally carried on by nonfarming groups. In Southeast Asia the Chinese perform this trading function; in India special castes or communities do the same. There is evidence that this relationship between farmers and traders was exacerbated by colonial rule, although it has also existed in Thailand. Generally traders are outsiders, peripheral to the patron-client system, since they have only a minor political role and low social status.

Sixth, rulers in the capital city have always been at the peak of peasant society, and the court official has always been superior. In precolonial days the ruler and court were the center of the entire system, and they played the highest role in all areas of society. There was a sharp, unbridgeable split between the government and village society. The government was the active force in society, including the economy; the peasant was passive. Government officials were of higher status; peasants, of lower. Education was limited to potential government officials, and those potential officials by heredity and education were provided with government positions. The villager traditionally could not aspire to government status. But, while he recognized the status superiority of the government official and, by indirection, the city dweller, he had little respect for the government official's knowledge of farming—and he had his own simpler virtues. The colonial experience supported this separation between ruler and ruled. After independence, once the possibilities of education became more widespread and class barriers weakened, one of the peasant's main hopes became to educate his son to enter the bureaucracy. At the same time, the government is regarded as the active force in initiating and approving change.

Seventh, as a reflection of the structure of society and its cosmology, decision-making sought to minimize disagreement and conflict. Age was associated with leadership; the role of father or village leader or ruler was strongest. Tradition was frequently the decisive element in a decision, and the achievement of consensus around the position of the leader or patron was more important than speed of decision-making. The colonial experience probably changed this style at the highest level, but the effect of independence has probably strengthened the influence of the peasant style of decision-making outside the village.

In the next chapter the effects of these characteristics of peasant society upon economic development are explored in a set of hypotheses.

CHAPTER 2 PEASANT SOCIETIES AND ECONOMIC DEVELOPMENT

LADY CICELY: *In my world, which is now your world—our world—getting patronage is the whole art of life. A man can't have a career without it.*
BRASSBOUND: *In my world a man can navigate his ship and get his living by it.*
— George Bernard Shaw, *Captain Brassbound's Conversion*, Act III

The business leader, as a rule, is the member of a social stratum other than that to which his employees belong. He is guided by the idea of economic progress, while his employees think in terms of their needs. Since his control has no relation to their lives, the business leader endangers the integration of the group with which he works.
— F. Redlich, "The Business Leader as a 'Daimonic' Figure"

Peasant society in its economic aspects gave rise to an economic structure which provided both a low level of security (in terms of food and employment) and status to all its members, in exchange for economic and political support to its rural and urban leaders. It was capable of some flexibility in terms of increasing output, or in terms of a greater flow of output from the country to the city, but its responses at the village levels were at least as much to the demands of its rulers and social structure as to commercial factors. This society was extensively penetrated by commercial forces, operating either directly through colonial rule or indirectly through the opening of the country to commercial influences. These commercial forces were moderated by an overlay of family and patron-client relationships and responsibilities which have continued to provide some security to the villagers.

The process of rapid economic development implies a greater stress upon expanding output of goods and services than is the goal of a peasant society. This need for increasing output calls for a greater specialization than is the norm in a peasant society; in the process of specialization, some individual security is sacrificed for the possibility of greater total output. Such specialization also implies far greater sensitivity of the entire system to both internal and external stimuli—in fact, "the number of reaction potentials increases faster than the opportunities for using them."[1] The greater sensitivity to external stimuli implies as a corollary an ability and willingness of society members to adopt old methods and institutions, and to develop new ones that are capable of responding rapidly and effectively to new pressures and opportunities. In effect this means replacing a society in which the present position and security of members depends primarily upon their past status and position, with a society in which the position and status of members at any one time depends upon their capacity to initiate. This in turn makes possible greater wealth for all the members of the society, but at the possible cost of wealth or position (or both) for any one individual.

Such a society requires an elaborate network which is sensitive to both external and internal pressures and opportunities, and which transmits signals to, and reactions from, interested individuals and institutions. The channels of interaction among the sectors of a developed society must be reasonably clear so that the signals are definite and reactions can be made speedily effective. In the economic area such a system may be provided through the market or some substitute.[2]

In this view of a developing society the stress is not on static results (e.g., a greater volume of saving or investment, or ultimately higher GNP) but on a process of a changing society, which by its changes provides the framework within and through which the results can occur. There are costs of such a society, with its greater

1. John E. Anderson, "Dynamics of Development System in Process," in *The Concept of Development*, ed. Dale B. Harris (Minneapolis: University of Minnesota Press, 1957), p. 38. This article presents a biological view of personal development that seems highly relevant to social development as well, since it stresses the system's response capability as the key to development.

2. By itself this says nothing about the relation of government to private enterprise. See on this Alec K. Cairncross, "The Optimum Firm Reconsidered," *Economic Journal* 82 (1972): 318–319.

degree of specialization and flexibility. A most obvious cost is individual security. At lower levels the minimum security of food and position provided by the peasant society is endangered; at higher levels the status and shares that have arisen from past inheritance and status are threatened by new people with greater initiative and ability to respond. Those at the highest levels may in fact be unwilling to weaken their present position and may seek to resist changes which may jeopardize it, or they may seek to use their superior position to insure that they reap most of the gains of change. At all levels there may be efforts to protect various groups against change by preventing the society's "nerve system" from freely transmitting signals; the effects of decisions can be cushioned in a network of protective devices to minimize those costs. Some of this protection may be a necessary condition of social stability in a period of rapid change. But misdirected protection can lead to the worst of both worlds: a rapidly collapsing peasant society and a would-be developing society which in fact does not permit the type of behavior that makes possible the economic goals of development.

What is the relationship between the characteristics of a peasant society, as summarized at the end of the previous chapter, and the flexibility required of an economically developing society? How does each characteristic influence the economy?

If we look first at the agriculture sector itself, the economic characteristics of the peasant have been well summarized by Robin Marris:

A man daily required to exercise judgment, to take risks and face difficult situations for which there are no exact precedents; the man whose short-run production function is never precisely known; who is a price taker faced with constantly changing prices: yet a man who not only has no influence over the equilibrium of his industry but usually sees himself, often fatalistically, as prisoner of fickle (i.e., frequently changing) fate? He is of course the yeoman farmer or peasant, before the advent of accurate weather forecasts, or of machines that cut laid corn, fertilizers that control fertility or governments that control price."[3]

3. Robin Marris, "Why Economics Needs a Theory of the Firm," *Economic Journal* 82 (1972): 324.

Under such circumstances it would be expected that the system would stress security, and the peasant society provided such security at low levels of output. It would not pay a peasant to introduce new technology for a higher yield if the risk and investment associated with that technology were high, while the expected yield increase was small or very uncertain. Failure would jeopardize his own food supply and that of his clients; success would depend largely on factors beyond his own control. Similarly, the peasant would not introduce a labor-saving device, because it would jeopardize the work and shares of other villagers for which he would be responsible anyway. Thus the economic costs of his initiative would include costs over and above his direct costs of investment and maintenance; there would be additional social and political costs of some significance. To override these known indirect costs the gains would have to be very large, and with a high probability of regularity.

In any case, since the margin above subsistence for a peasant was low, there would be few who could risk their very scarce capital resources in investments with uncertain and possibly long-delayed returns. Peasant society would be biased against technological change in the production of foodstuffs, and until the possibilities of gain were very high, or the risks of failure were reduced, the incentives to introduce new technology were outweighed by negative factors.

However, various loopholes permitted some response to new opportunities and market forces. First, the restraints and benefits of the patron-client system normally applied to food crops, not to commercial crops; if peasants could raise these latter and maintain sufficient food output for their own and their clients' needs, there was no reason for them not to take advantage of other opportunities. Thus many farmers did in fact grow cash crops such as jute or sugar when the opportunities arose, and still continued to meet their obligations. Second, when new areas were settled outside the traditional village, the restrictions might not apply; there were opportunities for trying new crops and techniques. In all the countries, output expanded to new areas. Third, the various governments built an infrastructure of irrigation systems and improved roads and railroads which permitted higher output of food grains and other crops, widening the area of production and market. Both of these reduced the risks of production and distribution at little or no cost to the individual farmer. In addition, all the governments had systems of crop research and extension; these developed and provided information to the peasants concerning new types of crops and new technologies of production, which the individual peasant could then try for himself. These factors all enhanced output; from about 1850 to 1930 total output grew, and total acreage cultivated expanded to permit an unprecedented and continuous population increase at roughly constant or somewhat improving living standards, while exports of agricultural products also grew (with continued profits for the colonial powers and trading merchants).

However, at the same time that empty lands filled up and populations grew, there was a tendency for reduction in size of landholding, increasing alienation of land, and growing indebtedness of the farmer. Many farmers found their resource position weakened; their capacity to take the risks associated with new varieties and technologies also diminished. With land ownership concentrating in the hands of larger farmers and traders, some of the traditional attitudes of patrons to clients broke down. This created a small group of farmers with resources to invest in potentially risky areas, and it encouraged a more commercial response to new technology, provided the possibilities of gain were large enough to overcome any social opprobrium.

Beyond the heavy weight of the risk element in relation to resources and obligation, the distribution of land ownership and income will have a profound effect on the future course of a new technology that promises to raise food output. This has been pointed out by Lefeber and Datta-Chaudhuri,[4] who have stressed that there must be markets for the additional output, and that in the Asian countries, where the great bulk of the population depends on agriculture, the largest share of the market must be the peasants themselves. A highly skewed distribution of wealth and income with low income and price demand elasticities would restrict the

4. See Lefeber and Datta-Chaudhuri, *Regional Development*, Ch. 4.

possibilities of expanding consumption of food grains in the rural areas; it would be necessary to find or develop significant foreign or urban markets for the additional outputs. Otherwise the increasing supplies would lead to oversupply and price fall, or to large stockpiles supported by an expensive price-support program. Either would threaten the collapse of a "green revolution."

Apart from effects from within the agricultural sector itself, Hayami and Ruttan[5] have made clear the strong positive relation between the growth of an industrial sector and the increasing output of agricultural products. A strong industrial sector provides reasonably priced chemical and mechanical inputs which farmers can use to increase their land or labor productivity, and serves as a market for agricultural raw materials. In addition, an effective public sector, by setting up research facilities and extension services, carries out the essential experimentation with new inputs and dissemination of results that farmers themselves are unable to implement; the government thus absorbs some of the essential costs of new technology. By its construction of irrigation, power, and transport systems, and by providing the conditions for efficient marketing of inputs and outputs, the government insures that the inputs are available, that they can be controlled in their application to the degree which the new technology may require, and that the outputs may be sold when desired. To the extent that the peasant society through its patron-client relationships determines the operation of the political system which controls the availability and allocation of public resources to research, extension, and infrastructure, as well as the functioning of the new institutions, it has a major effect on the spread of new agricultural technology.

The growth of the industrial sector is a key element in the economic development of the countries concerned. With respect to the development of agriculture, the industrial sector directly supplies inputs to agriculture, besides being a major consumer of agricultural products. But in the more general area of development, and the interrelation of the goals of peasant society and economic

5. Yujiro Hayami and Vernon Ruttan, *Agricultural Development* (Baltimore: Johns Hopkins University Press, 1971), esp. Parts 1, 2, and 5.

change, the industrial sector serves as a potential alternative employer of educated manpower. In the unchanging peasant society this latter role was taken by government. Reflecting pressures arising from the attitudes of peasant societies, the new governments in all these countries have greatly increased their education programs (and in turn the size of their bureaucracies) in response to the larger demand for government services and the greater supply of educated persons. This increase has been at a direct cost of resources which might have been used to employ these additional workers elsewhere in a more productive fashion, and there has probably been an indirect cost of reduced efficiency in government operations. It is doubtful whether employment of the educated in government bureaucracies can continue as in the past; other sources of jobs for the educated are essential. Industrial and related employment offers a major alternative.

The development of new agricultural technology and the consequent increases in farm output can stimulate industrial development. This stimulus could occur from the increased demand for industrial inputs and services related to the new techniques, and for manufactured consumer goods. It could also occur through the supply of additional farm outputs from the new technology, which could lead to a reduction in the relative prices of raw materials and foodstuffs and thus to greater industrial profits. Finally, a direct effect can occur by increasing the investible resources in the hands of the farmers who benefit from the new technology and are eager for new areas of investment in agriculture or industry; in the hands of industrialists or would-be industrialists who are interested in investing in industry; and in the hands of the government for investing in research and extension, in necessary education and infrastructure, and perhaps directly in industry. The flow of resources through these channels, and the effective operation of the system of signals which controls that flow, is essential for the growth of industry. If those channels are not functioning efficiently, as a result of either the income structure of the rural sector, or attitudes derived from peasant society which look down upon industrial activity and industrialists (whether private or government), or government decision-making behavior and policies which make industrial investment or industrial decision-making difficult, the potentially beneficial consequences of additional agricultural output on industry, and thus upon the entire development process, will be cancelled.

A key element in this entire process of development is an effective government sector. That sector's vital role in improving agricultural technology has already been mentioned. More important and more generally, peasants view the government as the only institution with the prestige to initiate major changes in direction and to introduce new institutions on a large scale. This prestige, derived from the values of peasant society, is reinforced by the prestige derived from contemporary intellectuals within the country who believe in socialism. But at the same time it is the government which most mirrors the qualities and demands of the peasant society, since it is, in one degree or the other, representative of that society. There is both a need and a demand for the government to undertake functions required for development: education; agricultural research and extension; police and protection; a framework of policies which can transmit the signals and responses needed for development, within which agriculture and industry can grow; establishment of new institutions to develop managers, transmit skills, and raise and distribute capital resources, all of which are needed in the process of development. There is also a continued demand for the government to play the protecting and redistributive role that is expected in a peasant society, thereby providing some of the security lost in the movement away from that society. The ability of any government to perform all these different functions is questionable; but the emphasis given to each, and the effectiveness in performing any one, will be strongly influenced by attitudes and methods derived from peasant society, and by pressures arising from the structure of that society.

The general themes set out in this introductory section are explored in depth in individual chapters on the Philippines, Indonesia, and Thailand. Each chapter begins with a description of peasant society of that country[6] to examine the extent to which it

6. Rather than repeating a separate caution for each country, it should be realized that each picture is based on a limited number of anthropological studies of

conforms to the general type already described. The impact of the national peasant society upon the political and bureaucratic functioning of the country is then explored. These considerations are brought together to examine peasant society's impact on the country's economic development by looking at two major economic issues: the peasant response to new technology in agriculture, and the relationship between that country's peasant social structure and its industrial policy and growth. The fourth country chapter looks at the relationship between India's social and political structure and its recent agricultural development and industrial policy, in order to permit comparison between the three Southeast Asian countries and India.

---

individual villages. However, these studies are of villages that may be considered reasonably representative of the major part of that country's population, while recognizing that each country contains large minority elements for whom the resulting generalizations would be far less valid. In my opinion, generalizations of a national character may be drawn from these studies; such generalizations provide useful insights in explaining the general character of a country's economic development, and they permit comparison among the countries.

PART II COUNTRY STUDIES

. . . what will the Philippines be a century hence? The storage batteries are charging little by little, and if the prudence of the government does not provide an outlet for the complaints that are accumulating, it's possible that one day the spark will fly out.

—José Rizal, "The Philippines a Century Hence"

THE PEASANT SOCIETY AND ITS HISTORY

Generalizations concerning the society of the Philippines, with its extended area and numerous islands, would on the surface appear quite dangerous. However, while there are significant differences, almost 90 percent of the people belong to eight culture-linguistic groups living in the lowlands; these groups show marked similarities in their history and culture. Approximately 85 percent of the population is Catholic, and another 10 percent of other Christian faiths; about 5 percent are Muslims, and a small remainder are of other non-Christian religions. The non-Christian population is concentrated in the south and in the highlands. While language and ethnic differences help determine how a Filipino regards himself, there is a very large degree of cultural homogeneity. Perhaps more relevant for our purposes, approximately two-thirds of the people live in rural areas; over half derive their incomes from the agricultural, forestry, and fishing sectors which contribute approximately one-third of the national output. Even though the role of the rural population has been declining since 1950, these percentages make clear the significance of rural society and its values upon the country as a whole. In Manila itself, the center of Philippine urban society, there is a sharp division between a "truly modern, cosmopolitan sector, and a sector which might be called 'subsistence urban,'"[1] in which more or less traditional methods of marketing, finance, manufacture and transportation, derived from a rural background, prevail.

The longest-standing social institution in the Philippines, far antedating colonial rule, is the nuclear family with a bilateral structure. "Both paternal and maternal relations are regarded as belonging to the family," which "gives the Filipino a ready-made social security system and a wide-range basis of political support." This has been described as "the basic productive unit in agricultural activities.... Social mobility is still familial, not individual.... Siblings display marked solidarity . . . reflected in patterns of contiguous residence, joint migration and so forth. . . . [Kinship provides a basis] in extending interpersonal relationships into the community and society.... [Kin groups] provide emotional, psychological and social security." Economically the family serves as the unit of subsistence; because output and earnings are shared, all members receive a minimum level of support. Socially the family protects any of its members from outside criticism and attacks, which may call forth a violent response. The closeness of the kin group also limits relations with nonfamily members; when such associations of a more than temporary nature do develop, they are often followed by the establishment of ritual kinship ties through a compadre system by which the outsider becomes godfather to a family child. In short, Philippine society has been described, in a particularly felicitous phrase, as an "anarchy of families."[2]

From the little that is known of pre-Spanish society, there was apparently no major state in the present area of the Philippines; the influence of the Great Traditions that centered in the major cities, with great courts and formal bureaucracies that we find in other Asian countries, appears to have been only minor. In the Philip-

1. See Sixto K. Roxas, "Tondo: Four Hundred Years of Urbanization," *Sunday Times Magazine* (Manila), June 20, 1971, pp. 20–22.

2. See Onofre D. Corpuz, "The Cultural Foundation of Filipino Politics," in *Social Foundations of Community Development*, ed. Socorro C. Espiritu and Chester L. Hunt (Manila: R. M. Garcia Publishing House, 1964), p. 417. Also see Robert B. Fox, "The Study of Filipino Society and Its Significance to Programs of Economic and Social Development," *Philippine Sociological Review* (Manila, January–April, 1959): 6, 7, 10, 11.

pines there were essentially local communities, usually along river banks, near the sea coast, or in the rolling hills below the central mountains. Each community might include several extended families, inhabiting one or more villages or barrios. Within these communities there was a gradation of social classes from chiefs to nobles to freemen to slaves.[3] The chief (*datu*) governed in peace and led in wars. The noble served in those wars and helped the chief build his home, shared in his feasts, and participated in his sport events. The freeman served the chief or noble, but he had the right to live in his own house on his own land, with exclusive rights to inheritance. His children could not be sold, nor need he move with his master. He helped his superior in sowing and harvesting, participated in his master's feasts, equipped his ship, and paid a tribute of rice. In exchange he shared in the feasts and the loot of war. The slave had no rights or privileges but to serve his master and be fed by him; he was regarded, along with gold, as a major form of wealth, and could be bought and sold.

This was not a closed society, although ancestry was a key element in determining one's position. But a slave could marry or buy his way to freedom; a freeman could be recognized as a chief by accumulating wealth and attracting followers; a chief or noble could become a slave by losing a war and being taken prisoner. There was a close interaction between power (defined as armed support) and wealth, but "wealth without power had little meaning."[4]

While these largely river valley, ocean-facing communities were not united under a large government, they apparently conducted extensive trade with other parts of Asia. "From time immemorial . . . merchants from the southern coast of China were already trading with the Philippine Islands. . . . We learn from [Chinese manuscripts] that the products which the Chinese sought were principally yellow wax, cotton, pearls, conch-shell, betel nuts and jute fabrics. In exchanges for these they offered porcelainware, refined gold, iron vases, lead, glass, colored beads and needles." In ad-

---

3. These are Western terms for more complex Filipino social types.

4. Frank Lynch, "Trend Report of Studies in Social Stratification and Social Mobility in the Philippines," *East Asian Cultural Studies* (Tokyo) 4, nos. 1–4 (March, 1965): 163–191, esp. 163–166.

dition to trade with China, the central power of East Asia, the Filipinos carried on trade with Japan, Siam, Indonesia, and India, as well as with the Portuguese before the arrival of the Spaniards. In the southern islands Islamic religion had been established by Muslim traders.[5] With such trade, as well as production for local needs, trading and artisanship were respected functions and means of achieving wealth and power.

Under the Spaniards this system changed, at least at the top. The Spaniards created a colony, the Philippine Islands, which they governed loosely from Manila; they converted the bulk of the population to Catholicism. Spanish rule in the Muslim south was always tenuous and subject to conflict, and its effects were minor. The difficulties of governing a collection of islands so many miles from Spain led to a policy that

everything outside the city of Manila was relinquished by the civil government into the hands of the missionaries. Spanish officials would venture out into the provinces only once a year to collect tributes. . . . Manila built up a massive ring of fortification around her, to protect herself against the Chinese living in the vicinity and against the Moslem pirates and the Dutch. Inside the walls natives and Chinese could not reside. Finally, with the establishment of trade with China and Acapulco the city was converted into one huge commercial entrepot, and all the Spaniards living there were soon engaged almost exclusively in the commerce of the galleons.

And so while Manila lived in comparative opulence and prosperity the Filipinos living in the fields and in the provinces were left to their old ways of life. . . . [The Filipino] did not learn the use of new products from Spain . . . Spanish customs, except those related to his religious faith, remained unknown, and the Spanish language was not understood. . . . The Filipino, in fact, became aware of the presence of the "Castilas" only when he had to pay his tribute or report for the [forced labor]. So there was no real contact between the native and the Spaniard. Instead there were two mutually unfamiliar castes, one of "Castilas" living within the walls and another of "Indios." And between the conquerors and the conquered were the Chinese traders and artisans and the . . . Mexican soldiers and sailors.[6]

5. Rafael Bernal, *Prologue to Philippine History* (Manila: Solidaridad Publishing House, 1967), pp. 39 and 50; also see entire issue of *Philippine Studies* 15, no. 1 (Manila, January, 1967).
6. Bernal, *Prologue*, p. 53.

The Chinese handled the limited trade between the Spaniards in the walls and the Indios outside the walls, but their numbers and movements were kept closely controlled by the Spaniards out of fear of rebellion. Since the Chinese frequently came without wives, there was easy intermarriage between the Chinese and Indios, and there arose a mixed group of *mestizos*, who were considered, and considered themselves, Filipino.

In the nineteenth century this changed. The galleon trade was abolished; Spaniards traveled freely in the country, lived outside Manila, set up businesses, and intermarried. The Indios were permitted to live in Manila. Many of the better off traveled to Spain to study and to live, returning with ideas of liberty; intermarriage between Spaniards and Filipinos also occurred. As part of the same movement of economic liberalism English and other non-Spanish aliens entered the country, established businesses, developed export crops such as sugar and abaca, and formed a commercial network of trading and financial institutions to handle the exports and manufactured imports; by 1894 the United Kingdom was the main trading partner of the Philippines. Similarly, free entry of Chinese immigrants was permitted after 1850, and the Chinese population rose from 6,000 in 1847 (out of a total population of about 3.5 million) to about 90,000 in the 80's (out of a population of about 6 million). The Chinese played a dominant role in many aspects of internal trade, both at the retail level and in the foreign trade area. In the latter field British firms frequently financed the Chinese traders, and one Spaniard complained that "from the commercial point of view, the Philippines is an Anglo-Chinese colony with a Spanish flag." At this time, too, while the fear of Chinese violence subsided, the strong Chinese economic competition to the Spaniards and mestizos gave rise to significant anti-Chinese feeling among the Filipinos and Spaniards.[7]

On the land itself the Spaniards in effect recognized the position of the chief, and his political power over his subjects was transferred to ownership of land. In addition, the religious orders were given

7. On this see Eugene Wickberg, *The Chinese in Philippine Life* (New Haven: Yale University Press, 1965), p. 72 and Ch. 6 for figures.

large grants of land; by 1900 it was estimated that friar lands constituted close to half of the total agricultural land in the Tagalog areas of Luzon. In the sugar-growing islands a large plantation was usually owned by a single proprietor.

The owner-cultivator system was the predominant system of farm operation. In 1903 about 80 percent of the 815,000 farms were operated by owners; this included the haciendas of the sugar provinces which were operated by planters, who employed laborers and supervised their work directly or through managers. The remaining 20 percent of farms were operated by tenants; by far the predominant form of tenancy was share tenancy, although cash tenancy was not uncommon, and on some lands (such as friar-owned) both types were combined. In share tenancy usually one-third of the produce was the reward for each factor of production—land, labor, and work animal-supplied; where no work animal was required, the tenant and landlord shared on a 50–50 basis.

It was customary in most regions of the country for the landlord to call upon his tenants for group labor at harvest time, to repair and build houses, ditches, and mills. Protracted work merited wages, while sporadic . . . labor was compensated by gifts from the landlord. . . . The tenant expected the landlord to defend him in all civil matters. . . . [The landlord looked upon his tenants] as poor relatives (which they often are) for whom he is somewhat responsible, and being recognized by the tenants as a superior personage.[8]

These tenancy arrangements were reinforced by the fact that the landlord provided credit for his tenant, with effective interest rates ranging from 50 to 500 percent per year; when debts were repaid in kind, the landlord took the rice at a price below the market price, sometimes reselling it to the tenant later at a much higher price. It was through such loans, with high interest rates and accumulating debt, that the landowner held the tenants on the land. This control was strengthened by the fact that the agreements were generally unwritten and the length of tenure was for only one planting season, at the landlord's discretion.

While political rule over the country was Spanish, this was cen-

8. John J. Carroll, *Changing Patterns of the Social Structure in the Philippines* (Quezon City: Ateneo de Manila University Press, 1968), pp. 7–29.

tralized in Manila, with the friars serving as the main intermediaries between Manila and the country. In the rural areas larger landowners, so-called *illustrados*, often of mixed blood, were dominant. There was a sharp split between the Spaniards and the Filipinos and "the failure of the Spanish regime to perform the basic service functions [of government], whereas . . . it forcefully collected levies . . . on people's property and labor,"[9] led to an alienation and estrangement of the government from the people. The Filipinos could only seek their own welfare and protection; this led to a further turning inward toward the family and a simultaneous withdrawal of transactions with the alien government. Eventually the result was a successful revolt against the Spaniards. The revolt, which began in 1896, was led initially by the artisans of Manila, but the leadership was taken over by the *illustrados*. It was followed by an unsuccessful struggle for independence with the United States, which lasted until 1902; the United States ruled the Philippines as an American colony until World War II. American rule in the economic field continued the trend of the nineteenth century—the establishment of free trade between the United States and the Philippines led to a massive expansion of Philippine exports of agricultural products in exchange for American manufactured goods. This increase in production was achieved by a great increase in cultivated land area. Most church lands were sold; land rights and landlord-tenant relations were legally confirmed by various surveys and laws. In the social field population had risen to over 19 million by 1948, shortly after independence, increasing at a rate of about 2 percent annually. There was a massive expansion of education at all levels, so that by independence there was approximately 60 percent literacy, with English spoken by many Filipinos. In the political field Filipinos were gradually permitted a large degree of self-government, and a constitution modeled in many respects on that of the United States was eventually adopted. But the government was in fact significantly different from that of the United States. Power *de jure* remained centralized in Manila, but *de facto* power was concentrated in the hands of the *illustrados*.

9. O. D. Corpuz, "Cultural Foundation," pp. 417–418.

These were the wealthy Filipinos, many of whom were *mestizo*, at the close of the Spanish regime. They had, by and large, little opportunity for political advancement in the Spanish scheme, and therefore had to go up the social ladder via nonpolitical avenues. In general, they were *hacenderos* or plantation owning families and real estate renters, with a number expanding the family fortunes in commerce. The American regime opened up the field of politics to this group. Its virtual monopoly of economic power and higher education immediately invested it with a practical monopoly of political leadership. . . . The roster of the higher bureaucracy and the membership of the pre-1941 Filipino legislatures are a veritable list of the *illustrados.* An even more striking demonstration of the existence of this elite would be a list of the family dynasties that make up the provincial and regional foundations of [the] political party system.[10]

In effect, this group "used the increasing self-government granted by the Americans to perfect a political system designed to perpetuate its political dominance."[11]

With some modifications since independence, this was the basis of the structure of power in Philippine rural society before the declaration of martial law in 1972.[12] Power was in the hands of large landowners, who were able to convert this economic power into political power through a patron-client social organization that extended from the barrios to the control of the political parties and the nonfarm sector of society.

The pressure of population growth since 1900 had resulted in a steady increase in farm tenancy. While in 1900 only about 20 percent of the farms were tenant operated, by 1960 approximately 40 percent were so operated, and it is estimated that this proportion probably reached 45–50 percent by 1970. Such tenancy is highest in rice farming; in 1960 the percentage of tenancy ranged from 70 to 85 percent in the rice-growing provinces of Central Luzon. While data with respect to the concentration of landownership or

10. Ibid, p. 414.
11. Frank Golay, "Some Costs of Philippine Politics," *Asia,* no. 23 (Autumn, 1971): 45.
12. Hereafter all description in the present tense will refer to the period before martial law was introduced in September, 1972. I have no way of knowing to what extent that event affected the social structure, although it clearly changed the functioning of the political system. However, I will not change the tenses, since to do so would only confuse the reader.

cultivation are generally lacking, some bits of evidence indicate a high degree of concentration. As one indication, while in 1960 the average size of farms was on the order of 3–4 hectares, the less than 1 percent of the rice farms which were over 500 hectares in size accounted for over 10 percent of the total rice hectarage. In a more recent sample study of 101 landowners in the two Central Luzon rice-growing provinces of Bulacan and Nueva Ecija, the bottom 50 percent of the landowners possessed only 6.2 percent of total rice acreage, while the top 10 percent possessed 72 percent.[13]

Not surprisingly, this skewed distribution of landownership is associated with a highly skewed distribution of rural family incomes. In 1965 the median rural family income was 1,359 pesos, but the 50 percent of all rural families receiving less than this income received only about 20 percent of all rural family income. In the rural areas the lowest 10 percent of all family income recipients received only about 2 percent of total rural family income, while the top 10 percent of rural family income recipients received about 30 percent of all family income (and the top 5 percent received about 20 percent). There is some evidence too that the distribution of rural family incomes has become slightly more unequal from 1956 to 1965.[14] Such a distribution of land and income, with its associated complicated systems of tenancy (largely sharecropping) and its related system of landlord-supplied or intermediary credit that provides the tenant or small farmer with credit for short-term production and consumption purposes at annual rates of interest which may reach 200–300 percent, is the economic underpinning of the rural patron-client system and its two-class social structure.

The social side of this system is glued together in part by family relationships (about one-third of the tenants are related to their landlords) and by an ethic requiring a redistribution of income in exchange for political support. In turn, this support from clients to

13. On the above see Carroll, *Changing Patterns*, esp. pp. 24, 99–104; U.S. Department of State, Agency for International Development, "Land Reform in the Philippines," mimeographed (Washington, D.C.: Agency for International Development, June, 1970), pp. 9–10.

14. See United Nations, Economic Commission for Asia and the Far East (ECAFE), "Distribution of Income and Wealth in the Philippines," mimeographed (Bangkok, 1971).

their patrons is the basis of power in the rural areas; such power is essential for prestige and influence, not only in the village but also on a provincial and even national scale. Wealth is a means of power, but a wealthy family without the power derived from support has little prestige and influence, as is shown most clearly by the case of wealthy Chinese in the villages.

The ethical basis for the patron-client relationship is the village belief that everyone has a right to live. Therefore, the patron family is obligated to provide its clients with at least minimal support in times of stress. The landlord-patron provides credit not only for production, but also for consumption and ceremonial expenses, as well as help for the education and job needs of his client-tenant. In exchange, the tenant provides

social and political assistance, for landlords often needed their tenants on ceremonial occasions, and were dependent on their support in various crisis situations, most often factional political disputes with other land-lords.... [The] obligations and responsibilities were reciprocal... [and] in moments of stress and celebration landlords and tenants would coalesce into mutually supportive groups.

Only slightly modified . . . this traditional pyramidal patterning of social relations continues today. . . . It is equally a model of political organization, though elaborated with smaller pyramids of reciprocal obligaton . . . between the poltical power holder and his ultimate constituency. . . . Should any party fail to maintain his upward or downward obligations those offended are considered fully justified in shifting their resources or allegiance to other rival groups or individuals . . . This pattern of interpersonal relations can be viewed as an interstatus redistribution system. While wealth and power . . . concentrate in the hands of a small group of persons, they are constantly sanctioned to use them for the benefit of their supporters. . . . [Popular] and personal regard (and thus effectively, political power in this "democratic" system) is founded on generosity in redistribution, particularly in times of stress for *either* those at the bottom or for those at the top of the power pyramids. Personal services and promises made and kept, and not ideolgical commitments or stands on particular issues, make a successful politician. Failure to provide favors or services . . . usually means rapid loss of support.

In this system one survives and succeeds on the strength of his vertical ties to those above and below. . . . For any particular individual these vertical ties are his most significant relationships. As a result, intrastatus alliances between relative equals are extremely fragile and tend to break when they conflict with interclass ties or obligations. . . . Horizontal solidarity is not characteristic of traditional lowland society.[15]

This system of relationships is supported by a set of psychological attitudes. Two of the key values in interpersonal relationships are "hiya," loosely defined as "shame"; and "utang na loob," defined as a "sense of gratitude," where each of the people involved knows his responsibilities or obligations. An individual's failure to fulfill the latter leads to a sense of shame, but the fulfilling of these reciprocal obligations is "strongly influenced by a system of ranking people, on the basis . . . among others, of belonging to the same political party, being barriomates or kin. Outside his immediate family the ultimate choice, for better or for worse, is his own."[16]

A major consequence of this pyramidal structuring of relationships is a very competitive and highly factional organizational structure. "Everybody wants to be boss. Labor leaders form splinter organizations if they can't boss their outfits. Student organizations proliferate . . . because every pretending student leader must be boss of one. Even politicians can't accept the truth that the other fellow is boss. That's why whoever is on top is cut to pieces."[17]

NATIONAL POLITICS AND GOVERNMENT[18]

Landé, in his 1965 analysis of national politics, stresses the outgrowth of the factional character of local politics into the national political structure. "Leaders of personal following in various villages and in the principal town of each municipality cluster together into competing provincial factions under the leadership of the men whose wealth and ambition are sufficiently great to make

15. David L. Szanton, *Estancia in Transition* (Quezon City: Ateneo de Manila University Press, 1971), pp. 84–87.

16. Mary R. Hollnsteiner, *The Dynamics of Power in a Philippine Municipality* (Quezon City: University of Philippines Press, 1963), p. 189.

17. Teodoro F. Valencia, "Over a Cup of Coffee," *Manila Times*, February 24, 1971.

18. It is obvious that with the introduction of martial law, the end of the existing party structure, and probable change in elections, many of these details have changed. But it is uncertain to what extent the general outline has changed or may change in the long run, except to eliminate competitors to President Marcos.

them aspire to provincial or congressional offices. Such provincial factions in turn form the building blocks of the national political parties." This political relationship is very similar to the reciprocal economic relationship between landlords and tenants, which is in turn based on the private wealth of the landlord. "The political leader's influence rests upon his ability to channel public funds into his village through the mobilization of followers or vice versa, and these funds are directed so as to maintain and possibly increase his following."[19] By association with the winning party, the local leader can get the public funds and jobs to retain a local following. In turn, the local leader who is wealthy can hope to build up a clientele by distributing his wealth. "[Persons] of wealth, either because they can deliver the votes of their clients, or because they can supply the funds with which a politician can buy votes, have a bargaining power vis-à-vis these politicians which far exceeds that of the ordinary villager, who has . . . [only] his own vote and maybe his family's."[20]

On a national level this is a major factor in the faction-shifting which characterizes Philippine party politics, as leaders and their followers continually switch to the party which seems best able to provide public funds. Such realignments are perfectly acceptable and occur at the highest levels.

Since kinship loyalties are the strongest and most dependable, there is a strong dynastic element in Philippine politics. Close members of the same family often hold key local, provincial, and national offices, thereby mutually supporting each other at all political levels. A distinguished columnist summarized the character of the Philippine political system in the following terms: "First of all, it is kinship oriented, not ideologically polarized. Second, it operates in the interest of patronage, not principles or issues, political or otherwise. . . . Third, it operates and prospers through familial alliances and federations of kinship blocs. . . . Personalism, loyalty and allegiance, are determined not by personal political beliefs but rather by outright blood relationship and personal closeness to the

---

19. Carl H. Landé, *Leaders, Factions and Parties* (New Haven: Yale University Southeast Asia Studies, Monograph no. 6, 1965), pp. 8, 12.
20. Ibid., p. 117.

protagonists involved."[21] The chairman of the commission on elections in 1971 declared "that elimination of the Political dynasties is so basically necessary that 'even if this reform alone is achieved by the new Constitutional Convention, the convening of the Constitutional Convention will not have been in vain.' " He stated that political dynasties led to a monopoly of power in a few families and were "the cause of compartmentalized justice, corruption and economic injustice" and "for overspending, fraud and terrorism in the election [as the dynasties], attempt to perpetuate themselves in power."[22] In turn, these dynastic relationships combine into regional geographic loyalties, center around a common language (or religion, in the case of the Muslim south), provide major sources of political support, and lead to major demands for regional distribution of funds.

Since the ability to tap public funds is the major source of power, it is not surprising that national elections are hotly and expensively contested. The president, senators, and congressmen are controllers of the public purse. Elections are expensive—it is estimated that 150 million pesos (about $75 million at the 1961 official exchange rate) were spent for all elections in 1961.[23] This equalled about 10 percent of that year's national budget, and about 1 percent of the GNP. The costs of election on a per capita basis in 1961 were higher than in the United States. Recently an obvious expert on this matter, ex-President Macapagal, publicly stated that "there is basis for the belief that 'on the average it costs from Pesos 200 to 500 thousand to run for congressman or governor, 1 to 3 million for senator and 50 and 100 million to run for president.' And he warned that unless arrested, this trend 'will make elective office a monopoly of the rich and privileged.' "[24] Alfredo Roces in two separate columns again puts this flow of funds into the broader personalistic context of Filipino politics. During elections, "the electorate becomes a demanding, grasping, opportunistic, patronage-oriented creature." Thus "an election is an expensive affair because

21. Alfredo R. Roces, "Political Division," *Manila Times*, April 5, 1971.
22. As reported in *Philippines Herald* (Manila), April 19, 1971.
23. David Wurfel, "The Philippines," in Symposium on Comparative Studies in Political Finance, *Journal of Politics* 25, no. 4 (November, 1963): 758–761.
24. As reported in *Manila Times*, October 4, 1970.

personal patronage and mechanics involves material tokens of support, whether it is for a sick person or a token given away. . . . The expense is not all in direct bribes or vote-buying, but because of this personalistic dynamics of patronage. . . . [Even] without . . . such illegal spending, money would still flow under our system."[25]

Teodoro Valencia relates these election expenditures to the government budget-making process when he points out that, in an election year especially, numerous appropriations are passed by Congress for all types of projects, but the funds are not made available. "There comes a time, however, a time like election time, when almost all projects are priority on the 'or else' basis." In order to find the funds, either special appropriations will be passed, or funds will be shifted by the president among budget items, or the government goes into deficit financing. In the 1969 elections 98 million pesos were legally transferred within the budget; during the first half of the 1969–70 fiscal year, which overlapped the 1969 presidential election campaign, the government had a deficit of about 600 million pesos with cash disbursements from the general fund exceeding operating receipts by 800 million pesos. One particular source of cash disbursement was the 160-million-peso barrio fund; within this fund 2,000 pesos were released to each barrio and about 50 million pesos were transferred from the fund to the executive office. (A similar barrio fund was voted in 1971 in time for those elections.[26]) Thus national elections serve as an occasion for the government to perform the redistributive functions expected of it, just as a feast provides the occasion for the village leader to perform these functions at the village level.

In a macro-economic sense the redistributive character of Philippine society has, as one of its major consequences, a peculiar, politically inspired business cycle. The effect of the large increases in government spending for elections, either through public works or by direct transfers, is to create a major boom every four years at the time of presidential elections and a minor boom every two years

25. Alfredo Roces in his column "Light and Shadow," *Manila Times,* September 5, 1969, and July 24, 1971.
26. See Valencia, "Over a Cup of Coffee," *Manila Times,* September 5, 1969; also news articles quoting Senator Aytona in *Manila Times,* February 3, 4, 1971; and editorial, *Manila Times,* May 2, 1971.

during senatorial elections. During these booms, foreign exchange reserves are drawn down. Wurfel writes:

During 1961 [a Presidential election year], the Philippines used up more than 75% of its foreign exchange reserves in large part because of the rush to collect funds from the kickbacks on licenses to purchase foreign currency. . . . Regulations originally designed to restrict imports, when manipulated for political gain, unleased [sic] a flood of imports and produced near disaster. Some inside dopesters claimed that 20 percent of licensed foreign exchange went into Nacionalista Party coffers. The businessman's motive was simple: no contribution, no license.[27]

The character of this 1961 experience reflected the foreign exchange control system existing from 1949 until 1962. After 1962, when the control system was ended, election years were still characterized by a large increase in domestic spending, but now also by an increase in government guarantees of foreign exchange credits to industry. The effect of this in the 1969 election was another business boom, characterized by a drawing down of foreign exchange reserves as both consumption and capital goods imports increased rapidly. After the boom of both these election years, with their drawing down of reserves, there was a period of austerity, during which exchange rates were revalued and government spending was held down.

Another obvious way in which the government plays the distributive role expected of it in Philippine society is by providing employment within the bureaucracy. Patronage is provided not only by spending, but also by directly providing jobs in the government. In 1945 the total level of government employment, including teachers, was 300,000 persons. By 1964 it had ballooned to 830,000, of whom almost two-thirds were unclassified—that is, they were appointed without any competitive examination, and thus were presumably appointed on mainly political or familial grounds.[28] While

27. Wurfel, "The Philippines," pp. 764–765. Sixto Roxas, "The Economics of Politics," *Business Day* (Manila) 2, no. 79 (January 16, 1969): 1–2 was one of the first to point out the political nature of the business cycle in the Philippines. See also Harvey Averch et al., *A Crisis of Ambiguity* (Santa Monica, Calif.: RAND Corporation, 1970), pp. 157–170. This study was subsequently published under the title *The Matrix of Policy in the Philippines* (Princeton: Princeton University Press, 1971).

28. The famous 50–50 arrangement of 1959 split all appointments to higher-paying government positions evenly between the president and Congress.

only about half the teachers were unclassified, approximately 75 percent of the national and local government employees (excluding teachers) were in this category. Mrs. Carmen Guerrero-Nakpil, a well-known columnist, has complained strongly about the "spectacular inefficiency" of government offices, based on her experience as the peso-per-year head of the Historical Commission. She stated that in that commission only eight out of eighty-nine employees "do any significant work." She describes the Philippine government as "the most labor intensive industry in the world: it takes ten people to do the work of one, and ten times as long" and suggests, half humorously, that government employment is a form of unemployment relief. In a subsequent column about the resignation of Secretary of Education O. D. Corpuz because "I am tired of everything," she describes again her experience with the Historical Commission, arguing that Secretary Corpuz had become tired for the same reasons she had. The Philippine civil servant believes that

a good boss should . . . be involved with his employees in degrees of relationship that range from that of parent to that of accomplice, but always in an intimacy that is repugnant to anyone accustomed to the more modern, impersonal ways of more developed communities. . . . I failed [in the Historical Commission] because I wanted to introduce change while remaining myself and refused to play "Mother" or "Pal" and violated the tenets of self-esteem and prestige and otherwise insisted on a thoroughly modern—all right, Westernized—developed, strict impersonal attitude while enforcing rules and expressing imagination and rationality outside of a traditional social structure which I believed to be feudal and indefensible even on pragmatic grounds. This is—writ large—also what happened to Secretary Corpuz.[29]

The effect of such a system is not only inefficiency but also corruption within the government. "The corruption of a particular public office, local or national, can be gauged by the behavior and the fortunes of the relatives and close associates of the public official. The public official either tolerates the corruption and the misuse of his office by relatives and friends . . . or else the official himself is the corruptor who needs the implementing agencies of relatives and confidantes." And the *Manila Times* printed an item

29. Carmen Guerrero-Nakpil, *Sunday Times Magazine* (Manila), March 7 and April 18, 1971, in her column.

that indicates a commonly held belief: "widely known businessman and entrepreneur reportedly suggested . . . that kickbacks should be standardized. . . . The kickbacks should be on a fixed percentage basis depending on the assistance extended by the government and its instrumentalities. This way . . . applicants for government assistance would know exactly just how much they will have to spend on their projects."[30]

In an attempt to get away from this bureaucratic inertia and inefficiency, a new president often appoints someone outside the bureaucracy to head those activities which he particularly desires to push. The appointee may be a so-called technocrat educated outside the country and associated with a modern business establishment in the city. The president at the same time may set up a new agency for this activity. But the purpose of this new agency is specifically to bypass the inefficient bureaucracy, and to reduce, if not eliminate, the inevitable political pressures in that area.[31] This also contributes to a proliferation of agencies, since they are rarely abolished, and succeeding presidents often have other priorities.

Under the system the president is extremely powerful, since he is at the top of the patron-client system. As winner of the national election, he is the source of most patronage, and his programs will have a major effect on the distribution of public funds. As party leader he plays a major role in determining who shall or shall not receive funds; as chief executive he is responsible, directly or indirectly, for national appointments, and if his party controls local governments, he plays a role in those appointments also. It is not purely coincidental that the president personally hands out the checks to be distributed to barrio leaders under the barrio fund. But the president's main source of strength lies in his control of the government budget. This control arises from the patronage character of the entire system.

Congressmen are elected and reelected largely on the basis of

30. A. R. Roces, *Manila Times*, May 5, 1971, in his column, and *Manila Times*, May 11, 1971, "Business Log."

31. O. D. Corpuz, "The President and the Bureaucracy," *Solidarity* (Manila), 3, no. 7 (July, 1968): 3–8. This short article gives a very informative picture of the changing character of the bureaucracy in relation to Filipino society, politics, and history.

their ability to channel funds to their districts. This is normally done through the budget, and a congressman hopes to win support by proposing items for the budget for his district. Under the normal procedure the president proposes the annual budget, and after discussion and amendments Congress passes a budget act. "The total income of government each year is fully appropriated in the annual budget act. Congress then proceeds to other laws appropriating more funds but without corresponding revenue-raising measures. But Congress does not repeal previous continuing appropriations and the invariable result is the accumulation of such bills. Currently more than 10 billion pesos of continuing and other appropriations exist to be funded from an already committed 4 billion pesos of annual income." This great overhang of continuing appropriations beyond the budget and exceeding annual revenues, as well as the legal flexibility in use of funds, in effect gives the president great power. He is able "to authorize government expenditures not strictly in accordance with any specific annual budget act. . . . The President therefore selects the projects which are to be funded from income, in accordance with priorities he adopts for any operating period."[32] In an election year he uses this legal power to help himself and his friends.

With such large funds and such powers an obvious question is, how could any president be defeated? In fact, until President Marcos's reelection in 1969, no president had ever been reelected. These defeats reflected the inability of the president either to achieve substantive results, or to satisfy the factional groups supporting him for the gains to be derived from that support. Past presidents (with the notable exceptions of President Magsaysay, who died in midterm, and President Marcos, who received credit for success in agriculture) have been vulnerable to criticism of failing to achieve results. A general pattern of a president's four-year term has been that the first two years are devoted more to new, substantive programs and less to programs to reward his followers and fulfill the promises made during the election. The second half is devoted to trying to satisfy the various regional and factional

32. O. D. Corpuz, "Philippine Public Administration: Performance and Challenges," *Asia*, no. 23 (Autumn, 1971): 30, 32.

elements among his supporters, in order to gain reelection. During this phase the programs of the first two years often evaporate into widely diffused expenditures with little result. At the same time, his limited budget resources (in relation to the promises he had made to his followers and to those members of the opposition whom he seeks to win over) inevitably mean that many of his supporters or potential supporters do not get what they feel they deserve. This leads to dissatisfaction that may turn to outright opposition, and eventually many factions turn to others who promise more. Thus there is a failure to meet expectations of both that segment of the public that looks for performance and the factional leaders. When this is combined with charges of corruption and graft beyond what the public will tolerate, the electoral response has been to "turn the rascals out." The voters of Manila are considered more likely than rural voters to vote on grounds of performance rather than faction; it is significant that, except in the 1969 elections, Manila has always voted against the incumbent. "The upsets of the President and his party are a negative repudiation by the electorate, not a positive endorsement for the [expected] minority candidate and his party."[33]

The main reservoir for presidential candidates is the Senate. Senators are themselves national leaders since they are elected at large every six years. In their elections they must set up both a national network of factional alliances and a well-established base of financial support. As a result all senators, regardless of party, consider themselves as potential future candidates for president or vice-president; all past presidents except President Magsaysay have been senators. Incumbent President Marcos was the leader of the Senate and president of the Liberal party in 1965, when he quit the Liberal party to run as candidate of the Nationalist party against incumbent President Macapagal of the Liberal party. In the 1969 election Senator Magsaysay, the late president's brother, left the Nationalist party to run as vice-president on the Liberal ticket. Since senators are such potential candidates, they are in turn interested in building up their own power bases within their home provinces, as well as nationally, and are frequently major critics of

33. O. D. Corpuz, "The President," p. 6.

the president. This criticism occurs within the president's own party before elections, since independence appeals to the voters, and is expected.

In contrast, congressmen represent districts; they are major channels of funds and patronage between the national government and their districts, if they are of the president's party. In any case, they are often interested in moving to the top of a hierarchy. While the president is strong, the power of Congress does serve as a serious challenge, even though the president's party may control Congress. The challenge arises out of the competition for future power. This competition between equals for status enhancement aborts attempts at cooperative action or movements; it is at the root of the political system, and extends from the village barrio to Malacanang.[34]

ECONOMIC IMPLICATIONS OF THE SOCIAL STRUCTURE

It would certainly be expected that Filipino peasant society, combining as it does a patron-client system with political power concentrated in a relatively small though factionally split and open group, a strong redistributive ethic, and a high degree of family-centeredness, would have major consequences for the economic policies adopted and the development process. Furthermore, since the characteristics of peasant society would be especially strong in rural areas, their direct effects on the peasant's response to agricultural innovation in rice production also would be expected to be strong. In addition, through their consequences on the character and implementation of public policies in the agriculture sector and for industrial development, there would be indirect effects upon agricultural development.[35]

Agricultural Development: Rice Technology

Historically, Philippine development has been based largely on the exploitation of the country's land resources to increase output

34. The Philippine White House.
35. See Ch. 2, above.

of foodstuffs for domestic use, and of export crops for foreign exchange earnings which permitted manufactured imports. In this process, increases in the physical productivity of land have played only a minor role.

The basic calorie intake of the population has been provided by domestic production of rice and corn and per capita production of these cereals has remained relatively stable since 1920. Over this period, the per capita area planted to rice and corn has shown no tendency to increase, which . . . means that yields (in the aggregate) also have remained relatively stable. In other words, Philippine agricultural development since 1920 [to 1965], has been essentially a process of expanding land under cultivation at a rate approximating the rate of population growth.

Since 1959, however, the marked decline in the rate of increase in cultivated area, the relatively lower yield of the land in the new areas, and the shift to corn production in those new areas because of its advantage over rice all underline the fact that the surplus land which in the past made possible the expansion of acreage has been largely exhausted. Even before the introduction of the higher-yielding rice varieties, the national average yield per hectare remained roughly constant only because rising yields in Central Luzon through new irrigation offset the declines in yields in the more recently opened areas. With respect to the two major export crops, there do not appear to have been any sustained increases in yields of coconuts, while a diminishing yield of sugarcane on new land has more than offset the increase in average yields due to technological improvements on the richer lands.[36] For these food and export crops future increases in output to meet both the internal consumption needs of a population growing at 3 percent per year, and the export requirements associated with continued growth of the economy, are dependent on significantly increasing the productivity of existing land.

Failure to raise yields in the past reflected both the lack of urgen-

---

36. The above is based largely on two secondary sources: Frank H. Golay and Marvin E. Goodstein, *Rice and People in 1990* (Manila: U.S. Agency for International Development, 1967), pp. 13–24 (quotation on p. 16); and George L. Hicks and Geoffrey McNicoll, *Trade and Growth in the Philippines* (Ithaca, N.Y.: Cornell University Press, 1971), pp. 196–203, 228.

cy of the problem, and the absence of technological innovations sufficiently attractive in economic terms to warrant their adoption on a large scale, when the risks were considered. Jocano examined the technological and social problems which thwarted the introduction of new seeds in a rainfed Visayan village in 1963. In the area of technology itself, the older seeds and technology had been adjusted to the regional rainfall pattern and its variations; with the new seeds a delay in, or failure of, rainfall had far more unfortunate effects on the crop. In addition, because of their growing cycle the new seeds were far more attractive to insects and rats than the older seeds. Both these factors discouraged use of the new seeds after the first trial.

Even more important were certain social factors. One of the most important arose from the fact that the appeal to introduce the new seeds was made by the extension workers to the younger, more educated, and presumably more venturesome farmers; when the extension workers left, the influence of the older farmers, who are highly respected by virtue of their age and experience, was against the innovation. But probably the most important limiting factor was the network of duties and obligations which a farmer assumes in relation to his family. "[The] more rice he has, the more relatives he has to support; the less produce he has, the less are his troubles. Weighing the two choices on the same practical level . . . most farmers commented 'having just enough is all right.' This was indeed the prevailing consensus of opinion in the barrio when I was there." In addition, in this village, where sharecropping was common, the sharecropping farmers lived on a very small financial margin. The new method required more money to purchase fertilizers and pay for laborers. While landowning farmers could afford to use the new method, the sharecroppers could not, because of the money and risks involved. "[One] failure . . . would mean one long struggling year; a peso for fertilizer would mean deprivation of other household needs. . . . The success therefore with [the landowning farmers] did not mean very much. The traditional method of farming assured the cultivators of at least six months' supply of food without the risk of losing it; a peso meant a dress for the child."

In fact, the efforts of the extension workers were criticized as "only helping the rich become richer."[37]

In another area in a village of Central Luzon, Takahashi observed in his 1963–64 study that almost all the cultivators were sharecropping on a 50–50 arrangement. They had little interest in the management of their farm and little incentive to raise output. Most seemed to depend for a large part of their income on off-farm earnings. Furthermore, the system of wage payment in cash or kind to hired laborers, most of whom were relatives of the tenants, was a disguised method of redistributing and retaining output among all the cultivators within the village. In fact, he felt that there was little difference between the share tenant and the wage laborer and that both were "much proletarianized." Thus he concluded that "the significance of farmland for [the cultivators] was not so much the means of creating profit from agricultural production but the basis of [proprietors'] guarantee for their livelihood."[38]

Yet within five years of both Jocano's and Takahashi's 1963 field work, which indicated apparent deep-seated social resistances underlying the peasant's reluctance to introduce technological changes in agriculture, the situation changed drastically, and Filipino farmers adopted new technology that significantly raised the productivity of their land. Takahashi, who revisited his village in April, 1971, was struck by the change in attitude and its results.

On a national scale, between the biennium 1964/66 and 1969/71 rice production grew at 4.6 percent per annum. It is estimated that the increase in yield due to the adoption of new high-yield varieties with their associated inputs was responsible for a 2.7 percent increase in output per annum (or over half of the total). In addition to this, and closely related to it, there was an increase in the amount of crop area irrigated from about 30 percent in the early 1960's to 45 percent in 1969/71. (In the 1950's irrigated crop area rose from about 20 percent to only about 28 percent of the total.) In spite of

37. F. Landa Jocano, *The Traditional World of Malitbog* (Quezon City: University of Philippines Press, 1969), esp. Ch. 15. Quotations from pp. 354, 353.

38. Akira Takahashi, "Proletarianization of Kasama Tenants," mimeographed (Los Banos, Philippines: International Rice Research Institute, August 19, 1971), pp. 1–4.

this marked increase in output, which brought the Philippines to the margin of self-sufficiency by 1969, the yield gains were, to quote an IRRI expert, "not . . . as great as might have been anticipated."[39] In the 1971 wet season, as a result of tungro, a virus disease which attacked both old and new varieties but which was possibly more virulent with the latter, there was no increase in output.

To what extent were those changes influenced by the character of Philippine peasant society, as it may have affected either the peasant's response directly, or the broader environment within which the peasant functions? In Chapter 2 it was argued that a major influence on the peasant's response was the farmer's lack of control over his environment, the risk thereby associated with new technology, and the resulting communal structure of society as a way of minimizing loss rather than maximizing output in a general low-productivity economy. It was also argued that this risk would be less for farmers with larger resources: more land, more capital, or better access to finance. The risk element for all farmers was in fact greatly reduced prior to the introduction of the new high-yielding seeds. This was achieved in a variety of ways.

First, much of the research and testing prior to the use of the new seeds was carried out at the International Rice Research Institute (IRRI), which had the benefit of some of the best international research experience in developing new agricultural technology. This by itself reduced the cost of research for the Philippines, while the range of seeds experimented with and the mass-production research technology of IRRI made possible the breakthrough. The farmer himself had continuous past experience with new seeds and was therefore accustomed to trying new varieties.

Second, the new seed technology did not obviously disrupt existing social patterns; in fact, it promised the individual farmer a greater output without changing his relationships within the village. The tests also promised potentially high gains, with yield in-

39. International Rice Research Institute, "Annual Research Review: Agricultural Economics," mimeographed (Los Banos: IRRI, February, 1972), p. 2; Randolph Barker et al., "Employment and Technological Change in Philippine Agriculture," mimeographed (Los Banos: IRRI, October, 1971), Table 2; quotation from R. Barker, "The Asian Experience with High Yielding Rice Varieties—Problems and Benefits," mimeographed (Los Banos: IRRI, October, 1971).

creases up to 100 percent, if the seeds were used in an irrigated water-control area and the entire package of new technology was adopted. On the other hand, if the new seeds were adopted without the additional inputs, the expected yields would not be less than from the old varieties.

Third, the government, by its policy of expanding the irrigated area, contributed to enlarging the area in which water control was possible, and thus the area in which it would be profitable to use the new inputs for reaping the potentially high yields. Fourth, the government price support policy guaranteed the farmer a satisfactory price for his outputs. In addition, before the devaluation of early 1970, the key ratio between the price of fertilizer paid by the farmer and the price he received for rice was less than 1.0, and thus favorable for the use of fertilizer. The existence of an effective fertilizer distribution system insured that the farmer could buy fertilizer if he wished to do so and had the funds.

On the national level the government had always given a high political priority to achieving self-sufficiency in foodstuffs. President Marcos, immediately after his accession to office in 1966, took advantage of the availability of a new rice technology to centralize and energize the existing bureaucratic machinery in this field by inserting in it his executive secretary, Mr. Salas, one of the most dynamic technocrats in the country. By his power, and by his close supervision of field operations, he played a significant role in implementing the rice and corn production program.

When new seed was introduced into a village, the first user was usually someone who had heard about the seeds from an outsider— possibly a larger landowner or commercial farmer in the region who had tried it and was attracted by its profit possibilities. The initial success of these outsiders, and the activities of commercial dealers in inputs, in turn encouraged smaller landowners and tenants to try the new varieties and the new inputs. Interestingly enough, the role of the extension workers did not seem to be of major importance.[40]

40. See Gelia T. Castillo, "Impact of Agricultural Innovation on Patterns of Rural Life," in Southeast Asia Development Advisory Group, *Agricultural Revolution in Southeast Asia* (New York: Asia Society, 1970), II, 16–18; Shigeru Ishi-

A crucial factor in the use of the new inputs, without which the potential yields could not be achieved, was the landlord. Various studies of the use of credit on rice farms show that the landlord is the source of over 50 percent of the short-term credit; clearly landlords supplied credit to their tenants to enable them to buy the required inputs. In Laguna credit to tenants rose four- to five-fold after the new varieties were introduced; it was supplied either directly by landowners, or by a rural bank, with the landowner serving as a channel to his tenant or as a guarantor to the bank for its loan to his tenant.[41]

The effect of these cooperating factors—international research, government actions and policies, landlord's credit, and farmer response—was that by 1970–71 close to 60 percent of the total lowland rice area had been planted in the new varieties; two-thirds of the irrigated area was so planted, and 45 percent of the rainfed area, since even on land without water control the expected yields were higher with the new seeds.

Unfortunately, there is no systematic detailed nationwide analysis of the effect of varying social systems or tenure arrangements on adoption. Owners of larger farms or commercial farmers with strong financial bases were the first adopters; but in the Philippines smaller farmers and tenants have followed rapidly. In fact, in one area that was closely surveyed, there was little relationship between speed of adoption and size of farm, and yield per hectare was higher on the smaller farms. There also seems to be little relationship between type of tenure and productivity of land, on the national level.

However, it is interesting that Takahashi felt that the shift from sharecropping tenancy to leaseholding in the village that he revisited was a major factor in persuading farmers to use the new varieties and the associated technology. He found that, following this institutional change, the use of the new varieties was encour-

kawa, *Agricultural Development Strategies in Asia* (Manila: Asian Development Bank, 1970), Ch. 2.

41. See the interview with Randolph Barker in Ralph Diaz, "Interviews on the Social Implications of the Green Revolution in the Philippines," mimeographed (Bangkok: UN Asian Institute for Economic Development and Planning, June, 1970), pp. 150–151.

aged by a marked change in the attitude of the farmers. "Cultivators, who used to give little attention to their crops, are now getting more and more concern[ed] with their farms. Almost everyday they attend their field, watch conditions [of] palay [rice], regulate water level. . . . Labor relations between cultivators and workers are becoming more contractual. Communal customs . . . through which a portion of output was distributed among neighbors are diminishing. . . . In short, cultivators are acquiring initiatives as farm operators. . . . They are getting more independence from both proprietor and village community, and are more attached to their land."[42] This too may be related to various IRRI studies which find that personal interest and management is a key element in determining a farmer's success with new seeds, although the IRRI studies did not associate such management with type of tenure.[43]

While Takahashi remarks on the reduced use of hired labor in his village, on a national scale there has been little evidence of displacement of labor for the Philippines as a whole. "Reduced labor requirements for land preparation have been more than offset by increased labor requirements for weeding and harvesting." In the harvesting and threshing the laborers normally receive one-sixth of the yield in kind under long-standing communal arrangements; it is not likely that they will readily accept either a reduction in their shares, or displacement by machines. But with the larger rice harvest from the new technology "there is a potential source of conflict between farm operators and harvesters to determine who has a claim to this added source of profit."[44] Although such conflict is more potential than actual at this time, there has been some evidence of increased mechanization of agriculture. In the past this resulted more from such government policies as an overvalued exchange rate, legal minimum wages for farmers, and a lending program supported by a loan from the International Bank for Reconstruction and Development (IRBD) to provide credit for tractor purchases, rather than from owner-laborer conflict over gains from

42. Takahashi, "Proletarianization," pp. 5–6.
43. R. Barker et al., "The Changing Pattern of Rice Production in Gapan . . . 1965 to 1970," mimeographed (Los Banos: IRRI, December 11, 1971), pp. 5–7.
44. See R. Barker, "Employment and Technological Change," quotations from pp. 22, 20.

the new technology. When the Philippines devalued in 1970, this had an immediate contrary effect on purchase of imported farm machinery. This does not indicate the role of policy in this area, but it points out the value of policy in supporting labor-intensive farming. This is especially important since the new rice varieties clearly require less labor per unit of output than the older ones, and in the longer run, if the Philippines reaches self-sufficiency, less labor will be required for total rice production.

There is no evidence from the one existing study that the gains from the new technology were limited to the landowners or larger farmers. In 1966, before the introduction of the new varieties in the one area studied, the net output was divided as follows: 43 percent to the landowner for provision of land; 37 percent to the tenant for providing carabao, tools and equipment, family labor and supervision; and 20 percent to hired labor. Following the introduction of the new seeds, the increased net was divided 43, 32, and 25 percent. In the particular area studied all groups gained absolutely; the labor group also gained relatively because of greater demand for hired labor, while the tenant, who paid the laborer, paid out of his share. These figures of course do not consider the potential longer-term gains to the landowner from rising land values; nor do they say anything about the daily wage rate for hired labor, which has not increased, and may in fact have decreased slightly in real terms over this same period.[45] The latter would certainly indicate that there has been little if any positive effect on the numbers employed in rice production for the nation as a whole.

Until now the experience with the new varieties has been too short to reach definitive conclusions with respect to the interaction between the new technology and the social and political structure. What is known, as of early 1972, seems to be based more on single-village or area studies and general impressions. But to summarize, there was no evidence that the adoption of the new varieties, and the gains arising from them, have been restricted to larger farmers. Second, the role of the government was important in the results,

45. R. Barker, "The Asian Experience," p. 12; Keith Griffin, "Economic Aspects of Technical Change in the Rural Areas of Monsoon Asia," mimeographed (Geneva: UN Research Institute on Social Development, January, 1972), pp. 16–18.

primarily through its programs of extending irrigation and price support, and less through its research and extension program. In the research area a key element was an international research effort, centering around the International Rice Research Institute located in the Philippines, and carrying on its experiments and testing in a local environment. Third, there was some evidence that the landowner, as the major source of increased credit to his tenants, has played a key role in making possible the use of the new technology. There was some question over the role of the land reform legislation on this; the possible higher rents after the introduction of new varieties and the attempt to persuade share tenants not to shift to leasehold may have encouraged the landowner to supply credit. On the other hand, this may have discouraged tenants from moving into the new varieties, since they would have to pay higher rents after leasehold, although the achievement of leasehold apparently provided a stimulus to adopt new attitudes.[46] Fourth, employment had not been affected *in toto* by the new technology and the associated greater mechanization of specific operations; but in the short run this seemed to have been more in response to government economic policy which made the mechanization profitable, rather than to other factors. Fifth, there was some evidence that the new varieties increased the possibility of conflict between different farm groups over such issues as splitting of gains and introduction of machinery, which may become more significant as relations between landowner and tenant or tenant and hired laborer become more contractual than customary. Sixth, a basic reason behind the extension of contractual relationships was the high cost of the new inputs, which made possible the potential high gains from the new varieties. There is less willingness to share on traditional lines, since sharing gains from these new investments promises to deprive investors of larger returns while it gives high returns to those who are not investing. Similarly, the new machinery and equipment is too expensive to lend out on traditional sharing lines, and both owner and user prefer more precise contractual

46. Apparently President Marcos, following his declaration of martial law, has taken steps to implement land reform by providing land ownership to tenants of larger farmers. It is probably too soon to evaluate the effects of this type of reform upon the use of the new technology.

arrangements. With respect to hired labor, in comparison to traditional relationships, such contractual arrangements call for greater direct supervision of hired labor by the cultivator and reduce any informal responsibilities for the laborer on the part of the cultivator. Thus the acceptance of a new production technology also weakens the constraints to its use from the communal arrangements associated with older technology. In the long run the possibilities of gain with the new technology seem to be creating a breakout of the former "limited good" horizons, as it shows possibilities of far higher gains than previously anticipated. When associated with new tenure forms, these potentialities probably contribute to an improvement in the management and care of the farm as compared to past practices in the Philippines; they have also led to a series of expectations of continued higher yields, and a demand for education and higher goals for the children and for new goods that can be revolutionary for future production and social arrangements on the farm.

But there are serious questions as to the past and future of the new technology. The actual achievements have never approached the potentialities, but the reasons for this are not well known. Certainly its use on rainfed lands is far less than on irrigated lands, and without still further expanded irrigation the possibilities on rainfed lands are severely limited. More recently the outbreak of tungro, a virus disease, has severely reduced production of new and old varieties; relatively little is known as to how to control its transmission, although some of the new seed varieties are more resistant than others.[47] Apparently the high cost of insecticide has also served to discourage farmers from purchasing both fertilizers and insecticides, and the lack of the latter contributes to the spread of the insects carrying the virus.

These recent developments raise an obvious question as to the consequences of the past lag in the land-reform program on the use of the new varieties.[48] If Takahashi's village is representative of

47. See the article "Tungro Comeback Feared," *Sunday Times* (Manila), March 12, 1972, p. 28; also discussions with R. Barker and G. T. Castillo, above.

48. Since President Marcos declared martial law, land reform has apparently been implemented especially as it affects the larger landowners and their tenants. But the information now available on this is slight; what follows is based on the situation prior to that action.

others, the shift from a 50–50 share-tenancy to a fixed-rent lease-hold with rents a maximum of 25 percent of net harvest would have a significant effect in developing new attitudes among farmers and a greater willingness to adopt new varieties. However, the secretary of agriculture himself stated in 1971 that

eight years after the passage of the Land Reform Code in 1963, there is little of substance in the accomplishments under the law. . . . So far, land reform has made a modest start in Central Luzon. Leasehold systems now cover some 200,000 rice farmers working in an area of some 400,000 hectares. . . . However, these newly converted leaseholders represent less than half of all tenants throughout the country. Moreover, only a few of these farmers have written lease contracts with their landlords, and only some 13 percent have verbal agreements. In fact, in most cases a disguised share-tenancy system continues, although it appears that a larger share of the crop is now given to the tenant. Agrarian reform, therefore, has far more form than substance in the Philippines. . . . The unsatisfactory credit situation, coupled with the lack of funds to acquire tenant-operated land for redistribution to cultivators [because Congress had deleted a land-tax provision in the original law] . . . has effectively crippled agrarian reform efforts to date.[49]

All who have written on land reform agree on the need to strengthen the rural credit system to replace the landlord if land reform is to succeed. With the introduction of a fixed-rent leasehold system, the first step under the land-reform procedure, the landlord is often no longer willing to act as a supplier of credit. Unless an effective alternative source is developed for these new leaseholders with government support, the entire program may easily collapse. The relationship between land reform, credit, and a poor harvest is made explicit in one village whose rice crop was hard hit by the tungro virus: "The major problem facing many farmers . . . due to the poor rice harvest is lack of credit to purchase fertilizer. This situation is particularly critical among many farmers . . . who have switched to leasehold and can no longer borrow from the landlord."[50]

Thus the possible effects of land reform on production would

49. Arturo R. Tanco, Jr., "Philippine Demographic Realities, Agricultural Development and Social Stability," *Asia*, no. 23 (August, 1971), pp. 104–106.

50. "Changes in Rice Farming in Selected Areas of Asia," General Information Memorandum no. 4 (Los Banos: IRRI, March 3, 1972), p. 3.

appear to be contradictory, but with credit institutions set up to replace the landlord, the effects can be quite positive. Without an alternative source of credit until the peasant can build up his own resources, one poor harvest could throw the farmer back into dependency on his former landlord. In turn, share-tenancy arrangements contributed to the farmer's ability to raise credit resources for the new technology, but the indirect costs would have been high, if the long-term changes in motivation which can be so stimulating for the continued increase in output do not occur.

Some individual cooperative credit organizations have been set up successfully, but on a national scale these have faced serious problems arising from the highly competitive social atmosphere and a lack of trust of outsiders, as well as from technical factors such as the quality of both staff and loans. Perhaps most important, the cooperatives have lacked the flexibility of landlords and money-lenders in offering consumption credit and market facilities.[51] The tie-in of cooperative lending with the new rice technology has led to an expansion of cooperative credit, but the role of such lending is still minor.

The experience with the tungro virus also raises two further questions. First, after unfortunate experience with tungro, will the farmer return to old varieties and old attitudes, or will he try new varieties that appear to be disease resistant? The answer is not certain, but initially it appears to favor the latter response. His hopes have been whetted and aspirations raised, and therefore he will probably not go back to the old levels of output without a struggle. On the basis of a very small sample, it further appears that he is experimenting with disease-resistant varieties.[52] The second question is: does the research, testing, and extension capacity exist within the Philippines to continuously develop disease-resistant varieties as long as the new varieties show susceptibility to serious disease? IRRI may help, but it does not normally deal with local problems. There is general agreement on the high quality of the staff of the University of Philippines College of Agriculture, but

51. See Gerald E. Korzan and F. A. Tiongsan, 'The Agricultural Marketing System—The Cooperative Dimension," mimeographed (Manila: First Asian Conference on Agricultural Credit and Cooperatives, December, 1970), esp. pp. 2–4.
52. Based on conversations in March, 1972, with G. T. Castillo and R. Barker.

there is some question as to the quality of the extension service; and there are problems of cooperation and coordination among the various government agencies concerned with research on rice production.

Thus, apart from the technology, key constraints upon continued increases in rice output apparently exist in the structure of government. Congress, heeding pressures from large landowners, so weakened the funding of the land-reform legislation that little had occurred in that area before late 1972. The government had not succeeded either in setting up or in stimulating others to set up an alternative large-scale source of rural credit to replace the landlord, although institutional sources are gradually playing a larger role. "[A] large portion of the farmers in the land reform areas who still relied on private sources were ineligible for institutional loans either because of their characteristically small scale which provides no repayment capacity or because of payment delinquency."[53] Credit is the key factor limiting the farmers' ability to use new resources and, unless new institutional sources are developed by the government, both the long-term success of any future land reform program and the use of new technology by smaller cultivators are in jeopardy.

In the past the government's own capability in the areas of research and extension has been doubtful in terms of administering programs, gaining the confidence of peasants, and achieving results. Many of these problems arose from the nature of the government and the functioning of the bureaucracy. Formerly these programs did not receive high priority, so the farmers are skeptical of the government. The last few years have shown that improvement is possible, but future success of the effort to raise output will call for levels of performance in both research and extension that have been unusual in the Philippines.

Industrial Development

The close relationship between industrial and agricultural development has already been stressed. Industry provides the inputs

53. Leon A. Mears and M. H. Agabin, "Finance and Credit Associated with Rice Marketing in the Philippines," mimeographed (Quezon City: University of Philippines, School of Economics Discussion Paper no. 71–15, 1971), p. 21.

to the agricultural sector at a price that makes it profitable for the farmer to adopt a more input-intensive technology; in turn, the increased output from a developing agriculture serves as a stimulus to expansion of industrial investment, output, and employment.

In the Philippines such a mutually supporting relationship has not in fact developed; this weakness limits growth in both sectors. It is not the purpose of this paper to trace past industrial growth in the Philippines, which has been done in several other recent studies.[54] Past industrial development involved the import substitution of consumer goods whose production was protected from foreign competition by direct controls initially, and later by high effective tariffs on final products and overvalued exchange rates; in turn, backward linkage to intermediate and capital goods output was discouraged by relatively free import of those products. With the low level of income and highly skewed income distribution in the rural areas,[55] the consumer goods industries that did grow up produced largely for the urban market, especially Manila, and were concentrated around Manila.

In 1965 median family incomes in the urban areas were almost double those in the rural areas; median incomes in the Manila metropolitan region were also approximately 60 percent above those in other urban areas. The concentration of incomes among urban families was more highly skewed than among rural families. Among the former the bottom 10 percent received only 1.2 percent of total urban income, while the top 10 percent received about 40 percent. In fact, the evidence appears to show an increasing concentration of urban incomes in the ten years from 1956 to 1965, in spite of the significant industrialization that occurred between 1948 and 1965.[56]

This concentration of the gains from industrialization and urbanization put a rather narrow limit on the further possibility of expanding industrial growth on the basis of the internal market,

54. Among others see Jeffrey G. Williamson, "Dimensions of Postwar Philippine Economic Progress," *Quarterly Journal of Economics* 83 (February, 1969): 93–109; John H. Power and Gerardo P. Sicat, *The Philippines* (London: Oxford University Press, 1971); Hicks and McNicoll, *Trade and Growth.*

55. On this see p. 39 above.

56. ECAFE, "Distribution of Income and Wealth in the Philippines," mimeographed (Bangkok, January, 1972), pp. 12, 18.

while the high-cost character of the "hot-house" industry that developed restricted the possibilities of export markets for the industrial products which were being produced. As opportunities were exhausted, it was not surprising that the rate of industrial growth, as measured by the value added in manufacturing in constant prices, fell from 10 percent per annum in the period 1948–56 to about 6 percent in 1956–60, and to less than 5 percent in 1960–68. From 1964 to 1968 the annual rate of increase of value added in manufacturing was less than in agriculture. The import-substitution policy, in the environment in which it has occurred and carried to the extent it has been, led to a misallocation of resources to and within industry. This has been a major contributing factor not only to the declining rate of industrial growth per se, but also to the observed decline in the rate of improvement of total factor productivity in the 1960's.

But together with any economic rationale behind the industrial development policies and the resulting character of the industries, both those policies and character have been strongly influenced by the peasant nature of Philippine society. Several aspects of that society—its family-centeredness and its suspicion of business, and the patron-client relationship which includes a role for the industrial entrepreneur—have been particularly important in shaping past industrial growth.

Carroll, in his pioneering study[57] of Filipino entrepreneurship in an urban setting, found that "a major share of the original capital for the enterprise was provided in most cases by either the entrepreneur himself or his family; the entrepreneur or his relatives held the office of chief executive (both at the start and subsequently.)" Where a firm started with several family groups within it, Carroll noted that there were frequent disputes over the management, and in several such cases either one group won control or the firm split. Because of the difficulties of working together, and the pressures toward the redistribution of resources to claiming relatives, Carroll noted "the prominence of foreigners, both Chinese and Westerners, among industrial entrepreneurs in the Philippines."

57. John J. Carroll, *The Filipino Manufacturing Entrepreneur* (Ithaca, N.Y.: Cornell University Press, 1965), p. 158; and his *Changing Patterns of Philippine Society* (Manila: Solidaridad Publishing House, 1968), pp. 95–97.

When examining a rural fishing community, Szanton found a similar heavy weighting of successful entrepreneurs from among minority elements in the society—Chinese, Protestant, or migrant—and women. In Philippine peasant society these groups are either not required or unable because of their positions to play the patron role, with its diffuse responsibilities, normally expected of well-to-do Filipinos. Thus members of these groups could concentrate on running businesses and on plowing back their profits, apart from "protective" contributions they might have to make in elections.[58] On a larger scale, Carroll found that his entrepreneurs tended to come from commercial or commercial-agricultural fields and already had experience in freeing themselves from the traditional network of claims.

As a way of spreading the managerial and capital resources of the family, a type of management organization has developed in the Philippines that is not unlike the managing agency system introduced by British businessmen in India in the nineteenth century. This system enables a small group, family or otherwise, to control several separate firms and permits the group to move scarce management and capital resources freely among the firms so controlled. An example of this is provided in the case of the Philippine Air Lines Corporation (PAL); the working of this system was described in an interview with the chairman, Mr. Toda, Jr.

The first question, of course, was about PAL's interlocking business connections with three Toda-owned corporations. There was nothing wrong about it, asserted B. Toda, adding that such a scheme was a normal operating procedure in other business enterprises. . . . The issue is not whether these are interlocking connections, Toda went on, but whether such connections proved prejudicial to the principal company, in this case, PAL. While most management firms got a 3% management fee, Rubicon (the Toda managing firm) gets only 2.5%. In other words, the hiring of Rubicon by PAL was to the advantage of PAL. Toda went on to cite five firms which hired management firms for a fee of 3%.

Concerning Aeroben [a separate purchasing firm also controlled by Toda], Toda said that PAL did not have the expertise and the time to canvass spare parts abroad. Another company has to do it. . . . and this duty involves a lot of research, canvassing and even haggling.

For all these troubles, Aeroben is charging PAL only a 10% commis-

58. D. Szanton, *Estancia*, pp. 89–100.

sion, according to Toda. Other purchasing firms charge between 20 to 25% commission (and some charge 30%) for such services.

In addition, the insurance for PAL is handled by a third Toda-controlled firm.[59]

The purpose of this quotation is not to criticize PAL; it is primarily to show how this system operates in the Philippines, in the case of PAL as the central firm in the Toda group, and two very closely related enterprises. It is apparently used by other groups also to allow a single family to manage and distribute resources among a wide variety of activities without losing control.

Similarly, many of the large industrial groups are associated with, or have as part of their system, a bank and/or insurance company, which frees them from dependency upon external sources for their normal financial needs.[60] A major reason for this is to prevent being squeezed by another group in the event of a serious financial situation. Furthermore, prior to martial law, many of the largest family groups—Lopez, Soriano, Elizalde, Menzi, etc.—had major outlets in one or more media fields (newspaper publishing, TV, radio) under their own control. Through these media they could wield extensive political influence, which strengthened their hands in their dealings with the government.

But the family-centered character of the firm also has a pronounced limitation: the growth of a firm or group is limited by its own resources, financial and managerial, plus whatever assistance it can get from the government or from foreign investors without diluting its control significantly. For those industries in which a larger size of the producing unit yields economies of scale and thereby significant reductions in cost, the desire to limit control to the family sets an upper limit on size that is frequently too small for most efficient operation. An effect of this family-centeredness may be to discourage entry into an industry entirely. If entry does take place, it can result either in the establishment of a high-cost small firm that a single family can set up and run; or if a larger firm

59. E. R. Kiunisals, "Questions about PAL," *Philippine Free Press* (Manila), August 15, 1970, pp. 8, 69–70.

60. Senator Aquino claimed that "some 50 families control the 43 commercial banks, with family members siphoning off the available loan funds." See Beningo Aquino, Jr., "Reform or Revolution," *Pacific Community*, October, 1970, p. 200.

is set up with outside financing, it often starts with an unduly high debt-equity ratio and is thus potentially vulnerable in a time of stress.

On a national level the reluctance of entrepreneurs to go outside the family for resources, together with the reluctance on the part of outsiders to take a minority equity position in a family firm, reduces the level of private investment in industry. Hooley found that household savings increased markedly during the 1950's, but the weakness of the capital market meant that the sale of equities played only a negligible role in the transfer of resources from the household to the private sector. "The lack of substantial growth in the equities market assumes its proper significance when contrasted with the growth of saving. With household saving approximately Peso 450 million in the form of financial claims in 1960, compared with Peso 103 million in 1952, a [deflated] peso equities volume of about Peso 27 million does not offer promise as a major outlet for household saving. . . . [He concluded] that the demand for good [marketable] equities considerably exceeds the supply."[61]

This need for additional resources has forced the would-be industrialist to turn to the government or foreign sources for funds. (These in turn interrelate, since foreign credits often require a government guarantee.) The potential industrial entrepreneur thus has to enter the political system for favors from somebody who can influence the entrepreneur's ability to get those resources.

The Filipino seeking to become an entrepreneur finds himself engaged in familiar political manipulation—to obtain foreign exchange, credit, items of reparation, tax exemption, and so on. Initially he is half businessman and half politician, and to the latter role he can bring to bear his long experience and skills. . . . Not surprisingly, the system is distinguished by the concentration of entrepreneurial recruitment from the traditional political elite, who enjoy obvious advantages by reason of their political influence and skills.[62]

In the light of the high costs of elections there is an obvious channel for exchange of favors—business firms cover a large part

---

61. Richard M. Hooley, *Savings in the Philippines, 1951–60* (Quezon City: University of Philippines Institute of Economic Development and Research, 1963), p. 68.
62. Golay, "Some Costs," p. 48.

of the private costs of electioneering in exchange for the favors the successful political figure can provide. One former leading Filipino politician, Senator B. Aquino (now in confinement), has been quoted as stating,

Every Philippine President spawned his own set of millonaires. [Before the Republic] Quezon did it, to fund his political machine, and the millionaires he created repaid love with love. . . . Under the Republic, the successive sets of millionaires have been identifiable with their respective gold mines.

The first set was the surplus property millionaires under Roxas. Then you had the immigration-quota millionaires under Quirino; the import-control millionaires under Garcia; and Macapagal's government-financed millionaires: the Todas, the Delgadoes who put up the Hilton. Under Marcos we have the money manipulators.

Of each new set, a few millionaires will survive the passing of the regime, the rest will sink back to obscurity. . . . Those who survive "institutionalize" themselves . . . where before, they were identified with a specific administration, now they can influence any administration.[63]

How this system works is exemplified in the recent history of the cement industry.

As early as 1967 when there were already nine cement factories, a DBP [Development Bank of the Philippines] official already recommended that the bank stop buying equity and guaranteeing the purchase of cement plants. That recommendation, which was based on serious market studies, was thrown to the winds. Since then, five more cement factories were supported by the DBP. . . . Now the cement industry is hopelessly overcrowded. [It] is threatening to raise the price to Pesos 6.50 per bag in the face of a glut if only to raise funds to meet maturing and past due obligations with the DBP. . . .

Why did the DBP allow the establishment of more plants?

"We are helpless," a spokesman said. "Politicians come to us contesting the validity of our studies and practically telling us to approve their projects," he said.

Don't they know that the industry is crowded and therefore their proposals are not profitable?

A ranking leader of the cement industry had a very frank answer: They are interested only in kickbacks arising from the overprice in the purchase of cement plants.

63. Quoted in *Now Magazine* (Manila), October 30, 1970. In his Pacific Community article he stated that loans from government financing institutions were largely made to about a hundred families.

He said the average cost of Peso 12 million per plant is invariably raised to Peso 18 million or a kickback of Peso 6 million. With a Peso 6 million "profit," some plants do not care even if the DBP seizes the collateral. . . .

The "raid" on DBP funds happens every four years, or every presidential election year. A junior DBP executive said that during national election years all sorts of projects are presented for financing to the DBP.

The projects are almost always poorly studied and overpriced, resulting in their failures, he said.[64]

In the cement industry, the DBP is exposed to the extent of 800 million pesos. A similar pattern, with variations peculiar to it, has apparently occurred in the textile industry, where the DBP is exposed to the amount of 400 million pesos. The tie-up of its funds in these two industries makes it difficult for the DBP to lend to other potentially more economic industries. Similar charges of politically oriented loans and investment have been made with respect to other government financing institutions, especially the Philippine National Bank, which is heavily involved in the sugar industry and the Government Service and Insurance System (GSIS). This resort to government funds and guarantees has also led to the high debt-equity ratio characteristic of much of Philippine industrial financing. For example, in the Iligan Integrated Steel Mills, Inc., formerly in serious financial difficulties, the owning family had only 55 million pesos of its own money in equity; $30 million worth of shares were held by foreign companies, while the Philippine government had invested about 700 million pesos in the form of direct loans, preferred shares, and guarantees.[65]

While the social costs of such "political" firms are heavy, the private political entrepreneur behind them can make substantial personal profits even if their output is low and firm profits low or absent. Among the sources of such personal profits may be kickbacks from the firm's suppliers, and payments for managing the firm, supplying inputs, or selling the output. These private gains not associated with production can far outweigh gains from effi-

64. A. L. Locsin, "DBP Fund Ills Traced," *Manilla Times*, June 2, 1970, p. 10.
65. A. Macasaet, "Government to Force Steel Combine," *Manilla Times*, April 1, 1971. (Before January, 1970, the exchange rate was about Peso 4: $1; in August, 1971, it was Peso 6.50.)

cient production; their gains are closely associated with the political power process in the country. This is not to deny that there are many production-oriented Filipino entrepreneurs whose operations would be efficient by any standards. In fact, the political entrepreneurs are attracted by the legitimate profits of the former group, and they seek to use their political influence to enter these apparently profit-making fields. Over the longer run this process may in fact develop a permanent group of reasonably efficient entrepreneurs whose cost of entry has been borne by society. But the method of entry will have saddled the economy with a legacy of high-cost industrial firms, many of which are neither able to expand in the narrow domestic market, nor to compete effectively against international firms either in the domestic market without protection or in the foreign market. Because of the close connection between politics and industry, "the political system up to the present has not been able to change industrialization policy to impose a needed process of rationalization. . . ."[66]

Thus an industrial structure which is able to provide low-cost manufactured inputs to the agriculture sector has not developed, nor has a type of industry which is able to expand significantly on the basis of the positive effects of increased food output. (Although the latter should be qualified in light of the relatively short period of increased food output, during which there was a large devaluation which substantially raised local costs of investment.)

Equally significant, while industrialization led to a marked upward shift in the proportion of national product produced outside of agriculture during the 1950's, that proportion remained almost constant after 1960. Similarly, the share of employment in manufacturing has remained virtually unchanged since 1956 in spite of the growth in manufacturing output. This is explained by the relatively capital-intensive character of the industrialization that has occurred. Some of this capital intensification can be explained by government protection policies favoring capital goods imports and by minimum wage legislation and trade union policies which may have discouraged industrial employment. However, another and possibly more significant reason is the family-centered char-

66. Golay, "Some Costs," p. 59.

acter of the industrial entrepreneurship and the close relationship of entrepreneurship to political power. The resulting highly skewed distribution of capital resources has led to a valuation of capital for its private possessors which is far below its social cost. Those entrepreneurs who have access to these resources are encouraged to purchase imported capital equipment which may be supplied through supplier-financed credit, whose use is encouraged by the working of the political system.

One of the results of this is that the share of payrolls within total value added produced by the manufacturing sector is less than 30 percent, while the share of profits is over 70 percent; in fact, the share to labor declined somewhat between 1956 and 1966. This in turn contributes to a phenomenon remarked by many: in spite of industrialization, the real daily wage rates of industrial workers have also declined from 1955 to 1968.[67] With such concentration of benefits from the industrialization that has occurred, it is not surprising that with industrial development the distribution of urban income over the same period has become even more skewed in favor of the top decile of urban income recipients.

Another consequence has been that the employment effects of industrialization have been far less than they might have been if industrialization of a more labor-intensive type had been encouraged. This has contributed to a level of visible unemployment in urban areas in 1967 on the order of 10 percent, and to apparently significant rural unemployment and underemployment. It is significant that this urban unemployment is apparently concentrated in the younger age groups and is on the order of 20 percent among younger males. In a context of high literacy rates among the young, a significant movement to urban areas, and increasing political dissatisfaction among young people in the urban areas, these characteristics of a high degree of concentration of urban incomes, a high incidence of poverty, constant or slightly declining real wage rates, rather high unemployment, and underemployment concentrated among younger age groups can lead to serious political problems in the relatively near future, especially if similar trends are occurring

67. See Hicks and McNicoll, *Trade and Growth*, pp. 63–65, 90–93; also Power and Sicat, *Philippines*, pp. 53–58.

in the far larger and relatively more passive rural areas. The fear of these political effects contributed to the introduction of martial law by President Marcos in September, 1972.

On the basis of this analysis we have noted the strong influence of a rural-based, patron-client system in Filipino society, with the characteristics of hierarchy, redistribution of output, and distrust of business noted in the introduction. One significant element in Philippine society reflecting past historical forces is the absence of a national tradition before the arrival of the Spaniards. This, together with the ineffective and exploitative character of colonial rule, contributed to the present family-centeredness of both political and economic behavior. The cultural additions from the colonial period, such as Catholic religion and political democracy, have been adapted to these characteristics of Filipino society.

This structure of society, combined with an outward-oriented, land-centered food- and raw-material-producing economy, produced sufficient economic growth to support a growing population at levels of well-being accepted by that population. Since independence, an industrial sector has been established by various of the more enterprising and wealthier segments of the landed power groups in the society, in combination with minority elements of the population. This industrial expansion has been undertaken by those elements which have been able to utilize their traditional political power in the industrial sphere. This has been responsible for the character of the industrial sector and for the policies supporting it. While the gains have been concentrated in a small segment of the population, these have been redistributed in the past by the political organization functioning though a patron-client system, to an extent that made it possible for the country to avoid a level of unrest that could overthrow its political system. (The introduction of martial law by the present president did of course overthrow it.)

In the field of politics, control has been concentrated in a relatively small group of leaders at the top of the system. Political democracy permitted both extensive criticism and change in the leadership, although this was described as a game of musical chairs. Furthermore, the democracy that existed and the deep Filipino interest in politics, in association with the patron-client system operating at the local level, made for widespread popular participation in elections. The government, too, served as the major channel by which the redistributive ethic associated with the patron-client relationship functions on a national scale. While this has directly contributed to inefficiencies in the public sector and in industrial development patterns, it contributed to political stability under the system as it existed before September, 1972. The *New York Times*, in a perceptive article on the Philippines in 1971, contrasted "the violence of public talk and . . . gesture and the general peacefulness of the country." The same article pointed out the imbalance of power and wealth between the rich and the poor. The author quoted Senator Aquino as saying that it makes little sense to discuss such policy issues with the voters on the ground that "the rural Philippines is most of this country, and the rural Philippines is today one notch away from what Magellan discovered. You can't talk economic sense to people who don't take part in the money economy."[68]

But the economic problems are serious, and major steps will be needed to deal with them. Population is growing at an annual rate of more than 3 percent; at the same time, the empty lands of the past have disappeared. This calls for a continued increase in agricultural productivity on existing lands. Since 1967 the combination of new seeds and technology, expanding irrigation, and government policies have resulted in a strong positive peasant response, and yields have increased significantly. But the increase has never been as great as possible, and in the past three years weather and disease have sharply reduced the rate of growth in output. One must hope that the change in the recent past has also led to a widening of the peasant's horizons, a rising of his expectations, and a sharpening of his interest in improving yields from his land. However, several major questions arise for the future. After the recent disappointing experiences, will the peasant continue to use new varieties? If the answer to this is positive, as appears probable, will the government be able to mount the effort in research and exten-

68. Henry Kamm, "Unrest in the Philippines Is More Talk Than Deed," *New York Times*, October 4, 1971, pp. 1, 18.

sion to develop and spread, on a continuous basis, new disease-resistant varieties? Given past experience, the answer to this second question is more dubious. A third set of issues relates to the farmer's interest in expanding his output and improving efficiency. This may well be related to a more rapid spread of land reform and fixed rentals than has occurred in the past. Apart from this, the demand for land reform arises from some of the issues of distribution of political power and income associated with the existing patron-client system. However, there seems to be strong evidence that landlords have served as sources of credit for farmers to enable them to buy expensive inputs. In some cases this has been done to persuade tenant farmers not to abandon tenant status, or to help them raise their outputs in order to charge higher rents once land reform is introduced. In either case the landlord's ability and willingness to provide credit may decrease. Unless an effective institutional system of credit is set up for the small farmer, whether legally independent or not, he will not be able to get credit without in effect returning to a "real" tenancy, even though nominally independent. The government must effectively raise resources for a credit program and transcend past political and bureaucratic limitations to implement such a program. It had not been able to do this effectively with land reform legislation before martial law was introduced. But without both land reform and credit, achieving continued marked increases in yield is more difficult. Without such increases in output, even maintaining a growing rural population on the land without a decline in its well-being will be difficult, even apart from the goals of raising farm income and feeding a growing urban population.

The growing labor force and the high rate of urbanization call for increasing industrial growth. The family character of enterprise, the close mixture of politics and economics in industrial policy, and the highly skewed character of income distribution all limit possible rates of growth. The acceleration of industrial growth calls for a rationalization of industry and an enlargement of domestic markets through income equalization policies that may not be compatible with past policies and the structure of political-economic power in the country.

The public sector is regarded as inefficient in much of its operation, although at specific times it has done well. Its ability to become more efficient and to expand operations in areas such as irrigation, rural credit, and agricultural research and extension may be crucial to development. In the area of taxation the proportion of taxes to GNP is comparatively low, but it has been increasing slowly. Overall the tax structure appears to be responsive to income; but a close examination shows that an increase of 100 pesos in GNP will raise income tax receipts by only about 3 pesos, and all tax receipts by only about 8 pesos. Furthermore, experience has shown that the major beneficiary of greater expenditures resulting from increased tax resources has been the personnel services, reflecting the pressures to increase the bureaucracy. Expenditures on economic development tend to get a relatively small share of increased tax resources, as compared to education and other welfare expenditures, or defense.[69] Certainly the 1971 congressional defeat of the proposal to continue the export tax, which would have transferred some of the gains of devaluation made by the large export groups to the government, indicated the difficulty of raising taxes on politically powerful groups; rumors of tax evasion and corruption in tax administration were widespread.

In the political field there had been indications that traditional patron-client voting relationships were becoming weaker, even in rural areas and small towns, by the time martial law was introduced. Among the older generation these relations had been cemented by mutural respect between the "big" patron family and the "small" client families. With a new younger generation of patrons, many of whom were raised in cities away from the villages, the bonds of respect are breaking down and old patterns of behavior are weakening. Gangsters were introduced into villages by competing families specifically to force certain voting behavior when the traditional ties of respect disappeared.[70] This trend may well continue, and in fact be strengthened, in the villages as contractual relations replace traditional ones.

69. Amartya K. Sen, "The Philippine Economy," mimeographed (Bangkok: ECAFE, 1971), pp. 30–31, and G. P. Sicat, "Aspects of Philippine Public Finance," *Philippine Economic Journal* 10, no. 1 (1971): 23–47.
70. In conversation with David Szanton.

In the urban areas, where the contradictions of the present system are more obvious, traditional relations had already broken down to a great extent before the advent of martial law. The discrepancies between the ostentatious displays of wealth and the manifest poverty were greater; the numbers of unemployed or dissatisfied were increasing. These were giving rise to demands for revolution by those who felt that the existing system was unsalvageable. In the past the connection between urban revolutionist and peasant has been marginal at best.[71] If these groups work together, the threat will become greater.

But there were also encouraging signs before the introduction of martial law. The problems raised in this chapter were known to many educated Filipinos, and they were working toward solutions at a variety of levels. The first student riots of early 1970, with their demands for reform, were sympathetically received by large parts of the population. Since then both the Catholic church and business groups created movements to change past national policies and to experiment with social change on local levels.

Social awareness was beginning to replace family-centeredness among some of the younger generation, both in politics and in business. In business some of the larger firms have become increasingly professionalized in management; some of the universities have high-quality professional staffs. Where this has occurred, performance is judged on merit and results, not on contacts. Both businesses and universities are supplying able technocrats to government. In some areas government performance has improved, and the criteria of performance are becoming more professional and less paternalistic. These same professionals are also actively advocating social reforms outside of politics.

In the connection between politics and economic life, in the past control was exercised by only a very few families. Recent industrial growth spawned new family groups; in the process the older ones were weakened, conflicting interests arose, and the relationships between specific business families and political leaders became more diffuse. While there are close relationships between the older

71. On this see Eduardo Lachica, *Huk* (Manila: Solidaridad Publishing House, 1971).

"sugar barons" and the new industrialists, some of the latter do not come from the former families—and the conflicts between them made it possible to achieve "reform-mongering" political coalitions.[72]

Among rural groups such elements as the Federation for Free Farmers pressed for land reform and opposed efforts to dispossess farmers. Farm cooperatives had started up, and some were successful where farmers recognized their potentialities. These rural groups achieved some successes and some change was stirring in the rural areas.

In the Philippines the framework of the old system, which had gradually weakened, permitted some time to achieve the reforms necessary for future economic development and peaceful political change. Some of this had been occurring—dramatically, but with some conflict and exchange in a democratic system. The introduction of martial law by President Marcos in September, 1972, represented a decisive break with the old system.

In fact, the introduction of martial law confirms the breakdown of traditional patron-client relationships on the national level. In the same way that force has been introduced in village and regional politics in the country as a whole, the army has now been introduced to replace the older system of national politics, based on mutualities of obligations and responsibilities. Apart from any considerations of personal power, it was argued that the old system had become so obstructive that it prevented the government from carrying out necessary economic and social reforms. After introduction of martial law President Marcos proclaimed various reforms—widening the area of land reform and implementing some new reforms, reducing the government labor force, and reducing crime and lawlessness. Able technocrats support this effort, but the question does arise whether President Marcos, who was a representative of the old system and reached power initially by his ability to control it, will in fact be willing and able to actually carry through the reforms that may be necesary. Is he a force for change, or an instrument of repression of needed changes?

72. In Albert Hirschman's well-known phrase from his book *Journeys toward Progress* (New York: Doubleday Anchor Books, 1965).

It is also clear that martial law polarizes the situation. The opposition can only flee or rise in revolt; it cannot openly oppose the president and hope to replace him in a peaceful fashion. If the president is unsuccessful in his reform goals, the introduction of martial law makes the possibility of armed revolution or direct army rule in a Latin American fashion even more likely. The chances for use of such force are greater than in the past, and the problems more urgent.[73]

73. I have not returned to the Philippines since martial law was introduced, so I can write little about its effects. However, for several recent reports, see Peter R. Kann, "The Philippines without Democracy," *Foreign Affairs* 52, no. 3 (April, 1974):612–632; Sydney H. Schanberg, "Troubles for Marcos," *New York Times,* July 5, 1974, p. 3.

I believe, therefore, that Java may fairly claim to be the finest tropical island in the world, and equally interesting to the tourist seeking after new and beautiful scenes; to the naturalist who desires to examine the variety and beauty of tropical nature; or to the moralist and politician who want to solve the problem of how man may best be governed under new and varied conditions.

—Alfred Russel Wallace, *The Malay Archipelago*

If you want to understand the economy of my country, study our culture and our political system; if you want to understand our culture and our political system, study our economy.

—Sajogyo, chairman of the Working Body of the Agro-Economic Survey of Indonesia

THE PEASANT SOCIETY AND ITS HISTORY

Indonesian society is multifaceted, and the character of its peasant society reflects a complex tradition and a long history. Discussion of this character is complicated by the fact that the present Indonesia is itself a complex of peoples, languages, and religions, with over 300 different ethnic groups and 250 different languages. However, these peoples can be divided into three major categories: the wet rice growers of inland Java and Bali strongly influenced by an early Hindu-Buddhist tradition, although of Muslim religion; the more purely Islamic coastal towns of northern Java, Sumatra, and those other islands which were the centers of the spice trade; and the various tribal groups especially located in the outer islands. The discussion in this chapter will be largely limited to the first group. While this would appear to be a drastic simplification, it is estimated that in 1969 approximately 77 million of Indonesia's 118 million people lived on Java. The few anthropological studies on which this chapter is based are largely confined to a small area of central Java, but there is reason to believe that the characteristics described are not unique to that area of Java, and that they have significant similarities to those found in other parts of Java, as well as in other parts of Indonesia and Southeast Asia.[1]

My analysis of Indonesian society starts with a look at the Great Tradition which serves as the basis of the Javanese world view, including the relation of the ruler to the subject, or of the court to the peasant. This is followed by a closer examination of the village segment of that society, both in history and at present. This section stresses the system of social stratification in the village and the functioning of patron-client relationships in their economic and political contexts. Apart from peasant stratification, another internal difference within Indonesian society arises from the relationship between those in the population who believe in the Javanese world view and those of a more orthodox Muslim position; this is explored briefly. Finally, the effect of Dutch colonial rule upon the changing economic patterns is examined to give a picture of the Indonesian economy at the end of the colonial period and to identify long-term problems.

Unlike what we know of the Philippines prior to Spanish rule, there is clear evidence of the existence of major states and Great Traditions on Java in the pre-colonial period. These states, the greatest of which were Srivijaya in the ninth century, Majapahit in the fourteenth century, and Mataram in the sixteenth century, were strongly influenced by Indian Buddhist and Hindu traditions; those traditions strongly influence contemporary Javanese and Indonesian society. Soedjatmoko describes the influence of this religious tradition on the structure of society:

A central concept in the Javanese traditional view of life is the direct relationship between the state of a person's inner self and his capacity to control his environment. Inner perfection, reached through detachment and the control of one's emotions and reactions, radiates, through the inner stillness thus acquired, to the world and influences it. And as social hierarchy is seen as a reflection of the cosmic order, one's place in the hierarchy reflects the degree of inner perfection and power one

1. See Robert R. Jay, *Javanese Villagers* (Cambridge: Massachusetts Institute of Technology Press, 1969), pp. 450–452.

has achieved. At the apex of this hierarchy stands the ruler, who rules by divine sanction and whose state of inner development is reflected in the condition of his realm. In this view territory is not the essential aspect of the state, but the court and the capital are. More than anything else they stand for the state itself.[2]

There is thus a universal axis—the cosmic center of the world, the ruler's inner self, and his palace.

The beneficent power of this universal axis radiates from the person of the ruler to each person in the surrounding population. . . . Proximity to the ruler through ties of kinship, marriage, or chance personal affinity, through royal office or simply through residental proximity were believed to strengthen the material and spiritual benefits an individual secured for himself through the ruler's power. Correspondingly, there was a physical clustering of the population in the proximity of the palace. . . .
Social rank was based on proximity to the ruler through the various kinds of affiliation: [kinship, voluntary submission, royal administrative office, other services such as domestic and craft service, and finally through residence within the ruler's range]. Other things being equal, the nearer a subject lived, the higher his rank, and the king's common subjects—the ordinary peasantry living out in the countryside beyond the circle of the court proper—represented the bottom of the social hierarchy. . . .
Finally there was a conception according to which access to and control over cosmic forces were differentially distributed in the society and that this distribution was exhibited in differential rank, which it also served to define spiritually. Accordingly all social relations were conceived as necessarily hierarchical.

In turn it was clear that proof of control over the cosmic forces was given by success in maintaining or extending one's power on earth; failure by a ruler was evidence of loss of cosmic influence.

The ideal man of this cosmology was one whose behavior reflected his inner serenity, and his position in the hierarchy, by his "control of his personal emotions, [his] calm demeanor under all circumstances, [his] outward grace of movement and speech, and [his] control of the elaborate ethic which served to express and fix relative individual rank."[3]

2. Soedjatmoko, "Indonesia and the World," *Australian Outlook* 21, no. 3 (December, 1967): 266.
3. Robert R. Jay, *Religion and Politics in Rural Central Java*, Yale University

This was a cosmology and code of behavior for the gentry (*prijaji*) and the court was an urban institution.

The Javanese aristocracy lacked the land-linked system of feudal obligation of Western Europe with its fief-holding agricultural gentry, or the rationalized Chinese bureaucracy drawing its officials from rural gentry as well as urban. They lacked even the solidified patron relations of the caste-organized India whence they borrowed so much of their world view. . . . [They] have not been able to turn themselves into a landed gentry. . . . For the most part [today] they are bureaucrats, clerks and teachers—white-collar nobles.[4]

There was a sharp, almost unbridgeable gap between the court and *prijaji* and the peasant (*abangan*), ruled to a greater or lesser degree by the court. The noble was "smooth" (*halus*); the peasant "rough" (*kasar*). "In the peasant the gentleman sees both a disturbingly barbaric parody of his own carefully controlled behavior and an attractive spontaneity and animal power. . . . In the gentleman the peasant sees both a summation of all that he wishes he could be . . . and a kind of self-important stuffiness. . . ." The peasants were considered to be permanently on the land, while the courtly *prijaji* remained *prijaji* by descent and tradition and were not tied to an area or piece of land. The relation of the *prijaji* to a piece of land was severed either because of loss of land by conquest prior to the colonial period, or by his obvious subordination to the Dutch or the shifts in his assignments after the Dutch achieved power. "Whatever bonds have existed between the villagers and the nobles have been brittle and opportunistic rather than permanent and traditionalized. . . . [The] *prijaji* have always found outward submission, exaggerated respect, and placating excuses easier to obtain from the *abangan* than actual obedience."[5]

But the *prijaji* were never more than a few percent of the Indonesian population. Traditionally the courts were supported by tribute from the peasants. While the source of power of the *prijaji*

Southeast Asia Studies Cultural Report Series no. 12, mimeographed (New Haven, 1963), pp. 3–5.

4. Clifford Geertz, *The Religion of Java* (New York: Free Press, 1964), pp. 229, 231.

5. First quote, ibid., p. 228; second quote, Clifford Geertz, "Religious Belief and Economic Behavior in a Central Javanese Town," *Economic Development and Cultural Change* 4, no. 2 (January, 1956): 155.

may not have been landed estates owned by them, they were in effect assigned revenue-collecting responsibilities for particular areas, and they served as the channels through which revenues from that area flowed to the king and court. The agricultural communities themselves were relatively independent of the court; they were ruled by groups of elders, with land held in some communal form. The community maintained some independence because at the time population was low relative to the land supply, and if the ruler or noble or even group of village elders sought to exercise severe control, the family or group affronted could move to a new area easily.

The Dutch recognized communal ownership of land, but they signed leases or rented lands for commercial cultivation by arrangements with the headman, who supposedly represented the village. "[The] more truly communal rights that had existed previously became personalized or more individualized with the strengthening of local leaders and control of land ceased in effect to rest with the group. . . . Another result of dealing with all land [in this way] was that it tended to encourage within the community itself . . . increasingly individualized forms of landholding and land use."[6] The culture system and the later corporate plantation system introduced by the Dutch contributed to the periodic subdivision of *all* village lands into small parcels, which established the conditions for the individualization of landholding. With growing population and increasing scarcity of land, this parceling process in turn led to the proliferation of tenancy and sharecropping agreements within the village, and an increasing social differentiation among the inhabitants of a village on the basis of their landholding.

In the economic area of rice production the traditional relationships among peasants working communal wet rice lands led to a set of land and work distribution mechanisms to insure that

intensive labor could be brought to bear on particular fields at necessary points in time as well as mechanisms of communal distribution . . . to maintain individual subsistence in periods of low labor demand. . . .

6. Margo L. Lyon, "Bases of Conflict in Rural Java," University of California, Center for South and Southeast Asia Studies Research Monograph no. 3, mimeographed (Berkeley, Calif., December 3, 1970), p. 9. The historical discussion owes much to this monograph.

The *abangan* village came to be comprised of a group of approximately equal status subsistence farmers, each with more or less identical . . . rights and duties, all locked together in an intricate system of mutual aid and assistance in order to make efficient wet rice agriculture possible. . . . The *abangan*, committed to world outlook which emphasizes a close interdependence among separate families in the same village, tends to share food equally when he has it and share its absence equally when he doesn't have it . . . out of a traditionalized mode of solving problems.[7]

In practice as land grew scarcer and went under individual control, landholding became the basis of differential social status within the village. By 1900

voice in village affairs, an obligation to perform village services, and a higher social status within the village all accompany landholding rights. The villagers who hold land, especially a piece of wet rice field . . . are considered the nuclear villagers. . . . They are generally the wealthiest villagers. . . . The village headman, the village administration, and sometimes the village teachers and religious leaders will all come from this group. . . .

Of lower status are those villagers who do not hold a piece of agricultural land, but own only a house and garden. These people either work in nearby industries, or engage in a handicraft, or work the land of others. . . .[They] may be consulted in village affairs when the village elders are seeking a consensus of opinion on some particular matter.

Lowest on the village social ladder are those people who hold no land and who own neither house nor garden.[8]

This trend of a simultaneous breakup and concentration of landholdings has continued. By 1960 the average holding on Java was less than 0.5 hectare.[9] Although a holding of 1 hectare is considered the minimum economic size, 51 percent of the 14.6 million farm proprietors had holdings of less than 0.5 hectare, and 28 percent held between 0.5 and 1.0 hectare. These 80 percent of all proprietors held only 50 percent of the cultivated areas in Java, with the remaining 50 percent held by the 20 percent of the proprietors with holdings of more than 1.0 hectare. Even more significant of the trend is the fact that approximately 60 percent of

7. Geertz, "Religious Belief and Economic Behavior," pp. 138–141.
8. Robert Van Niel, *The Emergence of the Modern Indonesian Elite* (The Hague: W. van Hoeve, 1960), pp. 22–23.
9. One hectare = 2.2 acres. In contrast to Java, the average size landholding in the Philippines is about 3–4 hectares.

the rural population were landless laborers in 1960. While these overall figures may be subject to large margins of error, they are supported by specific village data. Pelzer cites one village of West Java in which 44 percent of the households had no land of their own and another 48 percent had plots too small to provide a livelihood. Some people from these latter households had to work full time as tenants on land owned by someone else. In this same village half the land was held by the 2 percent of the families that owned more than 5 hectares each and employed the other villagers as laborers or sharecroppers. In a more recent study of the rural region of Jogjakarta in Central Java, Deuster estimated that 57 percent of the farm households owned no *sawah* (irrigated rice land) in 1959; only 3 percent of the households owned over 0.5 hectare of *sawah* each.[10]

It is apparent that land-labor relationships act as a basic divider of villagers according to personal rank. Those households able to do without wage work or share cropping concessions gain a personal rank markedly superior to households which are not economically strong enough to do this. . . . [Furthermore] wealth in the form of holdings of irrigated farmland is the commonest avenue for further advance in [personal rank]. . . . [It] yields the highest social regards, for it involves the landholder as a . . . patron of any beyond his close kinsmen who come to work on his land.[11]

The wealthier farmers

are almost invariably the influential men in the village and have tied to them, through links of kinship and neighborhood, various of the poorer villagers. The latter have obligations to support their patron politically, give him assistance and small gifts when he gives a feast, do odd jobs and run errands; and they must be available when he needs a large labor force. . . . Since success in farming depends largely on the ability to assemble a sufficient labor force, the patron must keep the loyalty of his followers. He must help them by lending or giving money and food or other supplies when they are in need, advise them in their dealings with the outside world, and allow them priority when alloting wage

10. The above data are from Lyon, "Bases of Conflict," pp. 17–18, 24; Karl J. Pelzer, "The Agricultural Foundation," in *Indonesia*, ed. Ruth T. McVey (New Haven: Human Relations Area Files Press, 1963), Ch. 4; and Paul Deuster, "Rural Consequences of Indonesian Inflation" (Ph.D. dissertation, University of Wisconsin, Economics Department, 1971), Chs. 4, 5.

11. Jay, *Javanese Villagers*, pp. 286–287.

labor, thus providing them with opportunities to earn cash. If he fails to do these things he loses their support, which in turn damages his prestige and endangers his economic position.

In addition, a wealthy man is expected to redistribute his wealth by spending it on various social occasions, in ceremonies associated either with his own family or with poorer relatives. A comparatively large farmer, with more than one hectare, is simply unable to work the land himself; he must give work opportunities to other villagers, as a work-sharing device.[12]

This influence of landowning carries over into village political leadership. "Community patrons . . . elected to rural office as well as those able to act successfully as leaders in organizing private associations are almost always from this [the landowning] side. Wherever leadership is present, therefore . . . it rests in the hands of this minority of independent [landowners], and most important, ties with urban society as well also channel down into the village through this minority in the community."[13] The village leader (*lurah*) and other village officials are chosen by elections in which patron-client relationships play a major role. While the posts are not hereditary, prior election does carry a great deal of weight. The position also carries with it a grant of land to reimburse the village leader for any expenses involved in the post, so it serves to bolster the landowner's previous strength.

In spite of the increasing social differentiation within the village due to the continuing division and concentration of landholding, there is a basic sense of social equality within the village. Farming is considered the most appropriate form of economic activity for the villager. Those who farm are considered equals in many respects, while villagers who engage in trade or other non-farming activities have lower social status than farmers of the same wealth. This sense of equality is reinforced by a belief in the communal character of the village which is stressed in various ceremonies

12. Quotation from Alice Dewey, *Peasant Marketing in Java* (New York: Free Press, 1962), p. 26; see also Selosoemardjan, *Social Changes in Jogjakarta* (Ithaca: Cornell University Press, 1962), p. 328. Also from conversation with John Bresnan and Theodore Smith in Jakarta in 1972.

13. See Jay, *Javanese Villagers*, Ch. 9, esp. pp. 267–269, 271–272, 286–288; quote on pp. 286–287.

celebrating the solidarity of the village community, and the fami-
listic character of the community leadership. While these functions
celebrate a past village unity, the most characteristic peasant social
function of today is the *slametan*, which in a period of shifting populations is a function of a neighborhood, rather than of a village or
family. This is a ceremony of the nuclear family and its immediate
neighbors—participation in it depends on the chance of residence.

[It is] the sacred communal feast of close neighbors designed to insure
the general well-being (*slamet*) of all who participate, most particularly
of the host. . . . In the *slametan*, the Javanese . . . does not request the
spirits to do anything for him, but merely pleads with them that they
do nothing to him [that might upset him]. . . . [It is a] brief, undramatic,
formal, and almost furtive little ceremony [; but even so, it] is but a
micro-model of the wider social order. . . . In the *slametan* the dependence of neighboring individuals upon one another and upon the crops
of their fields is symbolized, and the necessity for inter-familial cooperation, behavioral predictability, and deemphasis of individual pe-
culiarities are underlined. What food the group has is shared equally,
whatever deep-going emotions the participants feel are carefully concealed under a bland exterior, and everyone is committed to a politely
genteel behavior which can provide no surprises for anyone else.[14]

While the village has lost importance as a social unit, it remains
the basic political unit, with officials chosen by elections. Political
power within the village is associated with landholding and the
resulting client support, but the formal relationship of the village
leader (*lurah*) to the villagers is one of equality. The *lurah* is not
expected to command the villagers; he is regarded in many respects
as the head of the family and is expected to persuade rather than
command. Decisions at the village level are arrived at by lengthy
and repeated discussion to reach a consensus. If consensus cannot
be reached at the first meeting, more meetings will be held until
either a consensus can be reached or one is obviously impossible. In
the latter case no decision is achieved. The *lurah* is the link between
the peasant and the lowest link of the bureaucracy, serving as a
broker between these two elements of the society. The *tjamat*, who
is the lowest bureaucratic figure in touch with the *lurah*, in turn
exercises his power not by the sanctions at his command, but by

14. Geertz, "Religious Belief and Economic Behavior," pp. 138–141.

his prestige as a member of the bureaucracy, the contemporary *prijaji*, and his persuasive power. Open disagreement and a need to use force to compel obedience is a sign of weakness rather than strength, since it runs counter to the desirable behavior expected of high-status officials.[15] This role of intermediary may raise problems for the *lurah*, since there are often conflicts between the desires of the government and those of the peasants. Such a conflict is exemplified by a demand from the government for repayment of farm loans which the peasants consider to be gifts. In some villages the *lurah* has repaid these out of his own pocket to avoid antagonizing either the villagers or the government. Such conflicting pressures also give rise to the *lurah*'s verbal acquiescence to directives, while performance is avoided as a way of saving face at both levels.

The split between *prijaji* and *abangan* is a traditional one running through Indonesian society; it antedates the colonial period, but was then converted into the difference between the bureaucracy and the peasantry. Among the peasants, the stratification from differential private landholding began during the colonial period partly because of the economic policies of the colonial power. This difference is partially bridged by the ethic of equality within the village; however, it may at times be exacerbated when the differences between practice and ethic become too sharp. In addition, there are Muslim religious differences both within and among villages and areas of Indonesia. "The *abangan*, who are most numerous in the inland areas [of Java] where Mataram held sway longest, profess to be Moslems but are actually living still from the Javanese religious and philosophical tradition. . . . [In contrast] the *santri* concentrated in the North coast areas and part of the rural inland, take their Islam very seriously indeed."[16] Furthermore, among the *santri* themselves there is a split between the more orthodox group and a group strongly influenced by Muslim reform thinking of the late nineteenth and early twentieth centuries. This conflict between *abangan* and *santri* precedes the Dutch, since it

15. See Donald Fagg, "Authority and Social Structure" (Ph.D. dissertation, Harvard University, Department of Social Relations, 1958).
16. Soedjatmoko, "Indonesia and the World," p. 265.

was one of the elements in the conflict between the earlier coastal Moslem states and inland Mataram; the Dutch, fearing Moslem competition, favored the *abangan* strain while playing off each group against the other, and so it continues today. Within a village it may take the form of rival factions around a secular or religious teacher, or of entire villages following a dominant patron or *lurah*. On a national scale it has been the basis of strong political party distinctions.

Incidental mention was made earlier of Dutch influence upon the pre-colonial communal landholding system. But the effect of colonial rule extended to all sectors of economic activity, since the basic Dutch purpose was economic gain from the colony. While the major activity in the great pre-colonial states of today's Indonesia had always been farming, trade played an important role in the wealth of those states. They were major exporters of spices to other Asian areas prior to European entry into the trade; in fact, it was this trade that attracted first the Portuguese and then the Dutch. As the Dutch gradually captured political control of the various islands—a lengthy, piecemeal process characterized by diverse forms of imposed rule—they used their political power to force the production of export crops by the peasants and at a later stage invested themselves in large plantations. However, the gains from the trade itself were concentrated in their own hands. The consequences of those policies were great increases in the output of such commercial crops as rubber and sugar, the progressive settlement of all the land on Java by an ever-growing population, and the parcelization of land into steadily smaller private holdings. Geertz has described the effects of the "agricultural involution" arising from the Dutch-imposed sugar program of the first thirty years of this century and is rightly critical of the failure of Dutch policies to encourage a breakup of the patron-client peasant society and the "shared poverty" resulting therefrom.[17]

Those policies had major consequences for Indonesia's current economic problems. Although they did not break the patron-client peasant society, they strengthened the commercial orientation of

17. See Clifford Geertz, *Agricultural Involution* (Berkeley and Los Angeles: University of California Press, 1968), pp. 141–143.

the Javanese peasant. The Javanese peasant today is not a subsistence farmer. He produces and sells a surplus outside the village, and he buys a wide variety of goods from outside the village—food staples such as salt, sugar, oil, and spices; manufactured goods such as cloth, tools, building materials, flashlights, soap, bicycles, and fertilizers. Deuster found that in a recent year the farm households of the Jogjakarta region purchased from 20 to 100 percent of their consumption needs; for the production of their output 55 percent of their gross enterprise incomes went for purchased factor inputs.[18]

Second, as a result of Dutch policies the urban nobility that carried on the pre-colonial foreign trade were forced out of that commerce. Dutch policy was deliberately aimed at achieving a Dutch monopoly of foreign trade in the export of raw materials and the import of manufactured products. One of the first Dutch governors general wrote that the East India Company should be the wholesale dealer, the Dutch resident burghers the middlemen, and the Chinese the retail traders; Dutch policy was directed to that ethnic specialization of labor.

By the time of independence, large-scale trade was more or less in the hands of the five largest Dutch firms, which not only controlled general trade but also were by far the major force in the production and trade of estate products and minerals. The relative importance of Dutch and indigenous enterprises is shown by Van Niel's 1919 figures. In that year there were on Java 5,700 nonindigenous enterprises employing 323,700 indigenous workers, while the 3,200 indigenous firms emloyed only 13,300 workers.[19] These proportions did not change significantly over the next twenty years.

Between the Dutch and the local population the Chinese played a major role in internal trade. As a result of various East India Company policies, especially that of selling or leasing monopoly rights to Chinese traders, by the end of the eighteenth century the Chinese penetration in Java

had acquired the character of complete economic domination of the Native population in the field of agriculture and industry; . . . the Natives . . . were not protected against this [penetration] by any sovereign

18. Dewey, *Peasant Marketing*, p. 15; and Deuster, "Rural Consequences," Ch. 3.
19. Van Niel, *Emergence of Elite*, p. 267.

authority, either that of their own chiefs or that of the Company; . . .
on the contrary, the Company's policy . . . has effectively contributed
to the . . . Chinese penetration; the presence of the Chinese certainly
has not been to the advantage of the Native population . . . [which]
became tributary to the Chinese, whereby its . . . own economic development [was] greatly restricted.[20]

During the nineteenth and early twentieth centuries the Dutch
themselves entered estate cultivation processing and trading on a
large scale, with resources and power which left the Chinese only a
secondary role in the more capital-intensive areas of production and
trade. The monopoly leasing system was ended, and restrictions
were placed upon the alienation of native lands. But even at Independence, the Chinese had almost a monopoly of trade in the wholesale field, i.e., between the village bazaar and the export/import
trade proper. They controlled much of the milling and sale of rice,
and they handled much of the credit, both at the retail trade level
and within the village. The Javanese played no role in trade other
than in the very petty and local retail-bazaar trade. The situation
was somewhat different in the Outer Islands, particularly Sumatra.
Here a *santri* tradition operated to stimulate personal saving and
investment and indigenous investment in commercial crop production (rubber, copra, coffee, tobacco) of a non-estate type. A class
of Muslim entrepreneurs and traders in the production and export
of rubber developed and was competitive to the Chinese. (Estate
operations were largely under the control of Dutch and foreign
investors.) To a certain degree a similar Muslim group of entrepreneurs began to develop around the sugar estates in central Java
after 1915, but this group collapsed in the Depression of the 1930's.[21]

This collapse eliminated any large-scale Javanese entrepreneurship. The Javanese village ethos discouraged entrepreneurship
among the better-off peasants on the land, since cash-holding or
investment in business and trade were looked down upon as activi-

20. See W. L. Cator, *The Economic Position of the Chinese in the Netherlands
Indies* (Chicago: University of Chicago Press, 1936), Ch. 1. Quotation from pp.
23–24.
21. On the above see C. Geertz's *Agricultural Involution*, and C. Geertz, *The
Social History of an Indonesian Town* (Cambridge: MIT Press, 1965), esp. pp. 40–
43; and B. J. O. Schrieke, Chapter 1 of "The Causes and Effects of Communism on
the West Coast of Sumatra" in his *Indonesian Sociological Studies*, Part 1 (The
Hague: W. van Hoeve Publishers, 1966).

ties compared to either farming or gift-giving. Meanwhile, in the urban areas high mobility in the face of great population pressure on the land broke down any communal bonds other than those uniting members of the nuclear family. Thus in the towns there was little basis for the establishment of confidence beyond the immediate family.

Alice Dewey examines the relatively isolated condition of the Javanese trader, contrasting his environment with the more social environment of the Chinese. Among the merchants in villages

competition . . . is virtually free, and control of capital . . . is not concentrated appreciably in the hands of any one group. Therefore there is no economic base for the development of a patron-client system [as among the farmers]. Groups based on land and agricultural labor are absent since few traders own farmland or have the time to do agricultural work.

In towns where the majority of traders live there is less overlap between kin group and neighborhood group than in the rural areas. . . . A trader has a larger number of contacts than a farmer, and the ties formed tend to be highly individualistic . . . rather than channeled within and reinforcing a kin-neighborhood group. The demands of business, which force traders to travel [for lengthy periods] . . . further weaken local ties. Thus among traders there are no stable groups larger than the nuclear family. In fact, since in many sorts of trade an individual can operate more effectively alone, the economic base of the nuclear family itself is weakened . . . [ties] of kinship loosen very quickly. . . . Thus contacts with relatives in other trading centers tend to become unimportant for either social or economic purposes. For the Javanese there is no large organization such as clan or association which would serve to keep kinship relationships alive regardless of the specific interaction between the individuals. Among the Chinese [there are such groupings which] bring people together . . . [and] also provide a basis of common interest for those who are not actually close friends or kin.

In Modjokoto, the fictitious name of the town studied in the mid-1950's by Geertz and Dewey, even wealthy traders were not considered members of the upper class, since they operated in the market and were therefore socially inferior to the bureaucracy. A unifying element among the wealthier traders was that they were of the reform *santri* tradition; as such they were active in various social and economic organizations, including several cooperatives and (perhaps more important) the Masjumi party. But even among these better-off traders there was great difficulty in enforcing agreements. The poorer traders were far more isolated; they had lost their rural ties, and they had no wealth, nor had they been in the city long enough to be accepted by any other group. Thus they could only operate as individuals; even this was only possible because of the small-scale character of much production and consumption.

The result

is a lack of trust among urban traders. The ethical code is weakened, for rural values simply do not apply to many of the situations . . . and there are no sanctions to enforce those which are still valid. The lack of trust and the inability to predict behavior are probably most extreme among the poorer urban groups, but they are also characteristic of the wealthier ones outside of the [non-trading] elite. They are therefore restricted to small-scale individual operations. When they try to expand into large scale trade . . . they are at a severe disadvantage . . . for many Javanese who deal with others who are neither kin nor neighbors there is no effective social structure which can enforce the fulfillment of contracts.[22]

The one partial exception to this was that within certain large city trading groups there were apparently the beginnings of some limited group collaboration among the Javanese traders, who dealt with one or two major cash crops. The effect of this general lack of trust and cooperation among Javanese traders was that the Javanese trader was far less certain of the quality, quantity, and delivery of the goods he could offer, and was far less able to extend credit to buyers than his Chinese competitor. Finally, since he operated as an individual, he was far more likely to quit town to escape his creditors than the Chinese merchant—and thus was a far greater risk.

The indigenous entrepreneurs' inability to cooperate made any attempt to establish industry difficult if not impossible. In addition, Dutch policy toward industry was conservative, as shown by the unwillingness of the colonial government to encourage industrialization "as an objective in itself," regarding it merely as a supplement "to the income from sensitive agricultural exports and from other means of existence." As a result there was little industrial enterprise in the country at independence; most of whatever factory

22. Dewey, *Peasant Marketing*, pp. 27–49.

industry existed was Dutch owned, and the most important non-Dutch industrial entrepreneurs were Chinese. At independence or thereabouts income from manufacturing of all types was about 15 percent of total national income; employment in manufacturing was less than 10 percent of total employment (and only slightly more than 10 percent of this 10 percent was in the more capital-intensive sector, as distinguished from handicrafts).[23]

With such a concentration of control over the economy, a set of policies that stimulated neither indigenous industry nor entrepreneurship, and a continuous "sharing of poverty" in agriculture, it is not surprising that in 1939 the 97.5 percent Indonesian portion of the total population, very largely engaged in agriculture, received 69 percent of the total national income. The 0.4 percent European portion of the population engaged in trade, industry, estates, and higher public services, plus the foreign nonresident corporations, received 20 percent of the national income; the 2 percent foreign Asiatic (largely Chinese) portion of the population, with a near monopoly of wholesale trade and smaller industry, received 10 percent of the national income. Van der Kroef, like Geertz, concludes that "a very low and probably even decreasing level of welfare would seem to be the rule for the mass of the Indonesian population in the decades before the [postwar] Revolution."[24]

In the government, however, the Dutch left an effective bureaucracy down to the village for the functions which they considered appropriate. While the highest posts in the bureaucracy were in Dutch hands,[25] access to Western education both in the Netherlands and in Indonesia itself was gradually provided to the indigenous population, first on a very selective basis and then to a wider group. This in turn led to the recruitment of Indonesians, and to their promotion to government positions below the highest,

23. First quote from Justus M. van der Kroef, *Indonesia in the Modern World* (Bandung, Indonesia: Masa Maru Bandung, 1954), II, 16; Douglas S. Paauw, *Financing Economic Development* (Glencoe, Ill.: Free Press, 1960), pp. 206, 406; A. M. Siregar, "Indonesian Entrepreneurs," *Asian Survey* 9, no. 5 (May, 1969): 344–345.

24. Paauw, *Financing*, p. 207; quote from van der Kroef, *Indonesia in the Modern World*, II, 12, 18.

25. In 1940 only 221 of the 3,039 top civil service positions in the administration were held by Indonesians.

on the grounds of education rather than heredity. The extension of Western education also led to the rise of an elite group that objected to Dutch control of the society, and which sought Indonesian control of the society and economy. These political demands were associated on the one hand with the resurgence of a strong Islamic influence; Islam stood for everything that was indigenous (as opposed to foreign), including support of Indonesian (as opposed to Chinese) businessmen. On the more secular side, the boom and bust in the Indonesian economy during World War I led the Indonesian leaders to favor some form of socialism; the political success of communism combined with the efforts of Communist proponents led to the rise of a Communist party, which attracted supporters in areas where the social changes were particularly strong. During the 1920's, too, there was a split between religious and secular nationalism. Van Niel points out the rise of two contrasting Indonesian leadership groups by 1940: on the one hand there was a functional elite consisting of administrators, civil servants, professional men, and others; they viewed Indonesia's future "in terms of preserving the functioning, administrative state and society in which they were coming to play an ever more important role" and were willing to stay within the colonial system as long as independence did not seem possible. On the other hand a political leadership also developed, members of which were out of the colonial power system and aimed for a free Indonesia, although there were differences among them as to the type of social system favored. With the Japanese defeat of the Dutch in 1941–42, Japanese occupation with its recognition of the Indonesian political leadership, and the defeat of the Japanese in 1945, independence became a distinct possibility on which both the functional and political leaders united. Independence was declared in 1945, but only after a protracted military struggle did the Dutch accept the reality of independence in 1949. The achievement of independence by military struggle against a colonial power is unique among the countries considered in this book; it strongly colored future Indonesian development.[26]

26. On the above see Van Niel's *Emergence of Elite* in its entirety, and esp. pp. 82–91, 189, 242ff.; B. Schrieke, "The Causes of Communism"; and Bruce Grant, *Indonesia* (Harmondsworth: Penguin, 1967), Ch. 2.

NATIONAL POLITICS AND GOVERNMENT

As in the Philippines, the character of Indonesia peasant society and its development had profound consequences for Indonesian political and governmental forms and structures, and the policies emanating from that government. The similarities between the two countries are reflected in certain parallel developments. But the differences in the two countries' histories and social structures; the existence of a Great Tradition in Indonesia; the various and sharper splits within the Indonesian society between nobility and peasantry, between *abangan* and *santri*, between Outer Islanders and Javanese, between Chinese and local peoples; and the differing character of their colonial experiences and struggles for Independence all contributed to creating an Indonesian political system and set of economic policies different from that of the Philippines.

Following independence Indonesian political leaders generally accepted democracy as a political method and socialism, with major emphasis upon state action, as an economic ideology. Political parties emerged from the democratic system of election of government leaders. In accordance with Indonesian traditions and the centralized character of Dutch rule, the party leaders, organizations, and ideologies emerged from the cities. It was from the cities also that the finances came, out of the interconnections between party and government. In the absence of other organizational forms and horizontal structures (such as farmers' associations and trade unions) between the party and the peasants, the parties themselves served as the center of an entire stream of activities (*aliran*). In each village and larger area there were not only party branches but also, affiliated with the party branch, various women, youth, student, and veteran groups, all engaged in a wide variety of cultural, religious, and sporting activities.

The parties themselves relied for much of their mass support on votes from the rural areas which depended largely on patron-client relationships.

Mass following [on the national level] has proved to consist to a large extent of aggregates of people in the villages grouped around the dominating factors of their daily life; the village headman and the religious teacher. Popular vote in the villages was in the first place a show of allegiance to either of the two, or to both. Hence the surprisingly large turnout of the villages at the polls . . . larger even than in the towns. . . . Hence also the almost complete insignificance of campaign issues like corruption in government, high prices, economic development, etc. on the village level. . . . The numerical strength of the political parties as shown by the election results, or more precisely the political power of the particular elite groups leading those parties, is therefore not so much, and not only a reflection of the measure of acceptance of either ideology or leadership, but also a reflection of such groups' ability to manipulate the traditional power relationships within the village.[27]

These power relationships in turn revolved about the mixture of long-standing *prijaji*-peasant and *abangan-santri* differences. The *abangan* areas of Java supported the Nationalist (PNI), Communist (PKI), and Socialist (SI) parties. The PNI was especially strong among the *prijaji/pegawai* government officer groups in Central East Java; the PKI received support from peasant *abangan* groups, as well as from urban intellectuals and estate, public utility, and factory workers. The *santri* strength was concentrated in the Outer Islands, West Java, and Javanese coastal trading areas, and supported Muslim parties. Among these the reform Masjumi party received support from the urban and trading and religious reform groups in Sumatra and coastal areas; the more orthodox NU party derived its strength from the rural areas of Central and East Java in which there were orthodox religious schools and centers.

The one party which somewhat transcended these traditional sources of support was the Communist Party (PKI), which appealed to those rural groups adversely effected by the trends toward the minute division of land and increasing landlessness, coupled with concentration of land and power. Both trends were inconsistent with the old structure of village life and the old ethic of equality and sharing. "On the village level . . . increasingly substantial groups [no] . . . *longer fit into the old way of* life and social structure; often they are in latent or open conflict with the old village hierarchy. These groups . . . constitute a new dynamic or potentially dynamic political force." These marginal groups gen-

27. Soedjatmoko, "The Role of Political Parties in Indonesia," in *Nationalism and Progress in Free Asia,* ed. Philip W. Thayer (Baltimore: Johns Hopkins University Press, 1956), p. 132.

erally supported the Communist party and provided its rural support in the 1955 election.

The party and its peasant organization, the BTI, took the lead in supporting the rights of squatters on estate and plantation lands; in carrying out research at the village level on the situation of the peasants; in developing a peasant program of land reform stressing "land to the tillers" and agitating for passage of such a land reform law; in pressing for its implementation legally and then taking the lead in forcefully and unilaterally seeking to implement the law in the villages—both by increasing the tenant's share, and by taking over unoccupied or disputed lands. These splits over land ownership were especially strong since they were often, though not always, associated with the more traditional splits in the society. The Communists often represented *abangan* peasant groups against landowners from *prijaji* or *santri* groups, and the economic conflict was strengthened since it was occurring along more traditional lines of social cleavage. In fact, one result of the land reform struggle was increasing isolation of the Communists vis-à-vis other groups in the villages and in the government; because of this the Communist party sought to reduce both the demands for land reform and the number of unilateral village actions before 1965. The *santri* meanwhile sought to shift the issue from one of land reform to one of violation of traditional village religious ways of life. This conflict had already led to some violence and breakdown of local government in the rural areas of Java before 1965, and it is considered to have been a major factor behind the rural warfare and murder that followed the attempted 1965 coup.[28]

On the national level, the general absence of a middle class, and a village structure weakened as a result of population growth and widespread movement, made the government and its bureaucracy the central agency of social power, with the political parties partly competitive and partly supportive.

Power being widely dispersed within the bureaucracy [including the military] and within most of the parties as well, there was a thorough

28. On this see Lyon, "Bases of Conflict," part II; Jay, *Religion and Politics,* pp. 98–99; Guy Pauker, "Political Consequences of Rural Development Progress in Indonesia," *Pacific Affairs* 41, no. 3 (Fall, 1968): 386–402.

intermeshing of power relationships between the two spheres. By and large political leaders did not draw their power from class-delineated groupings. And they drew little of it from organized interests. . . . [The] most important unit of influence was a political-cum-personal clique, a group of leaders with personal followings and personal ties to one another. Such a group normally straddled parties and the bureaucracy. It often controlled a small party or a faction of a larger one, and it bade actively to obtain and keep positions of leverage within the bureaucracy. At the same time it articulated a wide range of interests on behalf of all those who chose to accept its leadership and protection, party members, civil servants and others with personal ties of any sort to the members of the clique.[29]

Ideologies and programs were not important, and the parties other than the PKI which sought to stress programs were weak. Power tended to gravitate to the bureaucracy in combination with the parties. In the early stages of independence the functional elite groups and urban intellectuals, represented by the PSI and Masjumi parties, with the strong support of Vice-President Hatta, were in control. They successfully negotiated with the Dutch, attracted Western support, allowed open criticism and a free press, increased food and industrial output, expanded exports, made available additional educational facilities, and routinized the administration. But they failed in certain important goals: eliminating squatters from foreign-owned estates, rationalizing the army, and reducing the civil service. The failure to defeat the Darul Islam and the fall in export prices following the Korean War weakened their popular support, the efforts to rationalize the army and civil service reduced their political support, and the substitution of prosaic administrative policies for the drama of the revolutionary period was widely regarded as a loss of *élan* and vigor.

After 1953 these functional elite groups lost some of their power to the more political solidarity-makers. President Sukarno increased his influence, and in 1960 succeeded in replacing the existing democratic system by a new system of "Guided Democracy" under his leadership. The establishment of Guided Democracy was in response to the political turmoil and rebellion of the colonels in the Outer Islands. This led to outlawing of the Masjumi and Socialist

29. Herbert Feith, *The Decline of Constitutional Democracy in Indonesia* (Ithaca: Cornell University Press, 1962), pp. 107–108.

parties; the other parties (the strongest of which was the Communist) and the army were combined in a National Front cabinet under the president, with an ideology—*Manipol*—based on village values of cooperation and "*Gotong-Royong.*" The new government stressed the image of Indonesia and the continuation of the revolution as its policy goals, with far less interest than the predecessor governments in economic growth and far more in foreign affairs. Although initially this unified government appeared strong, the coalition was too broad and the ideology too weak to achieve the desired strength or results, while the president brilliantly juggled the various elements in the coalition to maintain his personal position.

Decisions on national policy requiring joint action or support were reached by consensus; when consensus could not be reached, decisions were postponed or were undercut when made. Since the consensus was so wide in the range of beliefs included, policies were implemented only weakly if at all. While ministers representing the various groups gave lip service to decisions, those decisions could be ignored at the bureaucratic level or outside Jakarta. The decisions in turn lent themselves to undermining, since they were normally couched in language subject to a variety of interpretations to fit in the larger consensus ideology. On an operational level, to achieve consensus, the various parties and factions had to be given cabinet portfolios and associated patronage as the price of support; by 1965 the cabinet had grown to almost 100 members. The splits within such a large government and the difficulties of bureaucratic cooperation among the numerous ministries involved in the implementation of any single decision contributed to the weakness of the government. Finally, there was no way to hold ministers responsible for performance, since their real responsibilities were not to some broader "nation," but to their supporting *aliran*, which judged their success by their ability to provide patronage.

In many ways President Sukarno governed on the national level as the *tjamat* governed on the local level. His strength lay in his social prestige, which he sought to increase by dramatic gestures, and his sheer political ability to conciliate the members of his coalition. Like the *tjamat*, he also had the statutory powers of his office and the sanctions therefrom. But the sanctions were largely unusable because any attempt to use them against either the army or the PKI, the two other major elements of the coalition, could cause the collapse of the coalition and the entire government.

Under such circumstances policy consisted of once-over gestures in those fields in which the president could act more or less independently (such as foreign affairs), using the army to back up his gestures. In the economic sphere the major dramatic gesture that met both the nationalist and socialist images that the Guided Democracy set for itself was nationalization, first of Dutch and thereafter of most other foreign enterprises. At the local level, the government either forced out the Chinese or closely controlled many of their retail and middle-man activities in the distribution system. In the case of food and certain other major cost-of-living items, the army took over the distribution system, which contributed to the difficulties of distributing rice from the country to the city.

At the bureaucratic level the character of the parties and the interpenetration of party and government led, as in the Philippines, to a massive increase in the size of the bureaucracy and a decline in its efficiency. Figures as to the changing size of the bureaucracy over time are confusing because of the varying classes of employees included in or excluded from the data. However, it appears that in 1930 the number of civil servants (those with permanent status, including police officers) under the Dutch was 145,000; the comparable figure had risen to 600,000 by the end of 1953, to 807,000 in 1960, and to 1,160,000 by 1966. (These figures are exclusive of the number of people in the armed forces—which exceeded the number in the civil service—and of the approximately 750,000 workers in government-owned enterprises in 1966.)[30] By 1966 the number of government employees, excluding pensioners and rural workers, was estimated at 8 percent of the total labor force, in contrast to 1 percent in the pre-independence period. Some of this

30. See G. M. Kahin, *Government and Politics of Southeast Asia* (Quezon City: Aleman for Cornell University Press, 1969), p. 225; W. Brand, "The Manpower Situation in Indonesia," *Bulletin of Indonesian Economic Studies* 11 (October, 1968): 58–59, later quote from p. 59.

growth since 1940 can be explained by the greater number of government civilian functions, the development of the Indonesian army, and the nationalization of foreign firms in the late 1950's. But in 1968 it was "widely believed that as many as 30 to 50 percent of government employees may be surplus to the needs of an efficient administrative organization." This remark echoes comments of a similar nature made by President Sukarno and various ministers in the 1950's, but in spite of this recognition those governments were unable to reduce the number of employees.

Expenditures on these government workers, which reached 30-40 percent of the total national budget in the 1960's, contributed to the budgetary deficits and thus to the inflation of the Guided Democracy period. While the major contributory factors to these budgets deficits were the military costs associated with the Outer Islands revolt and the dramatic gestures of the West Irian campaign and the Malaysian confrontation, another significant factor was political pressure within a weak, coalition government. "Budget allocations [were] a key factor in the contest for power within the coalition. Hence there [was] a built-in tendency to raise, not lower the total expenditures. . . . Whenever the political problems of satisfying all the claims [became] insoluble within a predetermined expenditure limit, it [was] easy to simply increase the national size of the cake." At the same time it became increasingly difficult to expand revenues, because of political inhibitions to raising internal taxes, the weaknesses of the tax-collecting system, and the decline in foreign trade under pressure of higher taxes and other factors. Increased budgetary deficits were met by increasing the volume of money. "The government's resort to deficit financing since 1957 was, in effect, a means of putting off decisions of a politico-economic nature which might have caused dissension between elements within the government. A political balance was maintained, precariously at times, at the cost of economic equilibrium."

Between June, 1958, and June, 1962, the amount of money in circulation rose almost fivefold, rice prices in Jakarta over fivefold, retail prices for nineteen food articles sixfold, and the black market rate for U.S. dollars over tenfold. Thereafter the annual rate of increase of all these prices accelerated rapidly, so that in 1965 the money supply increased by almost 300 percent and the Jakarta price index by almost 600 percent.

The costs to the economy of this inflation were extremely high: in general there was a deterioration of the capital stock; a decline in per capita output, although total output is estimated to have risen at about 2 percent per year from 1960 to 1964; an increasing plethora of controls; a steady decline in real incomes of civil servants and a steady increase in double-jobbing and corruption to supplement incomes; an ever greater deterioration of business standards, characterized by an undercover alliance between businessmen who sought the privileges and licenses required for the operation of their businesses and the political, military, and bureaucratic figures who controlled those privileges and were willing to exchange a privilege for money (in part because such illicit funds increased somewhat their inflation-eroded budgets); an increasing regionalization of the country as local leaders protected their own regions and interests; a worsening of the urban situation combined with an increasing self-sufficiency and poverty in the rural areas.

In his examination of the consequences of inflation in the Jogjakarta area from 1959 to 1968, Deuster found that those groups which depended for most of their income on sources other than agriculture lost. Of those depending for their income on farming itself, the large and medium farmers and traders gained; in fact, the distribution of land shifted markedly in their favor. Farm laborers remained about even, while small farmers, who depended only in part on their farm income, lost in terms of income and land owned. In terms of attitudes, over 60 percent of those examined felt hurt by the inflation, with the white-collar group feeling it most adversely; only 14 percent felt that they had benefited, but this feeling was confined to larger farmers and traders.[31]

In the face of this weakness in Jakarta, the steady worsening of the economic situation, and the breakdown of social controls both

31. The best analysis of the political economy of the Indonesian inflation is J. A. C. Mackie, "Problems of the Indonesian Inflation," mimeographed (Ithaca: Cornell University Southeast Asia Program Monograph, 1967). The material in the previous three paragraphs is from that source; see pp. 7, 9, for quotations. See also Deuster, "Rural Consequences," Chs. 4–6.

in the cities and in the villages, the Communists, with the apparent tacit support of the president, sought to oust the army from the coalition by force in October, 1965. The collapse of the attempted coup led to the end of the coalition. The Communists were crushed and outlawed; President Sukarno, under continued but delicately modulated pressure by the army, was forced out of his political position; General Suharto took control. The *santri* groups were encouraged to lead in crushing the Communists, and in the rural areas they took a bloody revenge for the land reforms the PKI had earlier tried to carry out by force.

Since 1967 and the establishment of the new order, there has been political stability through army rule. This was confirmed in the 1971 elections when the army-led *Sekher Golkar* won the elections. From various accounts the rural elections were in many ways traditional, with the village leader determining the voting, although there was clear evidence of army pressure to achieve desired results. But the old social and religious divisions behind the former political parties still remain. The parties allowed to campaign in 1971 represented some of these divisions; the Communists are banned, though presumably the economic and social issues on which they had sought to win rural support still remain. Within the bureaucracy army officers now function in positions often parallel to those of civilian officers, creating some tension between the two groups.

The present regime is not a *santri* government; President Suharto apparently is sympathetic to *abangan* groups, and he has resisted *santri* demands for a strongly orthodox religious policy. In fact, there is some evidence of a spiritual revival with signs of splits from and within the Islamic religion, as *abangan* groups seek new religious forms while some Muslims themselves seek more mystical directions. President Suharto is playing a conciliatory role among the various *aliran* that is not unlike one of his predecessor's roles, but he is playing it without the dramatic gestures and the appeals to hyperactive nationalism that characterized his predecessor's policies. Instead army unity, the elimination of the Communists, the weakening of other political parties, and the greater role of the technocrats enables his government to make and implement policy decisions aimed at moderating religious and political strife and stimulating economic growth. These decisions are pragmatic, often responding to specific issues as they arise, rather than reflecting a more profound ideology. Perhaps that is sufficient. Many observers worry about the regime's lack of an ideology and (perhaps more important) its lack of a broad popular base. But after the emotional peaks of Sukarno, the more prosaic "ad-hocery" of Suharto may satisfy the short-run needs of the Indonesians while creating a climate within which the long-run goals of all postwar Indonesian governments—to establish an effective civil government and maintain Indonesia's national identity—may be approached more successfully than in the past.[32]

ECONOMIC IMPACT OF PEASANT SOCIETY

New Technology in Rice

All Indonesian governments have sought to increase rice output. Before independence this was part of the Dutch ethical program; since independence, as in the Philippines, the achievement of self-sufficiency in rice has been a major political goal set in part for psychological effect to prove real independence, as well as to save foreign exchange. The apparent wealth of the country makes self-sufficiency a goal which appears tantalizingly near. But in fact Indonesia has been a more or less consistent importer of rice, with the level of imports ranging from several hundred thousand tons to a million tons per year.

On Java the increases in output will have to be achieved by raising the yield per unit of land, since existing land is fully occupied; on the Outer Islands expansion of acreage is possible. The Indonesian peasant is hardworking and responsive to economic incentives, if the framework of policies is such as to encourage adoption of an appropriate new technology in which he has confidence, and if he has the financial resources to purchase the required inputs.

32. The above discussion owes much to articles by R. William Liddle, "The 1971 Indonesian Elections," and Clifford Geertz, "Religious Change and Social Order in Soeharto's Indonesia"; both published in *Asia*, no. 27 (Autumn, 1971): 4–18 and 62–84 respectively. It also benefited by the comments of Benjamin Higgins on an earlier draft.

But little Green Revolution has existed in Indonesia; in fact, per capita food production may even have declined during the 1960's.[33]

The Dutch carried out extensive research in rich technology during their rule, but the effect of this research on output was not very significant. Selosoemardjan describes the reasons for this failure in the Jogjakarta region: "The Dutch and Indonesian civil service in the pre-war period assumed a paternalistic attitude toward the village communities. They compared the relations between the civil service and the village community to those between a father and an eternally immature infant with only a limited experience of life and no idea of what he should do for his own benefit." In addition, there were frequent changes in the civil service personnel in the Jogjakarta area. Each incoming officer had his own ideas of what was technologically best, based on technical experiments in research stations. These ideas were transmitted by lectures from his office in the form of orders that the peasant should follow. The peasant reacted to all these lectures passively, listening politely to the *prijaji* but continuing to do that which he always thought best. The civil service made little effort to translate an innovation from the laboratory to the peasant's own field using the peasant's limited resources. In turn the civil servant, reacting to the peasant's passive response to his exhortations, often regarded the peasant as stupid or obstructive.

The Japanese in the Jogjakarta region also tried to introduce technological change; two examples were the line planting of seeds rather than broadcast sowing, and the use of compost fertilizer made in the village. These innovations were themselves good, but again the methods used to introduce them were not. Orders were given to the peasants; if these were not obeyed voluntarily, force was used to compel the peasants. At the same time, however, economic incentives were weakened because any increased output was forcibly confiscated by the military and thus did not benefit the farmer. While the farmers accepted what they were forced to in

33. Keith Griffin, "Economic Aspects of Technical Change in the Rural Areas of Monsoon Asia," mimeographed (Geneva: UN Research Institute on Social Development, January, 1972), p. 43, Table 13, shows a decline of 7 percent in per capita food production from 1960 to 1970, although there was some increase in the latter years of the decade.

facade-like efforts, the innovations were abandoned as soon as the Japanese left.[34] Unfortunately, since independence policy-makers have often clung to the policy goals of the colonial era: to reduce prices of rice to civil servants, and to keep land prices low for sugarcane production to feed government-supported or -owned sugar factories.[35]

Following independence many of the handicaps from a weak public sector, and the absence of an industrial base, shackled the program. Hayami and Ruttan have pointed out the key role of a public sector in building infrastructure, carrying out research, and disseminating the results through an extension service; of an industrial sector capable of supplying manufactured inputs; and of a distribution network capable of distributing the inputs and marketing the outputs.

The irrigation network, so crucial in controlling water for the new technology, deteriorated greatly. The reasons are complex; one of the most important was the deforestation begun during the war and continued thereafter. Perhaps more important was the weakening of the local tax base for irrigation and the general weakening of the entire government financial situation during a period of rapid inflation; these factors led to a marked weakening of the Department of Public Works and of the local agencies of irrigation maintenance and water control.

The departure of the Dutch in 1957, and the drastic reduction in research resources as a result of inflation, led to a marked reduction in the capacity to carry out research. The extension service, never very effective, became even weaker. With only a few extension workers functioning at the subdistrict level, it proved almost impossible for the extension worker to reach the individual peasant. In the area of marketing, the government eliminated the commercial distribution of fertilizers and insecticides as a result of its attempts to nationalize the marketing channels and replace the Chinese entirely. It also placed the rice mills, which were largely Chinese controlled, under such rigid rules that their usable capacity was

34. Selosoemardjan, *Jogjakarta*, pp. 230–241.
35. David H. Penny, "The Agro-Economic Survey: An Appreciation," *Indonesia*, no. 11 (April, 1971): 119–120.

much reduced. To replace the commercial distribution network, which also provided credit to the farmers, the government carried out a widespread expansion of the cooperative system to supply credit and some inputs, inserting the army as rice distributor. The cooperatives spread very rapidly but were so politicized that they were largely ineffective—and their resources were wiped out in the inflation. The army, which was directly given the task of rice collection and distribution, and the government monopoly which was given control of fertilizer distribution, had neither the flexibility nor the skills of private traders. During inflation the limited amounts budgeted for rice purchase proved inadequate, and the army was forced to resort to more or less compulsory collection of output in its efforts to meet largely illusory targets. Finally, the industrial sector has not been able to produce enough inputs to meet the needs of the rice sector.

Thus none of the conditions necessary for agricultural change has been present in Indonesia in recent years. President Sukarno's government, however, did import fertilizer when foreign exchange was available; these large amounts of fertilizer were distributed at subsidized prices. In 1963–64 the government encouraged the BIMAS extension program, which sent students to the fields to work with farmers in certain areas. National output of milled rice rose erratically from approximately 7.5 million tons in the early 1950's to about 9 million tons in 1966, which was somewhat below the rate of population growth. But it is significant that after 1960 total output in Java began to decline, reflecting the gradual decline in area harvested as the Javanese irrigation system deteriorated; increases took place outside Java, as a result of extended acreage. As inflation accelerated, governors of the Outer Islands restricted the flow of their rice surpluses to Java, in an effort to keep food prices relatively low in their provinces. This exacerbated Javanese urban food shortages and led to the importation of rice on the order of a million tons per year in the early 1960's, until the foreign exchange shortage sharply reduced those imports in 1963 and 1966.[36]

36. See Saleh Affif and Peter Timmer, "Rice Policy in Indonesia," *Viewpoints on Rice Policy in Asia,* mimeographed (Los Banos: IRRI, May 9–14, 1971), pp. 1–2, Table A–2. This is also a basic source on current programs.

The present government has laid great stress on increasing rice production. The goal of long-run self-sufficiency has been repeated, while in the short run increasing output to curb increasing rice prices was given high priority for inflation control. The rapid expansion of the BIMAS program was at first the main tool.[37] This made use of the students and the government extension service, but it was spread over a much larger area. The spread of an initially limited and flexible program weakened BIMAS, given the small number of qualified students and the weakness of the extension service. In order to circumvent this problem, farmers were required to take a uniform package of fertilizers and pesticides supplied on credit. The credit and inputs were bureaucratically distributed; there were serious problems of distribution, and many farmers found themselves receiving an unwanted input package too late to do any good; for it they incurred a more or less compulsory debt. Effects on production were disappointing, and much of the debt remained unpaid. In order to get around the weaknesses of the local BIMAS, foreign chemical firms were later introduced as the supplying and extension agencies. They were to supply fertilizer over a wide area and to carry out aerial spraying. Peasants in an area again received credits for a uniform package, and they were to repay a percentage of their output to the military collection and distribution agency, BULOG. While this program led to a greater use of fertilizer in the areas included in the scheme, the costs were high both to the government in the form of foreign exchange payments, and to the farmers in the form of more or less unwanted debts, a large part of which were not repaid because yield increases were less than anticipated. The National Fertilizer Survey results from a sample survey of farmers showed that between 50 and 60 percent of the farmers in West and Central Java who used fertilizer under these programs did not recover their additional costs. Much of this was due to inadequate water supply or pest attacks, both

37. On the BIMAS programs see in particular several articles by Gary Hansen: "Rural Administration and Agricultural Development in Indonesia," *Pacific Affairs* 44, no. 3 (1971): 390–400; "Episodes in Rural Modernization: Problems in the BIMAS Program," *Indonesia*, no. 11 (April, 1971): 63–81; "Regional Administration for Rural Development in Indonesia: The BIMAS Case," mimeographed (Southeast Asia Development Advisory Group Indonesia Panel Seminar, December 3–5, 1971).

beyond the farmer's control. For such farmers use of less fertilizer than offered under BIMAS was recommended.[38] There were complaints from farmers, as well as politically serious charges of corruption in administering this so-called BIMAS *Gotong Royong* (hereafter BIMAS GR) program, and it was ended in 1970.

During this period the government also adopted a rice price support program and fertilizer price policy to give the farmer a 1:1 fertilizer-rice price ratio to stimulate use of fertilizer. Meanwhile, to prevent undue urban price rises, BULOG was to distribute rice when rice prices rose above a certain level. This fertilizer price policy stimulated the use of fertilizer. While all these programs were costly, one benefit was the saturation of the rural areas with fertilizer, thereby contributing to increasing rice output, even though the results were less and the costs higher than anticipated.

In addition to these policy actions, steps were taken to improve technology. Fertilizer would have been of little value without new seeds. Initially the new IRRI varieties of the Philippines were used, but these were less suitable in Indonesia. Therefore Indonesian research in seeds was expanded, and various seed varieties better adapted for Indonesia were developed. These new varieties probably hold the key to expanding rice output in the future. As of 1971 new varieties covered approximately 10 percent of the total irrigated rice land in the country, and in Java the percentage has been higher.[39] In addition, the government has pursued an active program to rehabilitate existing irrigation works in Java, using imported food in some areas to encourage local rehabilitation efforts.

The result of all these efforts, together with an extended period of good weather, raised output from approximately 10 million tons in 1968 to 12.7 million tons in 1971. (Some of the increase also arose from a change in the method of estimating rice output. In addition, poor weather in 1972 resulted in relatively poor output.)

Perhaps more important for the long run with the ending of BIMAS GR, a new incentive-oriented program has been adopted. This retains the price-support element of the past program but relies on the farmer's own decision to use inputs in whatever quantity

38. From conversation with Ralph Cummings, Jr., Jakarta, March, 1972.
39. Ibid.

he wants. The rural banking system has been extended to the village level to provide the farmer with the credit he needs to purchase those inputs. In the first year 1.5 million farmers were given Rs. 15 billion in credit; the repayment rate was over 80 percent, far higher than in the past. This repayment was encouraged by the forgiveness of past debts, but it has been made clear that future credit will depend on repayment of new debt.[40] In addition, the government has begun a rural works program in some areas for which the participating farmer is paid in cash. This additional cash income makes it far easier for the small farmer to repay his loan, and is therefore an important part of any rural development program.[41]

Apart from freeing the farmer from bureaucratically determined uniform inputs, other companies—government and private—can now compete with the former government-owned fertilizer distribution monopoly. This will almost certainly improve the marketing of agricultural inputs.

The end of the great inflation and the general increase in output has enabled the government to reduce BULOG's role in rice procurement and distribution. Equally important, provincial barriers to rice movement have been reduced as prices have stabilized. In the rice-milling area extensive controls on the large Chinese-owned rice mills remain, and these mills operate well below capacity. However, many small rice-hullers have been distributed to Indonesian villagers. The controls on their functioning are far more difficult to enforce than on the large mills, and less acceptable. This has led to the far wider extension of machine milling at the expense of hand-pounding, and to reduced government interference in milling. While the economic costs are high in the sense that the large mills already exist and are more efficient than the small rice-hullers, the effects of the distribution of hullers have been beneficial. Controls can be bypassed, since the hullers are small and Indonesian run; these hullers are also more efficient than hand-pounding, even if less efficient than the large mills.

In addition BRI, together with the Ministry of Cooperatives, has

40. Conversation with Mr. Permadi, director of Bank Rajkat Indonesia (hereafter BRI), Jakarta, March, 1972.
41. Conversation with Richard Patten, Jakarta, March, 1972. I do not know how this and the credit program fared during the poor 1972/73 season.

begun to set up rural marketing cooperatives in conjunction with the village banks on a trial basis. If successful, these cooperatives can serve both as vehicles for credit, and to improve the conditions under which farmers sell their product. The first year's experience with the cooperatives has been described as unsuccessful. If the long-term effects are serious, this would be unfortunate.[42]

As a result of these policy changes and the continuation of an effective floor price, the environment for increasing rice output has been greatly improved, to give economic incentives a wider latitude.[43] Consistent with this was President Suharto's public statement in 1972, replacing the national policy goal of rice self-sufficiency by a new goal of improving the income and well-being of the peasant.[44] He recognized that this might be achieved by growing crops other than rice. But the government is only beginning to deal with the problems of developing an effective sector capable of producing manufactured inputs for agriculture.

From the little that is known of income distribution and the elasticities (both income and price) of demand, it appears that the increased output expected from current technological improvements can be consumed without long-term increases in stockpiles. The distribution of landholdings in very small plots, together with the system of sharing output, has meant that most farm families can consume more rice from the greater output. At the same time the increase in real urban incomes, as the economy once more moves forward and prices become stabilized, has resulted in a better flow of rice to, and probably a greater consumption of rice in, the cities.[45]

But this policy has not dealt with problems of land ownership, which served as the basis for Communist demands for land reform. It is difficult to determine what has been occurring on this issue, since it is seldom publicly discussed, but there is no reason why it should have disappeared.[46] It may be that this issue is not given

42. R. Shaplen, "Letter from Indonesia," *The New Yorker* (April 1, 1974): 59–60.
43. See Penny, "The Agro-Economic Survey."
44. Information from Saleh Affif, Jakarta, March, 1972.
45. See Affif and Timmer, "Rice Policy."
46. A recent talk by Eric Crystal about the island of Sulawesi makes it clear that issues of landownership and control are important there today. See the mimeo-

major significance today because of past Communist support, although the existing land reform legislation remains and is slowly being implemented. Evidence indicates that the gainers from the recent credit expansion program have been the somewhat larger farmers. While the average size of a holding in Java is 0.5 hectare, the average size of holdings of Indonesian farmers given credit under the recent BRI program is 0.8 hectare. This of course increases the disparity between larger and smaller, or landless, peasants. But the average holding of even larger peasants in Java is very small, and it is doubtful that further reductions in size by giving land to the tillers will yield economic benefits. In the long run failure to improve the lot of the landless laborers and tillers of tiny plots can only lead to further unrest. The continued subdivision of land in order to share poverty, whether carried out by traditional practices or by land reform, is unlikely to break through the ring of poverty on the land. Improved farm technology gives more time to solve this problem, and the effort to reestablish effective cooperatives is important, but the solution to this major problem is as much outside agriculture as in it.[47]

In part the government has sought to deal with this issue by encouraging movement of Javanese to the relatively underpopulated Outer Islands. But these programs have been failures in the past. Conditions outside Java have not been attractive in that infrastructure has been lacking, and farming practices are far different from those on Java; the programs have also suffered from inadequate funding and poor coordination among ministries. Annual emigration has not exceeded 50,000, and the number of emigrants has probably been exceeded by the number of immigrants. But mi-

graphed paper by Crystal on Sulawesi, prepared for the Southeast Asia Development Advisory Group's Indonesia panel conference, February 25–26, 1971. For more recent evidence that these problems of landownership have *not* disappeared, and that they may also be inhibiting the spread of the new rice technology in Java, as well as contributing to social tension, there are two later articles: J. Lelyveld, "Java Is Lush, But Not Rich Enough to Feed All Its 80 Million People," *New York Times*, August 28, 1974, pp. 27, 36, and R. W. Franke, "Miracle Seeds and Shattered Dreams in Java," *Challenge* 17, no. 3 (July/August, 1974): 41–47.

47. For a recent discussion of land reform see E. Utrecht, "Land Reform," *Bulletin of Indonesian Economic Studies* 5, no. 3 (November, 1969): 71–88.

gration would be no solution even if it were more successful. A study carried out by one of Indonesia's foremost economists and policy-makers estimated that if emigration from Java reached a level of 1 million people per year for a five-year period—a most favorable assumption—Java's population would still rise by about 50 percent from 62.5 million in 1960 to 95 million in 1990, even if human fertility declined by 25 percent while mortality continued its declining trend.[48]

Indonesia's major method of dealing with population pressure on the land must be one that has not really been tried. It involves developing the industrial sector enough to attract a significant number of workers from agriculture. If Hayami and Ruttan are correct, this is also a major requirement for sustained agricultural growth. The Dutch government was not interested in such a policy; governments since independence have been more interested but either have given it low priority or have adopted policies which have not had the desired effect. As a result in the late 1960's Indonesia had about two-thirds of its total population in the agricultural sector; the contribution of agricultural output to gross domestic output was among the highest in Asia, and the contribution of manufacturing employment to total employment was among the lowest.[49]

Industrial Policy

Indonesia should have favorable prospects for industrial development. While its resource base is still relatively unknown, it is believed to have abundant natural resources suitable for further processing, although these are probably more abundant in the Outer Islands than in Java itself. The large and relatively concentrated population, long accustomed to consuming manufactured goods, would appear to provide a good market for industrial products.

48. Widjojo Nitistrato, *Population Trends in Indonesia* (Ithaca: Cornell University Press, 1970), pp. 129–131; Ch. 11.

49. See *Annual Report of the Asian Development Bank for 1971* (Manila: Asian Development Bank, 1972), Tables 4, 5, pp. 137–138. Also from conversations with Wilhelm Boucherie, Jakarta, March, 1972.

But historically the colonial government gave little or no encouragement to development of industry, or of Indonesian entrepreneurs. In fact, Dutch policy encouraged Dutch and Chinese entrepreneurship at the expense of potential Javanese entrepreneurs—although some entrepreneurship developed in the Outer Islands.[50] In addition, the village ethos of sharing looked down on business practices in fields other than agriculture, while the *prijaji* ethic led to a strong preference for government employment. Meanwhile, the slow breakdown of communal relationships among the Javanese under the pressure of population growth and mobility broke down the relationships of mutual trust so necessary for larger-scale entrepreneurship, placing Indonesian entrepreneurs at a disadvantage to their Dutch and Chinese competitors.

After independence there was more discrimination against the Chinese. This reflected past history and the pressures of indigenous business groups, especially in the Outer Islands. All governments have acted to eliminate noncitizen Chinese from an economic role in the country and to force their emigration; naturalized Chinese have been allowed to function under a good deal of restraint, formal and informal, which has varied with the government in power.

Large Dutch and other foreign firms (the Dutch trading power was in the so-called Big Five firms) had a near monopoly of trade and production of estate and mineral products; this trade and production were often allied. Government policy toward these firms fluctuated prior to the present government. In 1957–58 all Dutch firms were expropriated, and from 1963 to 1965 all British and American firms were taken over as part of President Sukarno's foreign policy.

In order to replace these non-Indonesian business groups, various governments have tried to encourage local entrepreneurship. These policies had been played down, however, both for political reasons, because the businessmen were often of nongovernment parties, and for ideological reasons associated with socialism of the Guided Democracy. But perhaps most important, after 1960 the strains of the growing foreign exchange shortage made it difficult to divert

50. See above, pp. 91–95.

scarce foreign exchange to "train" indigenous businessmen, or to weaken successful nonindigenous businessmen who earned foreign exchange.[51]

It was politically necessary to take further steps to replace displaced Western and Chinese entrepreneurs. The Chinese-owned intermediary distribution system was replaced by the army, which was given control over the procurement and distribution of rice and other key consumer commodities. The government ran the nationalized enterprises and estates taken over from the Dutch and other Western groups; new government enterprises were established to import and distribute such manufactured products as fertilizer, and to manage some new large-scale industrial firms. These government-run enterprises have operated with varying degrees of efficiency, but they have usually functioned in a clumsy and expensive manner. They were often saddled with superfluous staff and hampered by political controls and bureaucratic rules which made operation on economic grounds almost impossible. During the inflationary period earnings of some army-controlled enterprises were apparently used not for productive purposes but to supplement the inadequate budgets of the military forces or of the provinces governed by military officers.

In addition to the government enterprises, the Sukarno government encouraged the growth of a new group of politically connected entrepreneurs; they took advantage of the detailed controls over foreign exchange and entry, and of the inflation, to set up money-making operations. Some entrepreneurs were formally outside the government, and some formally in it; the successful ones developed an effective understanding with the political leaders who controlled the licenses and permits, and who had the social status they lacked. "There are . . . sound grounds for an alliance between [these two groups]—a rather direct exchange of economic for social advantage. The government functionary gains the means to supplement his income and maintain his 'modern' style of life, while the businessman gains social acceptance, legitimation of his

51. See Frank H. Golay et al., *Underdevelopment and Economic Nationalism in Southeast Asia* (Ithaca: Cornell University Press, 1969); Ch. 3, "Indonesia," is by Ralph Anspach.

activities, and validation of his status." [52] The corruption resulting from this mixture of politics and economics was a way of life under the so-called Old Order; it contributed to the strong student dissatisfaction with President Sukarno, and to his ultimate overthrow. [53]

There have been a few specific studies of Indonesian enterprises and entrepreneurs since independence. The sultan of Jogjakarta, one of Indonesia's leading political and social figures, encouraged new business or industrial enterprises in or near Jogjakarta. [54] The first, started in 1954, was a tobacco farmers' cooperative which aimed at uniting individual farmers to improve their bargaining strength in dealing with tobacco buyers. Unfortunately, apart from the intrinsic problems of setting up such a cooperative organization, political interests overrode economic ones in certain major respects. Selection of management and staff was made on primarily political grounds, which resulted in poor decision-making. Thus, while the organization suffered from economic weaknesses, it finally collapsed for political reasons.

At about the same time the sultan also tried to start a sugar factory. Operation was delayed because of local political arguments over location; eventually it was begun in 1956 as a national undertaking, and it was completed in 1958. It broke down immediately upon completion because of serious errors by its East German construction firm, and it did not operate for a year thereafter.

A final example of ineptitude is shown by the experience of a former Dutch machine shop which was sold at the end of the war to the local administration, which then converted it to manufacturing iron tools. The new owners put in as manager an engineer who knew nothing about buying or selling, and the firm suffered heavy losses. The State Industrial Bank, the major creditor, then examined the firm and found that it had three times as many employees as required, and it suggested a reduction. This suggestion was turned down by the trade union and local administration; the bank there-

52. Fagg, "Authority and Social Structure," p. 151.
53. On corruption, see J. A. C. Mackie, "The Commission of Four Report on Corruption," *Bulletin of Indonesian Economic Studies* 6, no. 3 (November, 1970): 87–100.
54. For the three cases described below see Selosoemardjan, *Jogjakarta*, pp. 291–300.

fore refused to pay the remainder of a promised loan, which forced the firm to close.

"In all three cases there was no actual lack of capital, which was supplied by the government. Neither was there a lack of labor. But there was a lack of competent management. . . . The Sultan had assumed the role of entrepreneur, but he could fulfill only one aspect of this role, namely, to bear the risks of success or failure. He failed in the second part of the entrepreneurial role, in management." It was not possible to use foreign managers, given the policy of Indonesianization, and it was also "politically and socially impossible to take Chinese persons into the organization, even those who had accepted Indonesian citizenship. . . . The acceptance of Indonesian citizenship by individual Chinese may have helped them in their formal relations with the administration, but it has not changed the social relations between the Chinese as a minority group and the indigenous Indonesian majority. Having been favored by the Dutch, the Chinese are now disfavored."[55]

Geertz examines the beginnings of two quite separate entrepreneurial groups in Central Java and Bali in the mid-1950s. The Central Javanese group developed out of the traditional bazaar traders in one town: all the entrepreneurs were originally traders or traders' sons. They entered business specifically to meet the demands of a new urban lifestyle and to fill urban tastes, derived from Western influences coming through the main urban centers, rather than from court standards and tastes. They were united in the sense that all came from a particular social group practicing a particular version of reformed Islamic modernism; thus they were distinguished from other townsmen and traders by a religious practice which by its nature and separatism "makes economic achievement ethically significant." Most traders "belong to the same political and religious organizations; many of them are related either by blood or marriage; almost all of them have been close acquaintances of one another." But it is not an esteemed group—it is not accepted in the higher circles of the town because the members are not of the government, and it is not accepted by the peasants because the members are traders. However, the main

55. Ibid., p. 331.

problem of these businessmen reflects the sheer individualism of their efforts, arising out of the everyman-for-himself bazaar-trading mentality.

Almost all Modjokoto's modern enterprises are individual or immediate family concerns, and capital must be raised either through personal savings or (increasingly) through government loans; selling shares to villagers or large-scale borrowing on the open market is virtually absent, for the peasants' deep grained suspicion of traders effectively prohibits any relation between the two save that of the customary semihostile commerce. In Modjokuto even partnerships are almost non-existent . . . [as a result] Modjokuto enterprises seem to grow so large and then no larger, because the next step means widening the social base of the enterprise beyond the immediate family connections to which, given that lack of trust which is the inverse of individualism, they are limited.[56]

(This is similar to one characteristic of entrepreneurship already noted in the Philippines.)

The situation was almost the reverse among Balinese entrepreneurs. Here the entrepreneurial group came from the princely families at the very peak of Bali's Hinduized social system. The members of this group entered business not for reasons of social responsibility but in search of a new base for their political and social powers and status, both of which were being eroded by Westernization. These Balinese princely entrepreneurs had managerial ability—they set up a bus line, an ice factory, a tire recapping factory, a hotel, a weaving factory and a cooperative bank. Some of the required capital was raised by selling rice from their lands, but also by selling family jewels and other convertible property. In addition, these royal entrepreneurs used their social positions to raise capital by selling shares to, and getting loans from, peasants, civil servants, and small urban businessmen whose patrons they were; the labor employed in their enterprises came from families in similar subordinate groups. The entrepreneurs also saw their function "quite honestly, almost as much in terms of creating jobs as of earning profits."

In Bali the enterprises did not appear to have the problems

56. Clifford Geertz, *Peddlers and Princes* (Chicago: University of Chicago Press, 1963), esp. pp. 73–82, 121–141; quotes from pp. 122, 126.

arising from restricted access to capital which were found in Central Java; the princely family provided a large enough group from which to recruit managers for large enterprises. But because these Balinese firms were integral parts of the local political structure, it was difficult to prevent them from becoming politicized. There was great pressure "to divide profits rather than reinvest them, [and] to employ large staffs in an attempt to appease the rank and file," so they ran the risk of turning into relief organizations rather than businesses. But they also benefited from government favors. "In almost every case the success of Tabanan's noble entrepreneurs has partly derived from their ability to gain or demand support from the local wing of the national government. . . . The emergence, in Tabanan at least, of a unified elite of top civil servants and entrepreneurs mainly under the aegis of the Nationalist Party is fairly clear."[57]

Because they possessed less political significance than the sultan of Jogjakarta, and because Tabanan society had more unity than Jogjakarta's, these Balinese noble entrepreneurs were under less political pressure than the sultan. But both their experiences clearly show the mixture of politics and economics, and the risks thereof, in Indonesian entrepreneurship. An overall review of Indonesian policy from independence to 1967 concluded that

a considerable number of these businessmen [who were given one set of special privileges] were amassing wealth not by conducting regular business but mainly by acquiring the much desired import licenses and then selling them (illegally). . . . There were even many cases where an officially registered Indonesian firm in fact belonged to non-Indonesian citizens (mainly Chinese); the Indonesian owners and directors were used mainly as straw men in order to enable the firm to enjoy the [special] privileges. . . . [Following] the liquidation of the Dutch economic position [and the establishment of state enterprises], the Chinese role grew in importance. . . . This development was due mainly to the rather ineffective management of many of the state enterprises; a considerable number of the . . . executives not only lacked entrepreneurial dynamism but also efficient managerial skills. . . . [As] the disappointing experience with [various special programs to spur Indonesian industrialization] suggests, the failure of the Indonesianization and development efforts was due to a serious shortage of indigenous

57. Ibid., pp. 116, 123, 132.

Indonesian entrepreneurs—both as innovating risk-takers and as efficient managers—rather than to the shortage of capital and lack of opportunity.[58]

The effect of rapid inflation, followed by the necessary severe control of credit introduced by President Suharto's administration to curb it, greatly weakened or eliminated many private entrepreneurs. The present government has continued to use some of the large army-based organizations—especially BULOG in distribution and PERTAMINA in oil exploitation. These two organizations are considered to be fairly effective business enterprises headed by able and aggressive generals, but they have been subject to public criticism for supposed corruption, and the Commission of Four Report on Corruption examined their operations in some depth. The commission found them unwieldy in management, with weak financial responsibility and a need for government assistance; there was also some evidence of diversion of income to noneconomic activities. The Commission of Four recommended the gradual winding-up of BULOG and urged greater financial and managerial discipline on PERTAMINA's part.[59] As a follow-up to this report the president in 1972 appointed a three-man committee to oversee PERTAMINA. It is significant that this consists of several highly respected technocrats, who are regarded as above suspicion of corruption, but its powers are vague.

Other government-run enterprises have been inefficient, overstaffed, and uneconomic in their management. Since they may be performing economically useful tasks, and because they provide employment, they have been continued. But the government has evaluated their operations in an effort to improve their organization and management in order to make them cost and profit conscious, as a necessary step to putting them on a sound economic footing. If some of these enterprises cannot be made economic, serious consideration may be given to closing them entirely.

The development of nongovernment industrial enterprise is a far more difficult problem; on it the long-run future of the economy, and of the government itself, may well depend. In the five years of

58. Siregar, "Indonesian Entrepreneurs," pp. 345–347.
59. J. A. C. Mackie, "The Commission of Four Report."

President Suharto's government this has not been considered a major issue; in the second and subsequent plans, this, and the closely related problem of income distribution, are expected to be given much greater weight.

During the past five years the government's efforts to encourage industrial development have been directed primarily toward establishing a more stable environment for entrepreneurs by curbing inflation and correcting the errors of Guided Democracy. The government has been largely successful in curbing inflation; food processing and textile industries, which were operating far below capacity in 1967, were operating much closer to capacity in 1972 as a result of changes in regulation and an increased flow of imported raw materials, provided through foreign aid and greater foreign exchange earnings. In addition, private businessmen were allowed to play a freer role in trade and production. The major initial change in government policy occurred in the field of private foreign investment: for both economic and political reasons the government began to strongly welcome foreign investors. By the end of 1971 it had approved 129 foreign investment projects in agriculture, mining, oil, timber, and fisheries, as well as 260 projects in manufacturing. Some were in collaboration with government enterprises, but many were with private Indonesian businessmen.

However, there was an inevitable conflict on short-term policy goals. The control of bank credit required to achieve the prime goal of ending inflation served to depress those Indonesian industrial firms that existed, since many found it difficult to get continued working capital. Furthermore, the change in government broke some of the political-industry ties established under the previous regime, and many of these "hot-house" Indonesian firms failed. The government sought to counter this by making medium-term credit and other assistance available to Indonesian (as opposed to Chinese) entrepreneurs, in foreign trade, and in other fields.

But these programs are only beginning to get at the issue of encouraging Indonesian civilian entrepreneurs. Businessmen of Chinese origin in the private sector have largely monopolized the opportunities for establishing large-scale trading and industrial enterprise; the military has done the same in the public and semi-public sector. The close relationship between political power and business had encouraged this, since the military has always at least shared in power, and now largely controls the government. This political power had been used by the military to engage in trade and industrial enterprise. The businessmen of Chinese origin have historically been the ones with the experience, foreign contacts, and resources to be most useful, if a government desired financial support. The lives of such Chinese business firms often depended on their ability to work with the government (including the military) by providing government officials with either direct financial support or access to their experience and contacts. Because of their experience Chinese businessmen, either directly or through Indonesian fronts, were probably the major gainers from past programs, such as the medium-term credit program to help Indonesian businessmen. These problems may have been exacerbated by the entry of foreign firms into Indonesia under programs to encourage private investment. Many of these firms have found it worthwhile to collaborate with the military, because of their hold on power, and with the Chinese, because of their experience and resources.[60] This is beginning to give rise to what could become serious criticism of the neo-colonial patterns of development, with the gains concentrated in a small section of the local population—the military and Chinese—and the foreign firms. This critical attitude is strengthened by the associated development in Jakarta of a wealthy enclave, including entertainment facilities that cater to the new wealth, while the mass of the city's population remains in poverty. Jakarta, formerly characterized by its general quality of equality, is now beginning to resemble Manila, with its obvious disparities between the rich and the poor.[61]

In a country where there has been a strong ideological commitment to socialism and sharing, combined with strong antipathy toward and suspicion of Chinese, and in which there has been and

60. In Thailand, where similar development has progressed much further, it is not such a problem, since the Chinese are far better integrated there than in Indonesia.

61. See for example "Jakarta Getting a New Exterior," New York Times, May 14, 1972, I: 3.

is a strong student constituency sharply suspicious of corruption and desperately seeking employment in meaningful jobs, there are serious political dangers inherent in a continuation of these trends. These antipathies and dangers became obvious with the serious student riots during the visit of Japanese Prime Minister Tanaka. It will be necessary to take major, deliberate actions to encourage Javanese entrepreneurs and industrial enterprises, to maximize employment opportunities from industry, and to prevent the corruption associated with past industrial programs if the government is to succeed in future efforts to increase employment opportunities in the industrial sector and spread the gains to the general population. Unless such policies are adopted and successfully implemented, student groups or even the military could revive demands to severely control or nationalize foreign and Chinese firms. There is evidence that President Suharto and some government agencies are aware of this. The former Indonesian ambassador to the United States, Soedjatmoko, who has high prestige, had been appointed an adviser to the president, and to the planning agency, to suggest policies to deal with this problem in the Second Five-Year Plan, but it is uncertain how serious the Plan is on this matter.

A framework for overall industrial policy, and institutions to implement it, must be set up in the same framework as the agricultural policy which has gradually evolved during the past five years. Industrial policy must deal with such issues as the amount and duration of tariff protection in the initial stage of industrialization; the role of government-owned, frequently military-dominated, enterprises in production and distribution; the place of direct government controls on foreign exchange or imports; the establishment of medium and long-term credit institutions; the relative roles of foreign and indigenous entrepreneurs, and among the latter of those of Chinese origin and those of Indonesian origin.

It is not my purpose to discuss specific policies in these matters. However, as part of the discussion, and closely related to the politically sensitive issue arising from concentration of the benefits of past policy, one is struck by the absence of any policy to deliberately encourage small and medium-size industrial firms under Indonesian management. Short and medium-term credit facilities for

Indonesian-origin entrepreneurs should be provided; associated service facilities should be set up to provide entrepreneurs with technical and managerial training and services, as well as joint provision of expensive equipment and infrastructure. Industrial estates have been a useful institutional device for this in other countries. In addition, government-owned facilities and large-scale foreign enterprises should be required to train Indonesians on the job in management and technical skills, and they should be expected to subcontract at least some of their demand for manufactured inputs to small and medium-size firms if such are nearby. In fact, initially the government might provide insurance against loss to firms which carry out such subcontracting. For foreign firms the carrying out of a training program should be a condition of entry; failure to implement such a program, after independent review, should be grounds for termination of entry permission. For domestic firms, such a training program should be associated with any investment privileges.

Initially such a program should be confined to Indonesian, especially Javanese, entrepreneurs; as such entrepreneurs develop, the distinction between Indonesian and Chinese-origin entrepreneurs might gradually be ended. In the meantime, it is to be hoped that Chinese-origin businessmen will accept their Indonesian nationality and be accepted as Indonesians, so that the need for a discriminatory program will diminish.

In addition, on a broader scale, there is need for a deliberate effort to encourage labor-intensive industrialization if at all economic. Foreign investment per se will have only a minor effect on employment, since it is likely to be capital rather than labor intensive. (For example, a new textile plant requiring a 7 or 8-million-dollar investment will employ only 300 workers.) This may be obviated somewhat if the government begins to lay greater stress on employment creation as a criterion for granting foreign investment privileges. A program to encourage small and medium-sized local entrepreneurs and subcontracting should have greater benefits in this respect than the foreign investors program. In addition, the government might well consider whether the past program favorable to the welfare of industrial workers has not discouraged employment more than it contributed to welfare. But it would be politically difficult to change this latter set of policies unless changes were associated with strong efforts to increase employment and prevent greater income inequality in the country.

One element of any program to prevent manifest inequalities in income and wealth should consist of steps to deal with the corruption that currently exists, as well as to prevent further corruption. Some of this corruption arises from the characteristics of a patron-client system being transferred to contemporary environment; some arises from the erosion of government salaries and institutional budgets by inflation; some arises from the interpenetration of political and military elements into areas of trade and industry, under the guise of socialism, with related systems of control over both foreign and domestic trade. Even at this stage it should be possible to eliminate many of the controls on foreign trade, since the foreign exchange situation has greatly improved. Controls on internal trade, some of which were set up more or less illegally by local military leaders, can also be eliminated as food supply increases and the economy stabilizes. The sooner all such specific controls are eliminated the better; the same may be said for the withdrawal of the military from business and trade. The latter is a slow process, since the interconnection has been close in the past. But continued charges of corruption are likely without this divorce, and the damage of corruption to the government is serious in terms of reducing "support for the government among elites at the province and regency level."[62]

In summary, programs to advance industrialization more rapidly and to spread its gains to a much wider group are politically most significant. Steps are also required to prevent undue urban income inequality which, while still apparently less obvious than in the Philippines, is beginning to become obvious and to pose a potential long-term threat to the government. Such programs would provide jobs for the growing number of educated, who formerly sought work in a government which can no longer provide

62. On corruption see Theodore M. Smith, "Corruption, Tradition and Change," *Indonesia*, no. 11 (April, 1971): 21–40; quotation from p. 40. For an example of the high cost of corruption in customs, and the resulting delays, see "Inter City Hotels Use No Government Facilities," *Djakarta Times*, March 7, 1972, p. 3.

work directly; they would also provide work for the ever growing rural population, either landless or on diminishing plots of land. Thus it would be possible to break out of the poverty-sharing peasant culture, with the resulting involution of the economy, that has characterized Indonesian economic history.

The process would have profound social and political consequences. It would create classes of entrepreneurs and workers who, by setting up horizontal organizations representing their interests, would bridge the wide grap between family and government. This in turn could contribute to the development of a political system organized less along vertical lines rooted in traditional elements in society, bridged only at the top by a few political leaders and the military and civilian bureaucracy, and more upon political groups interested in issues and prepared to form coalitions cutting across the traditional vertical cleavages. There is no reason why such a development in Indonesia would or should take a Western political form. If it occurs in the fairly near future, it might represent a modification of the existing military-dominated party structure. It could provide the present military-cum-administrator leadership with some of the broader political support for its economic policies that it currently lacks, but which former President Sukarno temporarily achieved by his ultra-nationalistic appeals and personal style.

CHAPTER 5 THAILAND

There will be no more wars with the Burmese and the Vietnamese. There will be trouble only with the farang *[Europeans]. Take good care; do not fall into their traps. Whatever they have invented, or done, which we should know of and do, we can imitate and learn from them, but do not whole heartedly believe in them.*

—Deathbed statement of King Rama III of Thailand, 1851

Don't spit at the sky.

—A Thai aphorism

THE PEASANT SOCIETY AND ITS HISTORY

Of the three Southeast Asian countries examined in this book, Thailand is unique in several respects. First, it has never been under colonial rule, although it has clearly been influenced by Great Britain and France, the neighboring colonial powers. A Thai government has ruled what is now Thailand, with some border changes, since the late eighteenth century under conditions of general internal peace. Second, the Thai religion is Buddhism, although the Thai government and social structure has been influenced by the Hinduism transplanted to Southeast Asia. Third, Thailand is not a country of islands. This has contributed to its comparative ethnic homogeneity, to the ease of mobility within it, and to the relative uniformity of its government. The following analysis will be largely confined to the Thai-speaking population, the major ethnic group; however, it will also deal with the economic role of the Chinese ethnic community because of that community's great significance in Thailand's economic life.

Unlike the Philippines, but like Indonesia, Thailand has a Great

Tradition. Certain marked resemblances in the cosmology underlie the social structure and behavioral patterns in both Thailand and Indonesia. Basic to Thai cosmology was a belief in the "parallelism between . . . the universe and the world of man. . . . Harmony between [an] empire and the universe is achieved by organizing the former as the image of the latter, as a universe on a smaller scale." As the sun was the center of the universe, the king was the center of the empire. The king, by the ritual enactment of his role in various ceremonies, was the source of the people's life and prosperity; he was the father of the people, the center of righteousness and power, and the lord of the land. The central position of the capital in the empire reflected that role; within the capital the architecture of the palace and the arrangement of the court quarters all revolved about the king. In the traditional social structure everyone's role in the empire was determined by his or her relation to the king, as the center of the system. The king's position was proof of both his past accumulated and present merit. For others, high position and closeness to the king showed control over the universe and other people, and therefore proof of some merit, varying directly with rank. But the reverse also held true; natural disaster or defeat in war was proof of a failure to control the universe, and thus evidence of a lack of merit, and a justification for a change in superiors.[1]

This cosmological element which stressed the role of the king and state was combined on the personal level with a strong individualistic strain in Thai Buddhism. "All Thai are aware of the Buddhist injunction: By oneself is evil done; By oneself one suffers; By oneself evil is left undone: By oneself one is purified." This individualism is supported by a recognition that the individual lives in an environment that is highly indeterminate and subject to great chance, in which one must therefore avoid binding commitments to, or undue trust in, others. In order to control this indeterminacy the individual must govern his personal relations by an exchange of precise *quid pro quos*, while at the same time taking advantage

1. See Fred W. Riggs, *Thailand* (Honolulu: East-West Center Press, 1967), pp. 67–79; Robert Heine-Geldern, "Conceptions of State and Kingship in Southeast Asia," mimeographed (Ithaca: Cornell University Southeast Asia Program Data Paper no. 18, 1956), quote from p. 1.

of whatever external help he is able to marshal in dealing with this highly capricious world.[2]

The tension between the centralization of the state concept and the individualism of Buddhism was in turn strengthened by the character of the Thai economy before 1850; land was always abundant and manpower scarce.

All through Thai history the Thai were extremely conscious of the necessity for possessing large amounts of manpower, and were always devising ways and means of controlling manpower. Possession and control of manpower was vital for the survival of the society. . . . Thus, while certain societies might be more conscious of the importance of land and divide the polity into regions with definite boundaries, the Thai, extremely conscious of the importance of manpower, divided the kingdom into groups of men, each with a chief who served as responsible member of a staff-line, patron-client structure. The boundary of the kingdom, or of a province, was always left vague, while the population of the kingdom, or a town, and the numbers in a *krom* [a unit of power], were the main concern of the Thais.[3]

Since the ability to marshal manpower was the key element both in fighting the frequent wars that occurred between Thailand and its neighbors, and in building the necessary public works, an elaborate social system, in some ways closely resembling feudalism but in other ways significantly differing from it,[4] was developed. At the apex, consistent with the cosmology, the king in theory owned all manpower and land. In practice the king appointed nobles or princes (*nai*) to control the commoners (*phrai*) who made up the bulk of the population.

All *phrai* had to register and were assigned either to a noble or directly to the king; unregistered *phrai* were nonpersons. The function of the *nai* was to mobilize the *phrai* under him for service to the

2. The best discussion of this is Steven Piker's "Sources of Stability in Rural Thai Society," *Journal of Asian Studies* 27, no. 4 (August, 1968): 777–790.

3. The best study in English of Thai society before 1850 is Akin Rabibhadana, "The Organization of Thai Society in the Early Bangkok Period, 1782–1873," mimeographed (Ithaca: Cornell University Southeast Asia Program Data Paper no. 74, July, 1969). Much of what follows is based on this paper. Above quote from p. 77.

4. One major difference was that the relationship was not based on ownership of land; both noble and commoner could possess the lands they cleared or cultivated, without owning them.

king. This service might be as a soldier, or, if he were the king's *phrai*, as a laborer or corvée (which might last for four months out of a year). To perform this mobilization function the *nai* was given great authority over the physical presence, behavior, and services of his *phrai*. In turn, the *nai* was supposed to assist the *phrai* and protect him in any legal difficulties, to assist him or his wife financially by interest-free loans if the *phrai* was away from home, and to protect the *phrai* from other noblemen and from robbers by registering the *phrai*'s possession of land. The *phrai* provided direct services and gifts to his superior for these functions and services. Such gifts were an important part of the *nai*'s income, since he received no salary for his services; they represented a significant part of the total output of the land cultivated by the *phrai*. The relationship between *phrai* and *nai* was that of patron and client "in which one party [*a phrai*] offered gifts and services to the other [his *nai*] in return for aid and protection. . . . To each *phrai*, the *nai* adjusted his aid and protection according to the amount of gifts and services the *phrai* rendered him."[5] The king, as the protector of his people, was at the summit of the system. He was the court of final appeal to prevent abuse of the *phrai* by the *nai*, and he and his court were supported by the labor and the upward flow of gifts from the *phrai* through the *nai*. The system of relationships from king to the humblest person in the land was formalized in a precise hierarchy in which every rank was assigned a certain value (the *sakdina*) which expressed precisely, in terms of land, the number of commoners under one's control. The system of status of this *sakdina* system became in fact so deeply imbedded in Thai social life and behavior that, in the Thai language, "it is extremely difficult, if not impossible, to avoid the expression of relative social status of speakers. . . . All terms of personal reference—pronouns, titles and the like—carry with them definite connotations of social status. The linguistic function of social status in Thai is comparable to that of gender in English."[6]

While the system appeared quite rigid, there were significant

5. Rabibhadana, "Thai Society 1782–1873," p. 89.
6. David Wilson, *Politics in Thailand* (Ithaca: Cornell University Press, 1967), pp. 50–52.

elements of mobility. Unlike in European feudalism, the particular relationship between a noble and a commoner might be terminated relatively freely if either felt that he was not receiving what he expected, although the *phrai* would then be assigned to another *nai* or to the king. Furthermore, the *phrai* had three other options: he could escape to the empty lands if his superior was excessively demanding, although if he did so he would lose whatever minimal protection he in fact got from his *nai*; he could more or less voluntarily enter a relatively mild degree of slavery, which freed him from the corvée and which might be redeemed subsequently by payment;[7] or he could in effect renounce this world and its hierarchical system by becoming a monk. Thereby he would, at least temporarily, be relieved of the ordinary pressures of his life. Although horizontal movement was possible within the system, and some movement was possible outside it, upward mobility from slave to prince was very difficult. Except in times of war or irregular succession to the throne, the restrictions which arose because of requirements of family and knowledge made it very hard for commoners to become nobles.

For the noble some upward mobility was possible in peacetime, but this depended on his connections. Physical closeness to the king obviously could bring a noble to his attention and favor. Perhaps more important for the ordinary official, the ability to establish an informal client relationship with a superior officer other than one's formal superior offered opportunities for protection and advancement outside formal channels. In establishing such an informal relationship a quid pro quo arrangement, based on the exchange of gifts for services, would be set up.

Gains from any such relationships, whether formal or informal, were not one sided. The client gained protection and some services; the patron gained income directly, and indirectly political strength and wider influence from a larger number of clients. Two of the main political tasks of the king were to prevent any one noble from accumulating an unduly large number of clients, thus strengthening himself enough to become a threat, and to prevent competition

7. See Lucien M. Hanks, "Merit and Power in the Thai Social Order," *American Anthropologist* 64 ((1962): 1250–1252.

for clients from creating such division within the kingdom that its survival might be threatened in the event of an external attack. To insure his security the king sought to keep control over his subjects in the hands of himself and his family by limiting formal mobility and any informal or extralegal relationships among the nobles.

Another factor providing flexibility within the system as a whole was the role of the Chinese. They were deliberately encouraged to migrate to Thailand by being legally exempt from the corvée and the *sakdina* system. They were free to travel and settle anywhere within Thailand; they provided the labor for commercial agriculture and for the trading, shipping, and navigating functions necessary for carrying on foreign trade, monopolized by the crown. There were no limits on their right to accumulate wealth, and they were only required to pay a head tax. Their wealth made it possible for them to bid for the lucrative posts of tax farmers for the king; from the wealth derived from tax farming many could and did intermarry with Thais and become Thai officials and nobles, rising to very high rank. In fact, the rise of the Chinese to a position of power was a sign that by the mid-nineteenth century control over labor and labor's output from land was no longer the only source of power. Monetary wealth derived from trade was at least as effective an instrument for achieving status.[8]

Thus around 1850 the Thai social system contained various conflicts and tensions in both philosophy and practice. On the one hand there was a cosmology stressing the central role of the king and state, with individual merit reflected in a position near the king and with a high stress on hierarchy; on the other hand Buddhism stressed the role of individual effort and merit. There was a state with power theoretically centralized in the capital and the king, who owned people and land, with the people assigned to compulsory services or labor; in fact, power was diffused to a large number of nobles with specific positions to whom the commoners were actually assigned for service; the king sought to prevent any noble from achieving undue power, and to some extent to protect the commoners from the nobles. A two-class system of nobles and

8. Rabibhadana, "Thai Society 1782–1873," pp. 135–136, 162–165; G. William Skinner, *Chinese Society in Thailand* (Ithaca: Cornell University Press, 1957), pp. 96–98.

commoners (including slaves) allowed little movement between the classes in times of peace; however, significant opportunities existed to weaken hierarchical rigidities within each of these classes: among the nobles by establishing informal connections with more powerful noble patrons, and among the commoners by escaping to open lands or to a monastery, or choosing a form of slavery. Outside the Thai social structure, but serving as an additional source of wealth and power to the king, the Chinese performed nontraditional functions for the crown and thereby mobilized liquid wealth for themselves, which in turn opened for them new channels of power. This system, based on assigned labor, compulsory service, and restricted movement, functioned in a reasonably effective fashion with sufficient flexibility for a Thailand more or less isolated from world politics and trade. But in 1855 the signing of the Bowring Treaty by King Mongkut and the United Kingdom opened the country to more or less free trade. The old system could no longer protect the independence of the kingdom in a world of expanding colonial powers, nor could it take advantage of the new trading opportunities. During the reign of King Chulalongkorn (1868–1910) many of the major institutions were changed:

Slavery was abolished. Government corvée was entirely replaced by hired labor. The status of *phrai* . . . was deprived of much of its significance by the establishment of the regular army. The reorganization of the civil administration, which set up regular salaries for the previously unsalaried government officials, affected the basis of the organization. . . . [The] establishment of secular and Western influenced schools and higher education facilities also widened the avenues of social mobility.[9]

In the rural areas the introduction of a modern system of title deeds in 1901 confirmed the existence of private property, free purchase and sale of land, and free mobility of peasant and noble.[10] In order to reduce the kingdom's vulnerability to piecemeal division by colonial powers, the powers of the various local principalities were gradually reduced and control was concentrated in Bangkok.

During this great reform period a new relationship between the

9. Rabibhadana, "Thai Society 1782–1873," p. 1.
10. See especially Takashi Tomosugi, "The Land System in Central Thailand," *The Developing Economies* 7, no. 3 (September, 1969): 290–291.

state and the individual was established; it largely exists today. Politically the power of the king and the central bureaucracy was strengthened. National boundaries were defined, the powers of local rulers were largely eliminated, and all power was concentrated in Bangkok; the bureaucracy was nationalized and put on a basis of regular pay and promotion; a professional army was set up. In the economic sphere, however, the individual was given far greater freedom than before. Under the pressure of the colonial powers the whole country was open to trade, and anyone was permitted to engage in it. Agriculture and landownership were also open to all, anywhere within the kingdom; until the mid-1950s the size of new holdings from unclaimed land was limited to 50 *rai* per family.[11] With the ending of the corvée of Thai labor, there was a much greater demand for Chinese labor to construct public works and to perform the trade and service functions required in an expanding trade center such as Bangkok. The number of Chinese immigrants increased rapidly.

But although pay was regularized and promotion officially based on merit within the government, the patron-client relationship remained strong. Connection with the royal family remained a significant criterion for the top positions in the civil bureaucracy and the army; for other posts family and close relationships with a high-level official were, if not sufficient, then highly desirable advantages.[12]

In the rural sector the individual Thai peasant took up property, cultivated new lands, and greatly expanded rice output, attracted by the availability of imported manufactured goods brought to him by Chinese traders. But such economic individualism was tempered by strong feelings of dependency, since support of others was required to carry out the socially central religious and ceremonial functions, to produce rice, and to insure protection and security for himself and his wife in old age. The earlier formal patron-client system, including the alternative of slavery, was replaced by a far more flexible system which contained elements of the former patron-client relationship but which was limited to

11. One *rai* = about .41 acres, or about ⅙ hectare.
12. See below, "National Politics and Government."

one's family and village neighbors, including married relations. The need for dependency was met by "meticulously reckoned quid-pro-quo [relationships]. Prominent examples are: the networks for ceremonial assistance that crosscut village boundaries; cooperative harvest arrangements . . . and exchange of resources . . . and personal assistance among close relations." With respect to domestic security the system of brideprice, marriage, and matri-local residence functioned to establish a kindred relationship among connected peasant families. This provided the newlyweds with agricultural resources from the bride's family while the young couple matured, and it provided an assured home and food to the couple's parents when they reached old age. There was thus a narrow family-based patron-client relationship established among the kindred: initially the parents of the young couple served as patrons, but this was reversed over time as the couple took over the land and supported the parents. This security system, which did not restrict the individualism of the family, was based on conditions of almost universal landownership that existed until the first quarter of this century.[13] This rural system of kindred relationships was based upon a precise system of exchanges among equals and did not limit the ability of the Thai peasant to increase his landholdings or output. These relationships served to confirm the belief that "getting by in this world, especially in traditional agricultural occupations . . . [depended] largely on individual effort and diligence." But when the Thai farmer entered unaccustomed fields, "getting ahead, or coming to terms comfortably with non-traditional economic challenges, [was] thought to depend largely on how much others can be induced to do on one's behalf."[14] In relations outside the village, individualism was replaced by the need to become a client of someone more powerful.

The assumption of more or less universal landownership among the peasants on which this system was based was reasonable through the first third of this century. However, with rapidly growing population and exhaustion of the land, it is no longer as valid.

13. See Piker, "Sources of Stability," pp. 778–780; also Steven Piker, "The Post-Peasant Village in Central Plain Thai Society" (paper prepared for the 1972 meetings of the Association of Asian Studies, New York), pp. 3–5.
14. Piker, "Sources of Stability," p. 780.

Both Piker and Kaufman in their specific village studies have pointed out growing landlessness and the accompanying growth of wage labor and indebtedness in their Central Plains villages. On a more general level, by 1953 only about three-fourths of the land was owned by its operators in the Central Plains; this figure probably decreased from 1953 to 1968. In Thailand as a whole the average farm size decreased from 4.4 hectares in 1953 to 3.5 hectares in 1968.[15] While these figures indicate a higher level of landownership and larger holdings in Thailand than in neighboring countries, they also indicate that the abundant empty lands which long characterized the Thai economy no longer exist. With this transition one also notes development of new social relationships within the village. Piker describes this transition in a Central Plains village: "Landless families . . . no longer possess the wherewithal . . . to undertake the kind of reciprocal arrangements with others which, traditionally, have been the major source of assistance in times of need. Furthermore the income of landless families derives almost completely from individual wage . . . work; cooperative or reciprocal labor arrangements are virtually meaningless under these circumstances." Under such conditions the old age security element in these relationships also does not hold, since that was based on a quid pro quo between the parent generation and its children. The landless peasant now has no land to offer his children. Without land, the peasant works for wages and seeks to establish one or more client relationships with well-to-do landed neighbors. He benefits by getting some employment and food, a chance for low-interest loans, and permission to hang around the patron. In exchange, the patron gets some "free" services and congenial company. But these relations are non-kin based, amorphous, and short term; they are unlike the older relationships either within the bureaucracy or outside rural life. Since the landless peasant has no resources to offer for a bride, his children are independent in their

15. See Robert L. Pendleton, *Thailand* (New York: Duell Sloan, Pearce, 1962), pp. 166–171; Shigeru Ishikawa, *Agricultural Development Strategies in Asia* (Manila: Asian Development Bank, 1970), pp. 96–98, including note 121; Hazel V. Richter and C. T. Edwards, "Recent Economic Developments in Thailand" (paper prepared for a seminar on Contemporary Thailand, Australian National University, September 6, 1971), pp. 14–15. Also see Piker's "Post-Peasant Village," as well as Howard K. Kaufman, *Bangkhaud* (Locust Valley, N.Y.: J. J. Augustin, 1960).

marriage and immediate after-marriage arrangements and therefore assume no obligation for his long-term security.[16]

The assumptions of equality within the village are no longer
valid, and distinctions on the basis of wealth become significant.
Kaufman found in his village that

wealth plays an important, though at times subtle role in the community.
A farmer with money is in a position to exert pressure on many other
farmers. He is the *phujaj* in the *phujaj-phunauj* [big man–little man]
relationship. It is to him that others must turn in order to borrow and
to rent tools, to obtain cash loans, and land to farm. Once the transaction
is made, the debtor is obligated in many small ways throughout the
year. However, wealth without the proper behavior results in contempt
and malicious gossip, and receives only token respect during the poor
farmer's moment of need.

Large landowners are potentially in a position of great power . . .
[but they] do not exploit this power unduly since the prerequisites [*sic*]
of wealth are fairly simple. More wealth means more gold chains and
gold belts, and a more elaborate funeral. Tractors, cars and an elaborate
house are neither necessary nor desired. Great wealth might enable the
farmer to establish himself in Bangkok, but fear and illiteracy are strong
impediments against [such] a move. . . . Thus there is no major incentive
[in the village] for power as a means to wealth. . . . The village farmer
is not interested in power for its own sake; it exists as a prestige factor,
but within limitations. One cannot hope to rise higher than [commune
head] without the proper education, but with education, the farmer
tends to sever his ties with the village and move to the urban areas.[17]

It is not proper to use economic power to increase already abundant wealth or to appear to squeeze those without wealth. Moerman found that in the village of Ban Ping "some villagers perceive
and respond to economic opportunities more acutely than others.
Generally, those who save, invest, expand their production, and use
the market more efficiently than their neighbors are the villagers
who, for these and other reasons, are criticized as calculating, aggressive and selfish."[18] This is at least a contributing reason for the
role of the Chinese in the rural sector. The Chinese, and now those
of Chinese ethnic origin, have been and are the village merchants

16. Piker, "Post-Peasant Village," pp. 7–9.
17. H. K. Kaufman, *Bangkhaud*, pp. 35–36, 69.
18. Michael Moerman, *Agricultural Change and Peasant Choice in Thailand*
(Berkeley and Los Angeles: University of California Press, 1968), p. 144.

and moneylenders. Partly because of these Thai attitudes and partly because of the major Chinese role in foreign trade and rice-milling, the Chinese have inevitably moved backward into the village, not as landowners, but as traders and processors.

In conclusion, one can say that Thai rural society can be reasonably described as loosely structured. This description has been criticized as to both meaning and accuracy[19]—but if it does imply among the Thai peasantry an absence of permanent class relationships, a relatively high degree of equality, and a relatively high degree of mobility, it has been correct. However, as land has become scarce relative to population, with increasing indebtedness and landlessness, this description has also become less accurate. Although the latter tendencies were strong enough to permit Piker in 1972 to speak of the growth in the Central Plains of a post-peasant society characterized by the existence of a significant rural proletariat, in the form of landless wage laborers, this development appears to be confined largely to that region. Even in the Central Plains landlessness is far less prevalent than in the other Asian countries being examined; and for the entire rice-growing population of Thailand there remains enough sense of equality and individual mobility that it would be premature to speak of a two-class system. There is a functioning patron-client system, but it is less rigid than in the Philippines and is based on specific quid pro quos; if expectations are not met, the relationship can be freely ended.

Fragmentary data with respect to landownership among rice farmers support the above generalizations. "Information on the distribution of land ownership in 1965, by size of holding, among rice farmers in eleven provinces in the central plain [the area in which landlessness has proceeded furthest] shows that the top 20 percent had 34 percent of all the land concerned, while the bottom 60 percent had 40 percent. The concentration ratio worked out at 0.27 [a low figure]." However, the study also supports the observed tendency toward inequality, in two senses. First, incomes

19. See the discussion in H. Dieter-Evers, ed., *Loosely Structured Social Systems: Thailand in Comparative Perspective* (New Haven: Yale University Southeast Asia Studies, 1969).

of rice farmers are more concentrated than land ownership; second, when figures for all rural income recipients and all rural landholdings are examined, the concentration of incomes and landownership are significantly higher than for rice farmers alone.[20] This would indicate that income differentials arise from variations in fertility and farm location which reinforce differences due to size of holdings, and that the income derived from production of crops other than rice is significantly more concentrated than the income from rice farming.

While one might still speak of Thai peasant society as loosely structured, it would be an error to say that about all of Thai society, since mobility between the Thai peasant and the Thai government officer is still difficult. Status is very important, and the government officer is of distinctly higher status. It has been and still is difficult, given the importance of family background and the limited access to higher education, for a Thai to move from the ranks of the peasantry to those of the government, even though today there are more possible channels, including the army.

NATIONAL POLITICS AND GOVERNMENT

Although the accuracy of such a generalization is being challenged by increasing industrial growth and urbanization, it would still be reasonably correct to say that most Thai are either peasants or government officials. The traditional sharp line between these two groups remains.

Until 1932 the king was at the pinnacle of the government and the social system. The Revolution of 1932, which took place largely to increase government opportunities for educated Thai not of royal family, removed political power from the king (although he remains an influential figure) and placed it in the hands of the bureaucracy, of which the military is the most powerful component.

At the very top of Thai social structure, combining political

20. See UN Economic Commission for Asia and the Far East, "Economic Survey of Asia and the Far East, 1971, Part I," mimeographed (prepared for the March, 1972 meeting of ECAFE in Bangkok), pp. 117–119. Quotation, p. 119.

power, the highest positions in the bureaucracy, and social status, is a ruling group of about 1,000 members.[21] The topmost echelon of this group consists of the actual ten or fifteen rulers. This number includes the senior military commanders, a few civilian leaders, and a few people around the throne. The second level of the ruling group includes military officers mostly of general officer rank, special-grade civil servants, prominent members of parliament, some princes, and some particularly powerful businessmen. No landowners as such are included in this group. In contrast to the other countries studied, in Thailand the larger landowner has no political power as a member of an organized landowning group.[22]

The members of the top echelon wield their political power as leaders of cliques, each of which is based upon a network of personal ties centering about "the relationship between the leader and the follower. . . . [There] is a strong tendency for these ties to direct themselves up and down, while lateral ties . . . are not necessarily very strong," since the followers may be rivals for the leader's favor or for succession.[23] Political changes at this level come suddenly as one clique replaces another by what has become an almost normal, although unscheduled, method: the military coup.

In Thailand power begets power—"to him who hath shall be given"—since power itself is proof of goodness and virtue and attracts followers. Perhaps even more to the point, a leader is expected to be generous to his followers by rewarding them with jobs, privileges, or permits of one type or another; in exchange he receives the loyalty of those tied to him by opportunistic rather than kinship relationships. The reverse is also true. If power begins to slide from the leader of a clique, it falls at an accelerating rate, since the initial slide is evidence of a decline in virtue which

21. The above discussion of the top leadership is based largely on Wilson, *Politics*, esp. pp. 60–61, 116–117, 133–137, 160–163; quote from p. 60. This was written before the government changes in 1973. The tenses remain unchanged in this section of the text.

22. This important comparison was suggested to me in conversation with A. Siamwalla, visiting at Yale University in spring, 1972.

23. Quote from Wilson, *Politics*, p. 116. Hanks, "Merit and Power," and following him Edward van Roy, *Economic Systems of North Thailand* (Ithaca: Cornell University Press, 1971), pp. 114–116, use the term "entourage" to describe the entire network of a patron-client relationship, both in the village and in the government.

in turn results in less power to reward those opportunistic followers who quickly leave a sinking leader.

Formal authority rests with the prime minister and the cabinet; the ministerial position provides access to the potential rewards of power. The minister's constituency is his ministry; he fights for its budget and he protects its employees. His success depends on his relative position in the ruling clique, but there is strong competition among the ministries, since loyalties run vertically rather than horizontally.

In this top group the military leadership, which had traditionally combined civil and military functions, plays a very strong role. This is largely because the military is one of the few Thai corporate organizations which can mobilize large resources of men, capital, and power—and the army is the largest group within the military, and is thus the most important. The sheer fragility (or ego-centeredness) of Thai social structure militates against large corporate civilian organizations. The army by its very nature must be different.

In 1965 this top leadership of 1,000 directly controlled a bureaucracy of about 250,000 regular civil employees and an additional 150,000 employees in the Ministry of Defense, presumably officers and men of the armed forces.[24] Within Thai society, position in the bureaucracy serves "as the chief source of status, security and identity for Thai, above the level of the villages." This continues a tradition that goes back far beyond the opening of Thailand to the West. It is therefore to be expected that within the bureaucracy "the immediate source of authority is hierarchical status; and the substantive concerns of the [individuals] . . . are to some degree status-centered rather than achievement oriented . . . In this system the thrust must come from the top."

The hierarchical structure within the bureaucracy, as in the village, has a strong patron-client element. "Young and ambitious officials usually seek to establish an identification with a high-ranking patron. They support him by being helpful, informative

---

24. This discussion of Thai bureaucracy is largely based on Riggs, *Thailand*, and William J. Siffin, *The Thai Bureaucracy* (Honolulu: East-West Center Press, 1966). Employment figures from Siffin, p. 151; quotes from pp. 148, 167, 174, 246.

and deferential. He in turn is expected to obtain rewards for his followers, one of which is advancement. If the high official moves to a new organization, his proteges may also move."

Advancement in status is the major aim of the individual within this system, and it is also the key to material position. But status tends to take priority. "In general terms, wealth is no full substitute for rank. For some, wealth is a function of status and the perquisites that go with it. But wealth alone does not seem commonly preferable to high status. Thais who are shrewd and discerning in business affairs devote substantial amounts of time to bureaucratic careers, partly to protect or advance business interests, but also to try to reach the top class of civil service. And money alone does not necessarily provide easy access to that class."

This bureaucracy, located mainly in Bangkok, is the largest part of the small political public which Wilson estimated at no larger than 500,000 people. Since 1932 political parties have sometimes existed in Thailand, since the ruling group pays lip service to democracy, but these parties have generally been loose combinations of cliques grouped around a government leader, rather than independent parties with ideological bases. They have tended to compete for power with, as well as within, the bureaucracy. However, they could be weaned away from independence by the promise of reward; or, if they were competing for patronage, they would be swept away by a coup when they became annoying. Political struggles in Thailand have often been inter-clique conflicts over power and status. This in-house character of politics has usually resulted in low voting rates in urban areas, since issues were not presented that were important to more educated voters. However, as in Indonesia and the Philippines, "in villages and less urbanized areas there are face-to-face influences and status demands that . . . encourage voting. For instance, at election time it is one of the duties of the village headman to instruct the villages in voting procedures. Sometimes the district officer or other officials will supplement his efforts. In this way villagers tend to acquire the notion that failure to vote would be . . . at least a violation of obligations due within the status hierarchy."[25] The same observer therefore concluded

25. James N. Mosel, "Communication Patterns and Political Socialization in

that in Thai politics "there is no real threat from elites outside the formal structure of government . . . leadership of even a small clique is an almost certain guarantee of a ministerial post." Since most leaders of different groups are absorbed in the system, the membership of the elite remains remarkably stable in terms of the type of person included, although individual leaders may change.[26] The last elections under the 1969 constitution may have pointed toward some change in this pattern. While the chances of changing the government were slight, there was a vigorous opposition effort which sought greater democracy and closer legislative supervision of the administration. The opposition won a sweeping victory in Bangkok and played a critical role in Parliament until the 1971 coup dissolved Parliament and the political party structure. The opposition probably derived some of its strength from accumulated dissatisfaction against a long-standing government, but it may be even more significant of a growing political public reflecting wider educational opportunities, greater industrialization and urbanization, and urban and economic development outside Bangkok. The stifling of this opposition by the dictatorship that followed the 1971 coup, the rigidity of that dictatorship in response to the disquiet of students and other civilian groups over the changing international situation in Southeast Asia, and the charges of internal corruption and other domestic difficulties led directly to the unprecedented student unrest and violence that culminated in the overthrow of that dictatorship in October, 1973.

What have been the consequences of the government structure upon the character of economic policy-making? Both Siffin and Riggs[27] doubt the future ability of the bureaucracy, because of its patron-client character, either to mobilize effective support for domestic policy or to respond authoritatively to claims from within the society.

Transitional Thailand," in *Communications and Political Development,* ed. Lucian W. Pye (Princeton: Princeton University Press, 1963), p. 224.

26. James N. Mosel, "Thai Administrative Behavior," in *Toward the Comparative Study of Public Administration,* ed. William J. Siffin (Bloomington, Ind.: Indiana University Press, 1957), pp. 309–313.

27. Siffin, *Thai Bureaucracy,* esp. Ch. 10, pp. 253–255; Riggs, *Thailand,* esp. pp. 381ff.

A first and major consequence of government structure has been the concentration of power in Bangkok. This represents a response to the traditional role of the king and capital; as power was transferred from the provinces to the central government in the early twentieth century, Bangkok's role further increased. Throwing open the country to foreign contacts and trade had a similar effect, since Bangkok was the center of trade and the place where effective contacts could be made precisely because it was the center of government. Major units of the military have also been concentrated around Bangkok since 1932. Such combinations of political and economic elements have caused Bangkok to dominate the rest of the country. Ten percent of the Thai live in Bangkok, which has a population about thirty-five times that of the next-largest city, Chiang Mai in the north. Bangkok and the surrounding area form not only the center of government but also the hub of trade, finance, public utilities, and industry; the city is by far the major center of higher education and serves as a magnet for students. This magnetic effect is strengthened by the traditional fact that Thai students wish and expect to work in the government, centered in Bangkok; more recently, private nonagricultural opportunities for educated employment have also been concentrated there.

Because decision-making is concentrated in Bangkok, and because government employees wish to live in Bangkok, where their chances for promotion are greatest, assignments to posts outside Bangkok are often regarded as exile. This was a major reason for the neglect of distant areas in economic development policy— until recently, when the fear of rebellion forced greater interest. The obvious discrepancies between Bangkok and Thailand's outer regions, the difficulty of communicating local needs and desires from the developing outer regions to the centralized seat of power, and the rigidity of response of the center to those needs are believed by some to have contributed to rising political unrest in the outer regions.[28] Furthermore, the concentration of government leaders and the bureaucracy in Bangkok has led to economic poli-

28. Joyce Nakahara and Ronald A. Witton, "Development and Conflict in Thailand," mimeographed (Ithaca: Cornell University Southeast Asia Program Data Paper no. 80, June, 1971).

cies favoring the city. One rationalization for the rice premium has been that it permits lower rice prices for the bureaucracy and urban dwellers: certainly the steady shift of public and private resources as well as power to Bangkok has contributed to the massive construction that has drastically enlarged and changed that city over the past twenty years.

Those who know something of the government are aware of the fragmentation of responsibility and duplication of effort within the bureaucracy. One development adviser reports that "competing claims of alternative development schemes became competing claims of different segments of the government bureaucracy. There is no inherent machinery for resolving conflicts between ministries for funds; there tended therefore to be a process of settlement of the conflicts by compromise; with the result that no ministry got enough money to carry out the projects most urgently needed in the sector of the economy for which it was responsible."[29] In almost all reports on development programs, whether by Thai or external groups, a constant refrain involves the need for better coordination of efforts to avoid what may be conflicting policies and actions by two agencies with overlapping responsibilities.

It is of course difficult to verify existence of government corruption, and the borderline between corruption and legitimacy varies. However, there are frequent rumors of corruption. Some of these may simply reflect a carry-over of traditional practices of gift-giving to superiors from a period when they received no salaries. But civil service salaries have not kept pace with living costs, and this is blamed "for the prevalence [of] the 'tea money' system-payment of small bribes to expedite transactions with various government offices."[30] In addition there are the well-known connections (open or otherwise) of some leading government officials with business firms. Marshal Sarit and his successors were found to have large private resources, discovered after their deaths or exiles; senior officials have been prominent on the boards of directors of leading banks and industrial firms.

29. Wilson, *Politics*, p. 161.
30. James C. Ingram, *Economic Change in Thailand, 1850–1970* (Stanford: Stanford University Press, 1971), p. 302; see also note 34 below.

In spite of these problems, the Thai bureaucracy has not been ineffective. All observers agree as to the highly pragmatic and problem-oriented character of the Thai rulers, which arises in significant part from the fact that Thailand has always been independent and all governments have sought maintenance of independence as their first goal. This has probably led to better performance than in either the Philippines or Indonesia in limiting the expansion of the bureaucracy and controlling inflation. Thailand has a relatively smaller bureaucracy (recognizing the difficulty of comparison of the data). In 1932 there were 80,000 civilian government employees: by 1965 the comparable figure had grown to 250,000 officers. In addition 200,000 workers were employed in government enterprises and estates, and about 150,000 in the military forces. If we use the 450,000 people in civilian employment as the basis of comparison, less than 5 percent of the labor force in Thailand is employed in government. The Philippines has a population of approximately the same size, and a labor force supposedly 20 percent smaller (the difference being almost entirely in the female component); the bureaucracy of 800,000 civil employees is about 7 percent of the labor force. If a figure of 2 million is used for the comparable size of the Indonesian civil bureaucracy plus other nonmilitary government employees, 6 percent of the labor force is employed by the government.[31] Although in Thailand government employment has the highest status, the high respect in which farm life is held and the comparative availability of land for farming have kept the demand for such employment at moderate levels. At the same time, the strength of a long-independent government and the smaller size of the political public have enabled the government to better resist pressures to create jobs. The government also lagged in expanding opportunities for university education, possibly for reasons of bureaucratic defense. While future consequences of this lag may be unfortunate, it has served to restrict the number of applicants for government employment. However, even with this relative restriction of growth Ingram concludes "that many govern-

31. The figures on population and labor force are from You Poh Seng and Steven Yeh, "Aspects of Population Growth Policy," in Asian Development Bank, *Southeast Asia's Economy in the 1970's* (London: Longmans, 1971), p. 525, Tables A 7–8.

ment offices are greatly overstaffed, and the marginal productivity of labor [in these] is close to zero—if indeed it is not negative."[32] But other offices have been quite effective; the general level of bureaucratic functioning is certainly not below, and is probably above, that found in the other countries examined.

Likewise Thailand has been better able to resist inflationary pressures arising from structural elements in the society. The past strength of the government, derived from its long independence and the small size of the voting public, reduced the need for "pork barrel" projects to keep all groups happy. In addition, there has been a long tradition of conservative and anti-inflationary finance. This stems from the Thai government's genuine fear that financial instability might serve as an excuse for foreign intervention after the country was opened up. In addition, before 1939 the English financial advisers to the government were backed indirectly by the prestige of their own government and laid great stress upon conservative finance. Since the Bank of Thailand was set up in 1942 as a formally independent central bank, it has served as a major force against inflationary financing methods. Its formal independence has enabled it to attract a very capable staff and to remain free from undue political pressures. Its governors have always been men of great prestige and independence. It has thus been able to play a leading role in favor of a conservative internal monetary policy and a careful husbanding of foreign exchange reserves to insure that they would be used for development, rather than for political purposes. In such a policy it had the strong support of the commercial banks, whose financial managers had a similar background. The close relationship of many of the political leaders with the commercial banks generated political support for conservative monetary and fiscal policy.

In the following sections I explore the pattern of the development of agriculture in Thailand, especially the spread of new crops and technologies, and the development of industry. In both areas I examine not only the role of the pure Thai, but also the influence of the Chinese, whose direct role in government may be small, but whose mercantile and entrepreneurial role is large.

32. Ingram, *Economic Change*, p. 303.

ECONOMIC IMPLICATIONS

Agricultural Development

The opening of Thailand to world trade in 1855 led to greatly increased rice production, and a far greater increase in its export. Although production figures are not readily available, the area planted in rice rose from an estimated 6 million *rai* in 1850 to over 21 million *rai* in 1935–39. While little is known of yield per *rai* in this period, there is some evidence of a decline in yield after 1900 as worse lands were cultivated. However, a threefold increase in output would probably be a reasonable estimate. Over approximately the same period the volume of rice exports appears to have increased from about 1 million *piculs*[33] to 25 million *piculs*. In 1850 exports were about 5 percent of the total output; by 1907 the proportion exported was about half, and thereafter it ranged from 40 to 50 percent until 1939.[34] This increase in rice exports has been the major element in the commercialization and simultaneous monetization of the Thai economy, and it has been largely responsible for the expansion of agricultural production to the remote areas of the country.

Over the same period the population rose from roughly 5 or 6 million in 1850 to 14.5 million in the 1937 census. There is no regional breakdown for 1850, but most people would have lived in the central region then. By 1937 only about 40 percent of the country's population was living in that area. This population shift occurred together with a decline in the central region's role in rice production, which fell from about 70 percent of the total national area devoted to rice in the early twentieth century to about 55 percent by 1937.

The additional labor force needed to produce the greater rice output was met only partially by population growth. In addition there was probably some shift of labor into rice cultivation after

33. 1 *picul* = 60 kg. or 132 lbs.; 16.67 piculs = 1 metric ton.
34. Ingram, *Economic Change*, Ch. 3, esp. pp. 36–54. Ingram's book is the best book-length economic history of Thailand in English; it includes a good cautionary evaluation of Thai statistics. A provocative and more analytical analysis of Thailand's economic history from a radical point of view is Peter Bell's "The Historical Determinants of Underdevelopment in Thailand," mimeographed (New Haven: Yale University Economic Growth Center Discussion Paper no. 84, February, 1970).

1855. The indigenous labor which has produced consumer goods in the previously closed economy sought other employment as these consumer products were replaced by imported goods. But the quantity of labor from this source was probably not very large, since most rural Thai were probably in rice production already, either as full or part-time farmers. Most of the additional labor required to cultivate the newly opened land, therefore, was probably supplied by peasants who gave up some of their previous leisure to till more land to produce more rice and thereby earn for themselves more consumer goods. There is at least some evidence that from 1860 to 1900 the quantity of consumer goods (measured in terms of cotton textiles) available to the peasant in exchange for rice exports increased steadily. After 1900 the terms of trade of manufactured consumer goods against rice exports deteriorated until about 1920: thereafter they again rose and roughly stabilized at the 1910 level (still significantly more favorable than the terms of trade in 1850–60). This would support the notion of an improvement in the Thai rice farmer's well being once Thailand was opened to world trade.[35] One recent study[36] estimates that Thai per capita income in 1958, measured in British prices, was about one-third that of the United Kingdom—which would also support the impression of improved well-being after Thailand was opened to international trade.

The government's role in this entire process was crucial in that the policy changes described earlier made the entire development possible; apart from that, its direct participation was minimal. The

35. There is some contradictory evidence in that real wages of Bangkok laborers, measured in terms of rice, were apparently falling throughout much of this same period. Although these real wages rose after 1930, they still had not reached the 1850 level by 1950. One would expect a rise in peasant incomes to be reflected in higher urban wages. An explanation for these seemingly divergent trends may be that there was a sharp split between the farm labor and urban labor markets. The Thai farmer did not go to the city; the competitive wage for labor in Bangkok would not be the income or wage of peasants in rural Thailand, but the income or wage of peasants in that area of China from which the Bangkok laborers came. Why didn't the Chinese workers leave Bangkok to buy land and earn higher incomes in the country? While Thai laws permitted such free mobility, there still may have been de facto restrictions on Chinese acquisition of land. On this entire matter see James C. Ingram, "Thailand's Rice Trade and the Allocation of Resources," in The Economic Development of Southeast Asia, ed. C. D. Cowan (New York: Praeger, 1964), esp. pp. 112–120.

36. Dan Usher, "The Thai National Income at United Kingdom Prices," Bulletin of the Oxford University Institute of Economics and Statistics 25 (1963): 199–214.

key role was played by the millers and traders (largely Chinese), and by the Thai farmers. Initially British and American investors set up the large Bangkok rice mills and processed most of the exported rice, which they received from Chinese middlemen. However, by the end of the nineteenth century seventeen of twenty-three Bangkok mills were owned by Chinese, and by 1919 the Chinese owned fifty-six out of the sixty-six mills. The Chinese were not only the middlemen in the rural areas, but also rural moneylenders and traders. They controlled the flow of rice to Bangkok, and after 1919 they set up smaller local mills in the producing areas. The Chinese role in this rice trade was strengthened by the fact that the largest proportion of exports until 1940 went to China, Hong Kong, and Singapore, in all of which Chinese traders played the major role. In exchange, the Chinese traders imported and distributed the consumer goods whose availability provided the incentive for peasants to expand their output.

Chinese traders made large profits from this trade and apparently remitted large amounts to the mainland. Ingram estimates that remittances may have averaged $10–12 million per year from 1890 until 1941, or about $500–600 million in total, far in excess of government capital investments over the same period. He believes that over this period a substantial part of the money savings of Thailand was transferred abroad, so that by some definitions Thailand was a net capital exporter. If this saving had been invested in Thailand, the benefits for future Thai growth would have been substantial; by 1940 Thailand might well have had the infrastructure and industrial base it has been trying to build since 1950. (But if the remission of profits was a price that had to be paid to Chinese traders and middlemen for their services in the development that did occur, the cost might well have been justified.) It is difficult to criticize the government for doing something no other government was doing.[37] However, from 1860 to 1940 the government can be criticized for failing to tax the Chinese more

37. Ingram, *Economic Change*, pp. 204–205. I find criticism of past behavior on the basis of today's goals, standards, or theories of development unjustified. Growth was not a goal then, and capital exports were not restricted by any country. If the capital exports had been restricted, the rice trade and exports might also have been reduced, since an incentive for Chinese trading would have been reduced.

heavily (they were taxed less than the Thais for many years), thereby retaining a larger proportion of the profits in Thailand, and for not investing in infrastructure, such as irrigation works and schools, which might have been started in the late nineteenth or early twentieth century. Such projects were recommended at the time, and many other governments were investing in these activities—but with the favorable development that was occurring in Thailand, the need was not seen as urgent. This changed after 1950, and the government did adopt a major investment program for the construction of irrigation works and transportation facilities.

While the pre-1950 growth that centered around rice production and export was generally beneficial to the population, the future of Thai agriculture is in some question today.[38] Until 1950 the great increases in Thai rice output occurred primarily as a result of expanding acreage to outlying and lower-yielding lands. From 1950 to 1967 acreage planted still rose, but by only about 20 percent, while output went up by almost 50 percent. The main factor contributing to the yield increase was the investment in water control systems, resulting in better flood control, irrigation, and storage. But in spite of the increasing yield, Thailand's per acre productivity is still low compared to many Asian countries. From the scattered evidence available it appears that the national average yield per hectare in the mid-1960's only recovered to about the same level as in the first third of the century. While several high-yielding rice varieties have been developed in Thailand recently, they are still not used on much of the rice-growing area. Where they are used, it appears that they are being used more for their disease resistance than for their yield.

The increasing output of rice since 1950 is in large part con-

38. The discussion of recent trends in rice production in Thailand and of Thai government policy relies heavily upon the following sources: Delane Welch and Sopin Tongpan, "Rice in Thailand," in *Viewpoints on Rice Policy in Asia*, mimeographed (Los Banos: IRRI, 1971); Ingram, *Economic Change*, pp. 237–265; Takeshi Matooka, "Agricultural Development in Thailand," mimeographed (Kyoto: Kyoto University Center for Southeast Asian Studies Discussion Paper no. 27, 1971); Richter and Edwards, "Recent Economic Developments," pp. 11–22; Keith Griffin, "International Implications of the Green Revolution," mimeographed (Geneva: UN Research Institute on Social Development, February, 1972); conversations with Bhakdi Lusandanana, Bangkok, and Randolph Barker, Los Banos, March/April, 1972.

sumed domestically. While almost half of the output was exported before the 1930's, since the war exports have never reached more than 30 percent of production, and they are currently 10–15 percent. Much of the increased output is necessary to feed a population that has been growing at a rate of over 3 percent per year, at the same time that per capita incomes have been rising and urbanization increasing. But the effects of other nation's efforts to achieve self-sufficiency in rice, and the Thai government's policy, have also encouraged a shift toward other crops.

Various Asian countries had some success in increasing their own rice production and reducing imports prior to 1972. Ceylon, India, Indonesia, Japan, the Philippines, and Malaysia are in this group. To the extent that self-sufficiency is achieved by these and other countries, this trend will be continued; it resulted in a sharp decline in the world price of rice between 1967 and 1972. The effects of the poor weather in 1972 reversed this trend in the quantity and price of exports, but the reversal may only be temporary.

In addition, the Thai government's use of the rice export premium as a major, though decreasing, source of revenue reduced the returns to rice growers. With falling world prices, the premium was abandoned for most grades of rice, but potential benefits in the form of higher incomes for farmers disappeared as world prices also fell.[39] With higher world prices in 1972 the Thai government reimposed a rice export tax to control the increase of rice prices in Bangkok. When rice prices were falling between 1967 and 1972, the government's fertilizer price and tariff policy had kept domestic fertilizer prices significantly above world prices in order to protect a domestic high-cost fertilizer factory. The result was a 3:1 ratio in the price of urea to that of rough rice at the end of 1971. This ratio was higher than in any other Asian country for which such data existed, and was high enough to discourage farmers from using fertilizer. In turn, the effect of both falling rice prices and a high ratio of fertilizer price to rice price discouraged Thai farmers from using the high-yielding varieties.[40] In addition, the orig-

---

39. The rice premium has been very widely discussed; see Ingram, *Economic Change*, pp. 243–261, for a summary.
40. I do not know if this changed in the past year, when rice prices rose sharply;

inal new varieties were not adapted to the deep water character of Thai rice production in the Central Plains region.

These policies raised the profitability of other farm products relative to rice. Output and exports of maize and kenaf increased greatly; in addition, farmers shifted to oilseed and cassava production, while near Bangkok many farmers began to produce garden crops and fruits to meet that city's growing demand. While the area planted in rice rose by 20 percent, the area planted in other products rose by almost 400 percent from 1950 to 1967. In the former year about 85 percent of the entire planted area of the country was in rice; by 1967 this percentage had fallen to about 67. Much of this shift has been based on sound economic factors reflecting new foreign and urban demands; it is also likely that the newer lands, especially in the Northeast, which were more recently opened up to rice production, are relatively less efficient for rice and more efficient for other crops. Thus a gradual shift in patterns of farm production to concentrate rice output in the well-watered and fertile areas of the Central Plains and North, and to use the less-fertile outlying lands for other crops and livestock, would appear economic over the long run. This calls for major increases in the productivity of lands devoted to rice-growing, so that output in those areas could meet both the growing internal demand and an export demand which will probably remain in the neighborhood of 1.0–1.5 million tons if Thailand continues to maintain a significant comparative advantage in rice production. The export of rice has always been a major source of Thailand's foreign exchange earnings, and with appropriate policies it should remain so.

The Thai farmer has always been willing and able to respond to economic incentives. This may arise from a streak of individualism in the rural social fabric, comparatively widespread landownership, and the contribution of wealth to the possibility of higher social status. It has been shown by the expansion of rice production and is currently shown by the shift from rice to other crops. The middleman and trader, usually of Chinese origin, has provided incentive by informing the farmer of new markets, by offering an

---

but, as in other countries in the region, poor weather adversely affected Thailand's rice output.

attractive range of manufactured products in exchange, and by providing a reasonably efficient system of marketing. A recent study of the Thai rice trade concluded that the cost of rice distribution is low, with the Thai rice farmer getting 80 percent of the 1965 Bangkok retail price of rice.[41]

In the past government policy has set the framework within which the economic incentives might function; in more recent years the government's construction of irrigation and road systems has raised the productivity of the land and provided the facilities for moving output from more distant regions to Bangkok. (Output from the Central Plains normally moved by water to Bangkok.) But the benefits of this investment program for the rice-growing farmer were reduced both by the rice premium policy (which taxed rice farmers relative to others, and which particularly benefited urban groups) and by a fertilizer production and price policy which discouraged use of that key input. In addition, weaknesses in the government bureaucracy have reduced the benefits of government investments and the spread of new technology. Lack of coordination in planning and execution of irrigation projects, especially shown by the failure to construct terminal irrigation networks to the major systems, has reduced the benefits from the irrigation investment. While the marketing system has effectively spread technologies, their adaptation to Thai conditions and their improvement depend on an effective extension service cooperating closely with research. The weakness of the extension service, both in terms of its relation to agricultural research and in terms of its own quality, has hampered the spread of the new technology.

The adoption of the new rice technology will require expansion of rural credit. Rural credit institutions have been weak in the Thai system, with credit supplied largely by relatives and neighbors, or dealers and private moneylenders. Interest rates for such loans have been high, from 2 to 3 percent monthly; for the smaller farmer a common source of funds for production and consumption has also

41. See Dan Usher, "The Thai Rice Trade," in Thomas H. Silcock, *Thailand: Social and Economic Studies in Development* (Canberra: Australian National University Press, 1967). Usher found that the distribution costs for comparable products were a smaller proportion of the retail price in Thailand than in the United States or England in 1965.

been the pre-harvest sale of rice at prices 20–40 percent below post-harvest prices. Government efforts in rural credit have not been highly successful, despite programs to encourage private banks to provide rural credit and to encourage the growth of cooperatives. Private banks have begun rural credit programs, but this is a new field for them and will require time to yield results; cooperatives have had only limited success, which may reflect peasants' lack of confidence in each other and consequent difficulties of cooperation.[42] This issue has been raised earlier. But it is clear that the future of the small Thai farmer will rest on his ability to raise productivity so that his land will yield a favorable return. This calls for widespread use of high-yielding rice varieties, which in turn requires government actions along the lines indicated earlier; to provide favorable price incentives; to improve efficiency in the use of the country's water resources; to operate effective research and extension systems; and to develop a rural credit system that will make credit available to farmers for inputs required for the new technology. In addition, government by its own research and extension program, as well as by appropriate price policies, can encourage the development and use of new technology for rain-fed crop production, as well as for diversification to new crops and livestock production in those parts of the country where rice production is uneconomic. (The rice premium did of course encourage such diversification by making other crops relatively more profitable.)

Finally, the improvement of the well being of the agricultural population is related to the development of an industrial base that will provide the inputs required for the new technology at prices low enough for the farmer to be willing to use them. Development of industry is also necessary to provide jobs for those farmers who are losing their land. This has been proceeding rapidly in some areas. (For example, one recent survey of the Central Plains indicated that before 1965 about 80 percent of the farmers in the area surveyed owned the land they tilled, whereas by 1968 this percentage had dropped to 40. The previous owners became tenants

42. Tomosugi, "The Land System," pp. 307–308, contrasts Thai and Japanese experiences with cooperatives. On the problem of rural credit in general, see the papers in Tongroj Onchan, ed., "Agricultural Credit Problems in Thailand," mimeographed (New York: Agricultural Development Council, 1972).

paying about one-third of their output to landlords.[43]) This has changed the communal character of the village society and forced increasing numbers of villagers to seek work outside the village.[44] Fortunately, the process has been cushioned by the fact that empty lands were available elsewhere, and job opportunities outside agriculture have been growing at a rapid rate supported by a general economic growth. But both of these cushions may be weaker in the future. The empty lands are largely occupied; those that remain empty are the least productive, requiring large investments to make them attractive. New job opportunities in the cities grew rapidly with the general recent economic improvement, but they may diminish as the fighting in Indochina draws to a close and the American presence there declines. However, in the long run the structure of the Thai economy may benefit from the shifts induced by the smaller American role. Even during 1960–69, while real gross domestic product grew at a rate of about 8 percent per year, employment grew at an annual rate of only 2.5 percent, less than the 3.1 percent rate of population increase.[45] While unemployment is low, there was an increase in open unemployment from an estimated 87,000 in 1960 to 238,000 in 1966. (It may be assumed that this is entirely urban, with rural unemployment taking various disguised forms.) With the growing population and labor force and the trends in landownership, the demand for job opportunities outside agriculture will probably rise even more rapidly in the future. Industry will have to play the key role in meeting this need.

The Development of Industry

The government played a major role in industrial development before 1960, either by its own activities or by the policies it implemented. A variety of industrial plants were set up prior to 1940 to produce goods for particular government departments, of which those plants were part. (This was especially true in the Defense Department.) In 1954 the government sponsored and helped fi-

43. Onchan, "Agricultural Credit," p. 2.
44. See above, pp. 137–139.
45. Conversation with Jeffrey Romm, Bangkok, March, 1972; National Economic Development Board, *National Income of Thailand* (Bangkok, 1968–69); Seng and Yeh, "Aspects of Population," p. 562, Table B 5–6.

nance a National Economic Development Corporation (NEDCOL) to develop industries, but by 1957 this had collapsed amidst a welter of charges of corruption—"the men who started [it] were interested in exploiting government resources, not the resources of Thailand."[46] Many of these government-run enterprises were only incidentally productive; they were looked upon as sources of patronage and extra-budgetary income for the political leaders and agencies involved. Thus they were often drainers of resources rather than producers of income.

After 1958 the government turned increasingly to the private sector for industrial growth; by 1969 there were only 28 government-owned factories out of 46,000. The rate of growth of manufacturing and construction sectors exceeded 10 percent per year during 1960–69; the share of both as a proportion of GNP rose from 17 percent in 1960 to 23 percent in 1969. Employment in manufacturing also rose, but not as significantly. The 1963 industrial census gives a total of 481,000 workers (less than 5 percent of the labor force) in manufacturing enterprises; a 1969 survey estimated employment of 711,500 workers in manufacturing, plus 151,500 in construction.[47] The share of manufacturing employment in the total labor force was still below 5 percent of the labor force, which would indicate a relatively capital-intensive type of industrial development since 1963.

Of the more than 46,000 factories registered by 1969, almost 26,000 were rice mills. Less than 3 percent employ more than 50 workers each. The key policy instrument for recent industrial development is the Promotion of Investment Act of 1954, as amended in various years to 1965. The 1962 provisions grant a wide variety of familiar incentives, including some protection to industrial investment. This act contributed to the marked upsurge of industrial investment and output that occurred after 1963 in such fields as petroleum refining, cement, car assembly, and beverages, all out-

46. E. Ayal, "Thailand," in F. H. Golay et al., *Underdevelopment and Nationalism*, p. 308.

47. See Richter and Evans, "Recent Economic Developments," pp. 23–24; National Statistical Office, *Preliminary Report of the Labor Force Survey for the Whole Kingdom* (Bangkok, July–September, 1969), p. 31, Table 6B; NEDB, *National Income*, pp. 32–33, Table 7.

side the agricultural processing area. By the end of 1971 over 550 firms had been promoted under this act, and 435 factories were operating. Total investment in these firms was approximately $1.1 billion (their registered capital was about $350 million), and they employed 124,000 Thai workers. Thai businessmen supplied approximately two-thirds of the capital, and foreign firms, of which the most important were Japanese, the remainder. These firms are large by Thai standards, averaging more than 150 Thai employees, and there is some evidence that they are more capital-intensive than usual. Silcock argues that there has been a bias toward capital intensity in industry because of two social factors: possible private gain to top members of the bureaucracy from imports of modern machinery under supplier's credit arrangements, and the great prestige of capital-intensive equipment in the eyes of the government officials responsible for administering the program.[48] During this period one general orientation of industrial development policy was to substitute for manufactured imports domestic output behind a fairly high degree of tariff protection to meet the rapidly growing domestic demand. This resulted in the development of industries producing or assembling consumer and intermediate goods for the relatively high-income Bangkok population, or goods for government irrigation and road-building projects. But the new industry also had a high import dependence, a low backward linkage to other sectors, and a gap in the production of intermediate products and capital equipment. The Third Plan stresses creation of backward linkage and earning of foreign exchange as major criteria for stimulating future industry, with emphasis to be given to "export oriented types of industries or industries which use a great deal of local raw materials and labour to substitute for imports."[49]

The Industrial Finance Corporation of Thailand (IFCT) was set up in 1959 to encourage industrial expansion. This is in effect a government-sponsored but largely private financial institution,

48. Government of Thailand, Board of Investment, "Statistics of Promoted Investment," mimeographed (Bangkok, December, 1971); Dirk Stikker and Ryokichi Hirono, "The Impact of Private Foreign Investment," in Asian Development Bank, *Southeast Asia's Economy*, pp. 409–415, 443–444; Silcock, *Thailand*, Ch. 11, pp. 264–277; NEDB, *National Income*, p. 129.

49. National Economic Development Board, "Third National Economic and Social Development Plan: Summary," mimeographed (Bangkok, 1972), Ch. 1.

owned by a combination of local banks and foreign banks doing business in Thailand; it has received foreign currency financing by loans from the Asian Development Bank and the World Bank. The purpose of the IFCT is to make long-term loans and provide private equity financing for domestic industrial firms. After a somewhat lengthy starting-up period, during which lending was at a rate of less than $5 million per year, the annual amount of loans had reached more than $15 million in 1969; by the middle of 1971 the annual rate of lending was close to $20 million. On the whole it has followed sound practices but played only a small role, providing less than 5 percent of industrial financing during this period. A factor in this minor role may have been the reportedly strong disagreements between more conservative commercial-banking-oriented directors and more development-minded directors as to the appropriateness of long-term industrial finance. One must hope that this issue has been resolved in favor of the latter group, since otherwise there would be no need for an institution like the IFCT. One advantage of the IFCT, in part due to foreign investment, has been its relative freedom from bureaucratic pressures in making loan decisions. This has permitted economic (rather than political or other) factors to determine its lending decisions.

The expansion of the IFCT is also closely related to the general problem of developing a capital market. Thai industrialists, like those in the other countries, have been reluctant to sell stock to outsiders because they fear loss of control. When this is matched by investors' reluctance to trust their capital to strange hands, it results in serious problems of raising internal resources for large-scale ventures. It also leads to concentration of industrial control in family groups, often of Chinese origin, with their own banks, and operating in close conjunction with foreign investors and military leaders. This can create political problems, even though the benefits of growth have apparently been spread well in the urban areas.[50]

This is in turn related to the sensitive issue of the role of the ethnic Chinese in Thai industrial development, and the desire to encourage Thai entrepreneurship. The Chinese have traditionally

50. See below, p. 165.

filled the gap in the Thai society between the peasants and the bureaucracy. They were welcome from an early date and were exempt from the restrictions placed on both the Thai and other foreigners; in exchange they performed urban manual labor and most entrepreneurial functions. This meant that they migrated into the urban centers, primarily Bangkok, where they formed a clear majority of the population until their immigration was ended in 1949. In the villages they served as traders and middlemen.[51]

Assimilation has been far more rapid than in Indonesia or the Philippines. At least one reason for this contrast was the long history of Thailand's independence. Upward mobility in Thailand was assisted by identification as a Thai, since the ruling group was Thai. Therefore it was to the advantage of the Chinese to seek to be regarded as Thai, by intermarriage and training. In the other two countries a Chinese gained no social status in marrying a native, and there might in fact be a loss of status in relation to the ruler. Skinner argues persuasively that the rate of assimilation of Chinese into Thai culture has been equal to the rate of assimilation of Europeans into American society. He concludes that today a sizable proportion of the Thai elite is of Chinese ancestry. "The Thai have only to remain their sweet selves and follow a minimally sane policy through two generations to obviate the Chinese problem altogether."[52]

This quotation may be too optimistic, however. Even before the 1932 Revolution the Thais had been somewhat worried about the Chinese role in their country. Various nationalistic political leaders since then have been consciously anti-Chinese. This attitude grew stronger when political events and conflicts in China seem to have influenced the Thai Chinese community. Steps have been taken to stop Chinese immigration into Thailand, to curb if not eliminate Chinese education, and to limit Chinese business activity and prevent alien Chinese ownership of land. These policies have waxed and waned, but most recently the victory of the Chinese Commu-

---

51. The most thorough treatment of the role of the Chinese in Thailand is in the two books by G. William Skinner, *Chinese Society in Thailand* (Ithaca: Cornell University Press, 1957) and *Leadership and Power in the Chinese Community of Thailand* (Ithaca: Cornell University Press, 1958).
52. G. William Skinner, "The Thailand Chinese," *Asia* 2 (August, 1964): 80–92.

nists, the continuous fighting in neighboring Vietnam and Laos, and attempts to stir up rebellion in the Northeast and extreme south of Thailand have all contributed to some uneasiness, even though many Thai leaders have Chinese blood. One reason given for the November, 1971, coup in Thailand was "fears about the loyalties of the estimated total of three million Chinese living in Thailand" after Communist China's admission to the United Nations.[53]

A major reason for Thai criticism of the Chinese has been their dominant role in trade and industry. Their role in rice marketing and rural moneylending has already been discussed. In order to reduce the Chinese role in the rice trade, governments have nationalized some Chinese-owned rice mills and encouraged the establishment of credit cooperatives. But neither step has been significant, other than as a threat.[54]

The Chinese in earlier times played a major role in the development of rice milling, the major traditional industry. This investment grew naturally out of their role as middlemen in the rice trade. Outside this field, however, prewar Chinese investment in industry was small, partly because capital which might have been so invested was remitted to China.

Since the war, and the subsequent restriction on Chinese immigration to Thailand together with the Communist takeover of the mainland, the local Chinese have invested in Thailand. They have helped to develop the banking and service industries in Bangkok, and the manufacturing that has occurred. In fact, there has developed in Thailand a unique manner of pooling Chinese capital and entrepreneurial skill with Thai political and social leadership. The Thai political figure, often a military leader, is given a high position on the board of directors of the bank or firm, and the businessman, frequently of Chinese origin, is allowed to use his capital and entrepreneurial skills to run the enterprise. For the Thai political leader this combination provides access to extrabudgetary

53. *New York Times*, November 19, 1971, p. 3. The number used is a common figure which clearly includes the Thai citizens of Chinese origin, as well as the very small number of Chinese who are not Thai citizens.
54. On the Chinese policy of Thai government in the economic field, see Ayal's Thailand chapter in Golay et al., *Underdevelopment and Nationalism*.

income and jobs which he can use to meet his patronage obligations; for the firm it provides access to government contracts; for the businessman it provides protection and status. Politically too it has led to a pooling of political interest between the Thai political leadership and the Chinese business leadership, encouraging more rapid assimilation of the latter, as well as contributing to charges of corruption.

It is difficult to determine the extent to which this is a transitional arrangement. It depends on the expansion of the educational system in order to train more Thai in business. As increasing numbers of Thai become so trained, and as younger generations of Thai citizens of Chinese origin function as Thai within the society, occupational distinctions on ethnic grounds should blur.

Perhaps the most important economic question arising from this trend is whether and to what extent the Chinese move away from their economic orientation, so that the enterprises become vehicles for strengthening traditional Thai patron-client relationships rather than profit-making organizations. One recent study of assimilation of Bangkok Chinese (defined in terms of the language used by the parents) throws some light on this matter. This study found that although older and less-educated Chinese still believed in occupational distinctions on ethnic lines, for the younger Chinese, especially those educated in Thai schools, belief in these distinctions was far less. In fact, the present generation of Chinese students in Thai schools strongly preferred employment in modern, private business organizations—which they considered as neither Thai nor Chinese and in which both are employed—to entering a family enterprise. Such modern profit-making enterprises are not considered to have an ethnic bias, and are considered to be firms in which promotion based on objective performance is the rule. The Chinese in government service mix freely with their Thai colleagues and are oriented toward Thai values in their office work.[55] A second study of the Chinese born in the city of Ayutthaya found that the younger generation considered themselves Thai, were not confin-

55. See Boonsanong Punyodyana, "Chinese-Thai Differential Assimilation in Bangkok," mimeographed (Ithaca: Cornell University Southeast Asia Program Data Paper no. 79, March, 1971).

ing themselves to trade, and had assumed positions of leadership in a wide variety of the city's activities: "it is unlikely that they will maintain any degree of self-restricting exclusiveness if Thais do not exclude them."[56]

If this trend continues, the question of "Thai-ification" of industry will resolve itself without requiring further discriminatory steps by the government, unlike the Indonesian situation. Rather, the government's efforts might best be devoted to stimulating industry in general along the lines mentioned earlier, and to positive steps for providing more and better education at all levels. Stress should be on educating all Thai citizens, whether of Thai or Chinese origin, in skills useful for nongovernment employment.

Another important aspect of the long-term problem of spreading industrial gains is the concentration of industrial growth in the Bangkok area. Bangkok has always been the center of government and service activity. Since 1963 the increase of jobs in manufacturing and construction has been far greater there than in other cities; by 1969 25–30 percent of all industrial firms, and one-third of the total number of employees in industry and construction, were employed in the Bangkok area. (If employees of rice mills were excluded, the proportion would be far higher.) Approximately two-thirds of the large enterprises set up under the Promotion of Industry Act by the end of 1971 were located in or near Bangkok, and approximately 80 percent of the value added in manufacturing is derived from that region.[57]

The apparent effect of this development on income distribution has been interesting and somewhat contradictory. Among urban families there has been a greater equalization of incomes during the 1960's, and the concentration ratio decreased between 1962–63 and 1970. However, the difference between urban and rural income levels has widened over the same period, as the mean rural family income fell from 42.5 percent to 40.8 percent of the mean urban family income. In addition, the relative degree of income inequality among regions has become wider. From 1961 to 1966

56. S. F. Tobias, "The Chinese in Ayutthaya," *Chulalongkorn University Social Science Research Institute Journal of Social Science* (July, 1971): 76.
57. NEDB, *National Income*, p. 129; NSO, *Labor Force Survey*, p. 31; BOI, *Statistics of Investment*; conversation with J. Romm, Bangkok, March, 1972.

per capita incomes in the Central Plains (which includes Bangkok) rose from 154 percent to 166 percent of the national average; in the south the proportion rose by about the same percentage, but in the north the proportion remained roughly constant, and in the northeast it fell.[58] This concentration of development gains in the Central Plains and southern regions, especially metropolitan Bangkok, further exacerbates regional discontent and contributes to political unrest in the outer regions. When this is combined with a breakdown of agricultural employment sources and long-standing communal relationships as more peasants lose their land, and a feeling in the outlying areas that Bangkok is insensitive to their problems, the political issues can become threatening. Solutions to problems of regional discontent are not easy, but they will necessitate various measures both to provide industry with incentives to locate in the outer regions and to discourage further clustering of industry in the Bangkok area. Over the past decade various smaller towns have been built up in the outer regions, partly as military bases. An infrastructure now exists in those towns, and specific actions, such as provision of preferential credits to businessmen setting up firms there, might encourage the spread of industry catering to the consumption and production needs of farmers in outlying areas. This would also reduce the impact of decreasing military expenditures on the local economies. It is most encouraging that the development that has occurred in the urban areas has apparently contributed to greater equality of urban incomes; if this trend extends outside the Bangkok area, it will have a beneficial effect upon the society. At the same time in the political field there is a need for the dominant political groups in Bangkok to become more responsive to the requirements of the outer regions and their leaders.

Thailand's internal problems are potentially serious, but certainly not comparable to those of the Philippines and Indonesia. Externally the situation in Indochina and the existence of a strong Communist China create a felt threat to the country. This has contributed to a degree of reliance upon an outside country (the United

58. ECAFE, "Distribution of Income and Wealth in Thailand," mimeographed (Bangkok, January, 1972), pp. 9, 21, 49–50.

States) that appears unusual in Thai history, and to the series of events from 1971 to 1973 which led to the overthrow of the previous ruling military group. The overthrow of the old military dictatorship may lead to a substantially lower reliance on the United States, as well as a movement to a broader-based constitutional government.

Thailand has been remarkably successful in maintaining its political independence and social characteristics, while adapting selected institutions and even commodities of Western culture to Thai requirements as seen by its leaders. In the process there has developed a uniquely Thai-Western culture, based primarily on Thai social characteristics. The only country in Asia with more success in such selective adaptation of Western culture is Japan, if measured in terms of economic growth, although not in terms of political stability or peace. It is to be hoped that Thailand will retain this capacity to choose, and the flexibility it implies, by not imposing unduly rigid controls in the political and economic fields, while at the same time retaining an approach toward living and a set of social relationships that are humanely satisfying and reasonably equitable in Thai eyes.

For Thailand the type of isolationist policy adopted by Burma is probably not possible in either political or economic terms. Thailand must continue to look outward in its economic strategy. But the success of that strategy may require changes in existing economic institutions and bureaucracy, and in current policies. Such changes have occurred in periods of crisis. The greatest change occurred under King Mongkut in the mid-nineteenth century and resulted in opening the country to trade; under King Chulalongkorn in the 1890's there was a major reform of the bureaucracy that has permitted it to function effectively since then. Flexibility in other matters has continued since. However, the rigidity of the recent military government, as shown by its scrapping of a constitution that permitted greater popular participation and its subsequent repressive actions, led directly to unprecedented student violence and the overthrow of that dictatorship. Unless subsequent governments permit greater public participation to deal with national problems in ways not encased in such tradition, they too will face the risk of popular uprising. In this respect it is significant that the royal family's prestige and influence have been strengthened by the October, 1973, student uprising. "The traditional power centers—the military, the bureaucracy, and the Chinese-dominated business elite—remain intact and apparently ready to defend their interests."[59] The ultimate results of that uprising are thus still uncertain. It may have served as the first step in a transition to a government that retains certain traditional characteristics, but which is more responsive to public demands arising from a changing international situation and the effects of internal economic pressures.

59. James M. Markham, "Slowly, Thailand Feels Her Way toward Democracy," *New York Times*, June 1, 1974, p. 2.

CHAPTER 6   INDIA

I therefore find that someone like me lives in two worlds—the world of inter-national business and modern technology, and the world of yesterday. There is a constant search to see how far I have got from the older world; what deep influence that older world still has upon my modern world.

—Prakash Tandon, "Maturing of Business in India"

SOCIAL STRUCTURE AND ITS INFLUENCE

I do not intend to discuss the Indian social system and its implications for economic development in the depth devoted to the other countries, since I have devoted an entire earlier book[1] to that subject. The purpose of this chapter is, first, to summarize some of the points made in that book concerning the complex Indian social structure and its effects on economic growth, taking into account some of the more recent literature; and second, to explore the effects of that social structure upon Indian agricultural and industrial development since 1965, within a framework of analysis comparable to that used for the three Southeast Asian countries. This will make it possible to compare the effects of rural social structure upon economic development in India with those effects in Southeast Asia.

In India the basic social institution is the family. In rural areas the joint family, bringing the brothers together in a single household, is the form considered desirable and is probably most general. The family is the principal unit of production and consumption; it is a unit before the gods; it is a social unit on the main occasions of life; and it is the basic unit in the wider organizations

1. George Rosen, *Democracy and Economic Change* (Berkeley and Los Angeles: University of California Press, 1966). See especially Chs. 2, 4 and Appendix B.

of village and caste. The father is the center of the family and the key in decision-making, but in all important decisions there is close consultation with the brothers, and if possible the decisions are reached through consensus. However, for a variety of reasons related to economic and social factors, the nuclear rather than joint family may in fact function. Very poor families tend to be more of nuclear form; for urban families whose wealth is not in the form of land, there are advantages in smaller size.

The family is also the basis of relationships within the village, since the family is the key to the *jati*. Because it is family based, the *jati* is quite precise, and its composition is known to all in an area. It serves as the unit of social relationships in the village, and village *jatis* are the building and functional blocks for the caste system. On a national, as distinct from village, basis caste structure is quite amorphous.[2]

In traditional rural India economic relationships among villagers functioned through the *jajmani* system, in which each village *jati* had a distinct occupational specialization. The precise economic relationships and obligations among *jatis* were carefully delineated. A similar set of relationships, with their obligations and precise terms of conduct, also existed among *jatis* in the social and religious spheres; these intertwined so that status in one sphere supported ranking in other. Together all were unified in the wider system of caste, wherein each *jati* knew its own position and its relationship to others in the village and area. But as one proceeded farther from a village and a particular language area, the precise distinctions that were recognized in that village became less clear, and titles and ranks shifted. A clean caste that was dominant in one area could well be subordinate in another.

In the rural areas caste dominance was traditionally derived through landownership, and while the dominant caste varied from area to area, it was always a "clean" caste. Around the dominant caste members in a village (if not themselves Brahmins) revolved the Brahmins, who performed the ritual functions; the actual

2. On the family, *jati*, and caste, David G. Mandelbaum's *Society in India* (Berkeley and Los Angeles: University of California Press, 1970) contains an inclusive review of the literature and thorough analysis.

workers on the land, who might not necessarily be the owners, since the owners might be ritually prohibited from actually laboring in the fields; those families performing specific and "clean" nonfarming functions (carpenters, metalworkers, traders, and others); and finally the families engaged in handling the waste and dead matter of the village, who were members of the religiously "unclean" castes. The families of the landholding castes and the Brahmins had the highest status. Each landholding family was the patron for a group of client families. The landholders were responsible for producing the crop; at harvest times the crop was distributed among the clients according to shares determined by custom and tradition, and enforced by known mutual obligations. It was a system in which everyone knew his position. If there was any output, everyone got a share consistent with his status.

Within most villages there were caste councils consisting of older villagers of a single *jati*; these councils were usually of an informal nature and settled purely local issues for a particular *jati*. Formal regional councils were generally set up to deal with issues of significance beyond a single village.

Village government was carried out by a village council, often consisting of an informal group of leaders of the local "clean" caste councils. Leadership in the village council was usually exercised by the economically more powerful of the dominant caste members, since they had the resources to perform the favors required in order to establish a political network of supporters. As within the joint family, the purpose of the council meeting was to achieve a consensus; this might prove difficult and time consuming if the dominant caste was split into factions. Apart from serving as the local government for village matters, the village leadership was also to represent the villagers in dealing with the outside world. But these relationships were kept as distant as possible, since the outside world was distrusted, and therefore to be manipulated rather than worked with.

The Indian social system, with the rods of caste running through it, appears rigid when compared with the more loosely structured social systems of Southeast Asia, but it has always had built-in elements of flexibility. The most important is the ability of a clean *jati* to gradually assume the character of a higher caste, by a process termed "Sanskritization." For example, a group of families of a clean lower *jati* might improve their economic position by moving to a new area and becoming landowners. They could then try to become recognized as of higher caste by adopting the characteristics of a higher caste: for example, by adopting a new mythology and high-caste ritual observances.

The foundations of this traditional system were undermined, first by the British and then by the changes introduced after independence. Under British rule the laws and legal systems changed; British courts provided legal channels outside the caste system, and the British hierarchy was outside caste. Economic opportunities outside agriculture expanded greatly, and urban trading and industrial centers sprang up where traditional caste relationships and hierarchies were now inapplicable, and frequently unrecognized. Western education provided new paths to high position and status (especially for Brahmins) and undermined the intellectual foundations of the caste system among the educated. Under the influence of Mahatma Gandhi there was a strong movement to break down barriers between clean and unclean castes; the new Indian constitution following independence refused to recognize traditional caste differences. Although caste relationships were weakening as the basis for rural economic and social relationships, most peasants "honored or appeared to honor their customary obligations. All along, moreover, medium and small landowners continued to conform to them. The growing number of the landless relied upon them for their security." In addition, in both rural and urban areas and among people with varying degrees of education the caste system showed ability to adjust to the new demands and opportunities associated with wider political suffrage and industrialization. More traditional caste councils were transformed into caste associations on a state and national level, not only to deal with religious problems, but also to serve as vehicles for mobilizing political strength in elections, and for pressing political claims thereafter.[3]

3. For the quotation see Francine R. Frankel and Karl von Vorys, "The Political Challenge of the Green Revolution," mimeographed (Philadelphia: University of Pennsylvania, Department of Political Science, 1971), p. 6; on changes in the caste

As in the other countries studied, traditional patron-client relationships tended to govern village voting relationships, the structure of political parties in the rural areas, and political operations at the state level. The following summary description of Punjab politics of 1966 can be applied to other states as well. "[All] major parties in the State were factional coalitions built on extensive and localized patterns of vertical mobilization. The leadership of the secular Indian National Congress, the communal Akali Dal, indeed, even the Communist Party of India, was recruited from the upper-caste landowning classes. . . . Although the Harijans [former untouchables] . . . benefited from constitutional guarantees assuring them of proportional representation in the State Legislature, they were given only token representation in government ministries and excluded from effective power."[4] At the national party and government level these traditional local political forces were moderated and bounded by the influence of groups thrown up by the struggle for independence, as well as by the national political leaders who functioned originally through the Congress party, and the members of the bureaucracy and army. All of these national groups transcended in their attitudes, goals, and methods of operation the specific caste politics of the states. On a national scale all political and government organizations represented an uneasy and shifting coalition of both of these elements, and the resulting policies and actions were compromises.

India is a political democracy, functioning as a federal republic. Eighty percent of the people live in rural areas, and in rural voting the traditional elements described above have played a key role. In addition, the state governments have the constitutional responsibility for much of the agricultural legislation. In the state governments the power of the dominant landholding castes is very strong. In order to understand agricultural policy one must understand the pattern of rural landownership. In 1960–61 the 42 percent of rural households with farm holdings of less than 1 acre operated 1.3 percent of the total cultivated acreage; about 45 percent of rural

---

system see Lloyd and Suzanne Rudolph, *The Modernity of Tradition* (Chicago: University of Chicago Press, 1967), esp. Pt. I.
    4. Frankel and von Vorys, "Political Challenge," pp. 13–14.

households with holdings of 1–10 acres operated about 39 percent of all cultivated acreage; 13 percent of households with over 10 acres each operated almost 60 percent of all acreage. (Within this latter group the less than 1 percent of all households that held over 50 acres per household operated 11 percent of total area cultivated.) This inequality is moderated by the fact that farm households with holdings of less than 10 acres tend to hold a larger share of irrigated acreage. The equalizing effect of the traditional output-sharing system in distributing cereal output is indicated by the appreciably smaller degree of inequality for rural consumption than for land-holdings, and the even smaller degree of inequality of cereal consumption than total consumption. But while recognizing these qualifications, it is estimated that 150 to 160 million people in rural India (about 40 percent of the rural population) had per capita incomes below a minimum poverty line of 200 rupees per year during the 1960's.[5]

Within a village the farm households with larger holdings are usually those of the dominant caste. They have greater political power, arising largely from their traditional patron relationship to those villagers with either smaller or no holdings. In the early period following independence the major policy of raising output sought to strengthen cooperation among the villagers. On the one hand this policy sought to utilize traditional relationships within the village; on the other it sought to lessen the disparities in land-holding and income that had developed during the colonial period. Community development programs were introduced; land reform and protection of tenants were advocated; cooperatives were set up. But these programs failed to achieve their goals of reducing disparities and restrengthening traditional institutions and relationships, or of encouraging the use of new technology and greatly increasing output. Output did rise, but less that had been hoped for; the larger farmers benefited more from the new institutions, and traditional relationships were more or less maintained. Since

5. On the above see A. Vaidyanathan, "Some Aspects of Inequalities in Living Standards in Rural India," mimeographed (paper presented at the Indian Statistical Institute Seminar on Income Distribution, New Delhi, 1971), pp. 12–13; B. S. Minhas, "Rural Poverty, Land Redistribution and Development Strategy," *Indian Economic Review* 5, 1 (April, 1970): 97–128.

the larger farmers held power in the state government, it was not surprising that effective land reform usually ended at an early stage with the abolition of *zamindars* and other groups who had supported the British and lost power after independence; further legislation to protect the rights of tenants, limit the size of landholdings, or consolidate landholdings has been largely ineffective. Meanwhile, direct taxation of farmers has been substantially reduced since independence, so that "in India upper-income rural people pay only about one-third as much as urban people in the same income bracket";[6] high price supports for output are also maintained.

The influence of traditional patron-client relationships upon the functioning of the Indian government at the bureaucratic level may also have been strengthened after independence. Prakash Tandon, one of India's leading industrial executives and a subsequent holder of high government positions, contrasts the approach of the modern professional Indian industrial executive with that of the government official:

[The executive's] training in management and technology makes him essentially an applier of modern techniques of change; the [government] administrator's training is patterned on an old system and his practices are older still. The change he has introduced in his systems is practically nil, and he is conscious of it, though curiously helpless. But all this puts the Indian executive into a kind of conflict with the society. . . . As the only trained applier of new technologies, the Indian executive has the task before him of creating production and growth in a society which is traditionalist by nature and, being essentially democratic, able to enforce its reluctance to accept the pace of change commensurate with the growth it wants. . . . [The Indian executive is an] interesting all-India type who rises above the ties of caste, religion and region. This in a way brings him into conflict with his family and the society, because his values have moved away from the purely local. He is less dependent upon his relations, and also less supportive of the weaker members of the family, contrary to our old tradition. . . . [His] interest centers on his own family, his children's upbringing, his own self improvement. . . . [As regards the society] he is in conflict with the society's tender-mindedness. . . . He is by no means the tender-minded

6. For the quotation see Uma Lele and John W. Mellor, "Jobs, Poverty and the Green Revolution," *International Affairs* 48, 1 (January, 1972): 25–26; on general agricultural policy see Francine Frankel, *India's Green Revolution* (Princeton: Princeton University Press, 1971), pp. 3–5.

type, nor is he the man who would take each time the soft options that the society usually tends to do in face of the hard choices. . . .The executive is taught and expected to choose, consistent with his means, the very best in the resources he employs in order to give the maximum production, the best and the cheapest product, and the highest return in profits. . . . All this requires conditions of merit and purity of administration, and here the society and leadership disagree with him, because they want the personal and technological decisions to be based upon regional, hierarchical, and not result-oriented considerations.

Tandon then cited several examples of this latter characteristic, based on his own experience in Indian government.

I said [to a secretary, the highest Indian civil servant] that no one seems to disagree with me [in government]; they all agree with what I say, and if I disagree with myself, they also disagree with me, and we always seem to end up by agreeing with me. [The secretary] patiently explained to me that I had to remember that I was now in a different society from the international business in India; I was in the heart of the Indian administration, and if I wanted people to disagree with me I had to teach them to disagree, and I might not find this easy. We [the Indian government administrators] have a strictly hierarchical tradition of the elders and seniors always being in the right.

For the next example Tandon cited a conversation with Prime Minister Gandhi in which she stressed the importance of introducing the merit concept in the state corporation Tandon was then managing. But Mrs. Gandhi also pointed out the great difficulty she herself had in achieving this, by giving an example of her search for a man to fill a top government position. She thought she had found

absolutely the right person, the right merit, the right qualifications, the right experience; until one of her senior colleagues said to her, "Madam, there are other more important considerations in life than merit". . . . [This] must have been one of her main problems, of how to bring new values to those who have been used to the old ways; and yet want products and results of new values.

The duty of the [political] leaders is . . . to throw a bridge between the society's desirable and the manager's possible, and try to make the society accept a little less and pay a little more as the price. . . . [The] leadership has a very important role to play, to approach the society for the adjustments which are necessary for achieving the goals it sets and to ensure the needed resources for the manager. I am not so sure that our leaders always do that today. One can only come to the conclusion that in our search for growth through industrialization . . . we are anxious to go forward, but at the same time anxious not to give up what we possess. Thus we go through a period of experimentalism at all levels.[7]

In the area of industry the Indian social structure and attitudes have influenced industrial development in two ways: through the direct functioning of industry, and through government policies. Within industry itself Indian business has been family and caste oriented, and this has apparently contributed to the growth of past industrial enterprise. Milton Singer, in a highly perceptive study of Madras industrial organization, has pointed out the "structural and organizational parallelism between joint family management and business management," and consequently the direct extension of the principles of the management of the rural joint family household to the industrial firm. The joint family provides a nucleus of capital, a pool of management, a structure of authority and succession, and a vehicle for continuity that meets many of the requirements of industry. Thus there has been a mutual adaptation of joint family and industrial firm organization to achieve an effective form of industrial organization in Madras.[8]

In addition, the existence of the caste system permits the Indian firm to transcend narrow family limits to capital and management skill. A family of one caste or community is quite willing to hire officers and raise capital from other families of the same caste or community: at the same time other families in that caste will have experience useful for, and will be willing to risk their own capital in, such enterprises. Thus the business castes and communities (such as the Marwaris, Chettiars, Banias, Jains, Sindhis, and Parsis) are large enough to assemble both trusted managerial skill and sufficient capital to effectively finance and manage large enterprises. In the earlier days of Indian business history the managing agency system introduced by British businessmen provided British and

7. Previous three quotations from Prakash Tandon, "Maturing of Business in India," *California Management Review* 14, no. 3 (Spring, 1972): 77–79.

8. Milton Singer, *When a Great Tradition Modernizes* (New York: Praeger, 1972). Ch. 8, "Industrial Leadership, the Hindu Ethic, and the Spirit of Socialism," is relevant to this question.

Indian entrepreneurs with a legal institutional form for mobilizing and shifting scare capital and managerial resources, while retaining control in a small group or family. Today this legal form is gradually being ended, but that ending will have little impact on future industrialization. The existence of a social system and an institutional form which made possible large-scale Indian entrepreneurship meant that there was never any need for the colonial power to introduce external population groups (such as the Chinese) to perform an entrepreneurial function, nor was there any significant motivation for such groups to migrate to India. Indian businessmen are largely natives.

But the caste system also had certain limitations as a growth factor. Tandon points out that the Indian family firm system provided no room for professional managers outside the family or caste. In 1937, when Tandon joined a British firm as its first Indian manager,

> Indian business still only recruited its kith and kin, or men of their own caste; and at least for its top positions still continues to do so. It is a significant fact . . . that I can today count a dozen leading *foreign* companies who all have Indian chairmen. Among all purely Indian companies there is not one chairman whose name is not the same as the company's. Even Tatas is still headed by a Tata, though their company is . . . wholly professionalized at the top. As for the Birlas, Sarabhais, Mafatlals, Ruias, Jains, Kotharis, Singhanias, Dalmias, Lalbhais and all others, their top executives are always of the family.[9]

Tandon feels that in such family-controlled firms the criteria for decision-making and promotion are too often similar to those he finds in government, and unlike the criteria of a professional manager who stresses growth and efficiency. The multinational corporation that functions in India has provided opportunities for the latter in the past.

Perhaps as important as the limitation this caste or community orientation may place on future growth within individual firms or family enterprises is the attitude in other elements of society that may arise as a result of the caste or family origin of such industrial groupings. The traditional Indian industrialist often has a family and caste, if not personal, background in moneylending or trade; his business practices may reflect that background or be blamed

9. Prakash Tandon, "Maturing of Business," pp. 77–78.

upon it. In addition, because many Indian firms are run by people of the same family or caste and appear closed to outsiders, suspicion is inevitably created. In turn those outsiders, especially high-caste outsiders to whom trade has never seemed respectable, distrust the businessman. (Although, in South India especially, many Brahmins are entering and succeeding in industry as opportunities in more traditional fields, such as government, are being restricted.) The rural peasant also often sees the industrialist as a Marwari moneylender, whom he frequently considers to be dishonest and exploiting. Among high-caste Indian intellectuals this basic distrust contributes to a belief in socialism and controls; among even the well-to-do-peasants it results in an inherent belief that businessmen (other than themselves) must be controlled. The effect of these ideologies and beliefs when translated into policies and legislation is to overlay the functioning of large-scale private industry with legal and bureaucratic controls that make flexible and speedy operation difficult. (There may of course be other more immediate reasons for such controls—war, or shortage of foreign exchange.) Thus, while the conditions under which Indian business functions are different from those in the three Southeast Asian countries considered here, the existence of a similar distrust of businessmen derived in part from similar traditional peasant attitudes and social structure results in similar problems for the businessman, even though in India the businessmen are of indigenous, rather than Chinese, origin and the legal forms of control are different. Likewise, Indian businessmen tend to respond to the government in a fashion that is similar to the response in the other countries.

All too often the large businessman must serve as a client of government.[10] He is heavily controlled and limited in what he can invest, but he is often dependent upon government contracts for orders, and on government permits to invest and obtain scarce resources. He almost invariably gets into politics, since the political parties and leaders that make the decisions require funds for elections. While the businessman may wish to avoid politics and the

10. On this see Stanley A. Kochanek, *Business and Politics in India* (Berkeley and Los Angeles: University of California Press, 1974).

government official may normally keep him at a distance, at election time his contributions are encouraged. If sufficient, such contributions at least provide access to political and bureaucratic leadership, and at most they may contribute to favorable decisions with respect to the allocation of licenses or scarce foreign exchange on which any businessman's future may depend.[11] Thus arises an incongruity: business interests are too weak to be considered, and frequently may not even be consulted, by government leaders on broad economic policies; but on specific matters of projects and permits they are deeply involved in resource allocation.

The remainder of this chapter explores the relationship between these aspects of Indian social and economic structure and resulting economic policy upon the character of the Green Revolution in India, and the recent trends of industrial development.

THE NEW TECHNOLOGY IN AGRICULTURE

In the early 1960's it became clear that although past policies to expand agricultural output had achieved some successes, the results were not those hoped for or required in the context of total Indian development. The need for increasing food-grain output became critical when the decline in output caused by unusually poor monsoons resulted in near-famine conditions from 1965 to 1967. This led directly to a new strategy of agricultural development which focused on increasing agricultural output in those areas and farms that had the greatest potential, by providing a framework of policies and a supply of inputs that would make it worthwhile for farmers to take advantage of the gains in agricultural technology, especially from high-yielding seed varieties. This so-called High Yielding Variety Program (HYVP) was applied to a variety of crops—wheat, rice, maize, millet, and sorghum.

The adoption of these new varieties of wheat was very widespread from 1966 to 1970. One study showed that by 1969/70 close to 95 percent of the wheat farmers surveyed in the Punjab were using the new varieties, and that they had planted 95 percent of their

11. Of course this is not peculiar to India. The recent American experience with election funding at both the national and state levels shows similar factors at work.

irrigated acreage to these varieties. But adoption in other states was less in both respects. In neighboring Haryana and Uttar Pradesh the proportions were above 50 percent for farmer participation and 85 and 65 percent respectively for area covered; in Bihar and Rajasthan both proportions were below 50 percent and falling. The total area sown to wheat expanded by about 25 percent in 1964/65; the yield on acreage sown to the high-yielding varieties was about double that on the same acreage in 1964/65, with the average yield per acre on all wheat land rising by about one-third. From 1964/65 to 1969/70 wheat output rose by 8.8 million tons, which was 80 percent of the total increase in output of the five crops over the same period. The new high-yielding rice varieties were much less acceptable than the wheat varieties and were used mainly in the less important dry season rather than in the wet season. The small increase in production of rice, the most important food crop in India, as well as in the production of the three minor crops, indicates the relatively limited character of the Green Revolution in India. Progress in the new varieties of crops has been largely confined to wheat and has been limited to only a few northern states. As a result of this discrepancy in gains from the new technology, wheat output rose from 16 percent of total cereal production in 1964/65 to 28 percent in 1971/72.[12]

Wheat output tripled its previous compound rate of growth from 3.3 percent annually during the 1952/53–1964/65 period, to 10 percent annually from 1964/65 to 1969/70. Perhaps the most significant measure of the gains from the new technology in wheat is that even in the very bad monsoon year 1972/73, the total wheat output of 26 million tons was more than twice that of the best year prior to the introduction of the new technology, when output was 12 million tons. This output and the stocks accumulated from the previous years made it possible for India to avoid a disastrous 1973 famine that might have been unavoidable without the new tech-

12. The summary above has been taken from the draft study by Bert Lockwood, P. K. Mukherjee, and R. T. Shand, "The High-Yielding Varieties Program in India, Part I," mimeographed (New Delhi: Government of India Planning Commission and Australian National University, 1971), Chs. 1–3, 6. The most recent published review updating the status of the Green Revolution to 1973 is Wolf Ladejinsky, "How Green Is the Indian Green Revolution?" *Economic and Political Weekly* 8, 52 (December 29, 1973): A133–144.

nology.[13] But the rate of growth of output of the other foodgrains and cash crops in fact decreased, and the increase in wheat output has thus enabled total crop output to recover to the long-term trend of cereal output which existed prior to the very poor crops of the mid-1960's. (There was an almost 5 percent increase in rice output in 1970/71, but the effect of the new varieties, as distinguished from weather, on this is uncertain.)

The great increase in wheat production occurred in the Punjab, where use of the new varieties was greatest. This process has been examined in some depth in the Ludhiana district of that state, and it is possible therefore to look with some confidence at the causes and effects.[14] The new Mexican varieties of wheat introduced in 1966/67 offered Punjab farmers the chance to raise their net incomes by 70 percent. The Punjab was fortunate in that it already had a very good irrigation system, which is one of the keys to water control required for effective use of the new varieties. In addition, for four years after 1966 there was a massive increase in the number of privately owned tube wells, which permit even better water control; a threefold increase in the consumption of chemical fertilizers; an extension of the new varieties to 65 percent of the total wheat acreage; an almost 50 percent increase in per acre yield; and a doubling of total wheat output. This was accompanied by mechanization that would make possible even greater efficiency in wheat farming.

One of the main economic and social characteristics of Ludhiana and the Punjab is the relatively large farm size, compared to other parts of India. In Ludhiana in 1961/62, 80 percent of cultivating households operated holdings of 10 acres or more, and these 80 percent account for 90 percent of the total cultivated area in the district. These figures are higher than for the Punjab as a whole, where only 37 percent of the rural households had over 10 acres each in operational holdings, but this 37 percent accounted for 74

13. Dharm Narain, "Rice, Policies and Problems," in IRRI, "Viewpoints on Rice," mimeographed (Los Banos: IRRI, 1971); Ladejinsky, "How Green," p. A–134.

14. See Frankel, *India's Green Revolution*, esp. Ch. 2; Frankel and von Vorys, "The Political Challenge," pp. 11–26 (pp. 15–16 contain the figures given in this paragraph).

percent of the cultivated area. Farm size in the Punjab far exceeds
that in India as a whole, where only 13 percent of rural households
have holdings of 10 acres or more, or in the other wheat-growing
states of Uttar Pradesh and Bihar, where 80 percent of farm households operate holdings of less than 10 acres and the size distribution of farms is far closer to the all-India average.[15] Another
characteristic of Ludhiana and the Punjab in general is a relatively
high degree of industrialization, especially small-scale industry; 65
percent of the population is employed outside agriculture, which
contributes in turn to the large farm size. In addition, the population of Ludhiana is largely Sikh—one of the most economically
aware and hard-working communities on the subcontinent. Literacy in this district is relatively high.

Eventually almost all Punjabi farmers adopted the new technology, but the larger farmers adopted it first and reaped the largest
gains. Farmers with twenty acres or more were more likely to have
the in-place capital investments in private tube wells and the more
sophisticated equipment so useful both for reducing the risk in
introducing the new varieties and for maximizing the gains. In
addition, they were more likely to have either the financial resources or the access to credit that would enable them to buy relatively large quantities of fertilizer and other current inputs to maximize their expected yields. The gains came not only in the form
of higher current income, much of which was reinvested in additional land and equipment, but also in the doubling and tripling of
land values that followed the increases in output.

Small farmers adopted the new varieties more slowly. They
lacked the capital equipment initially, and they had to borrow from
rural credit institutions and cooperatives to buy the equipment
and inputs. Their debts have increased, and they have been more
constrained than large farmers in the use of optimal quantities of
fertilizers and other inputs. In addition, economies of scale in introducing tube wells and adopting mechanization are available only to
large farmers, or to small farmers in a group. Thus the gains to
small farmowners have probably been slight.

15. Frankel, *India's Green Revolution*, pp. 17, 45; Frankel and von Vorys, "The
Political Challenge," p. 12. Also see above, pp. 173–174.

Many small farmers are either pure or partial tenants; the use of leased-in land increases as size of holding decreases. Following the introduction of the new varieties, cash rents were increased by 50 percent, and where sharecropping exists landlords have insisted on higher output shares. Such higher rent shares may still give the tenant a higher absolute return, but with such higher sharing the partial tenant, who often lacks the resources to use optimal quantities of the inputs, may find the new varieties uneconomical, unless he goes into further tenancy or sells his own land at the current higher prices. Pure tenants of course do not have this last option.

About 15–20 percent of the people in Ludhiana are landless agricultural laborers. Even in 1961, well before the new wheat technology was introduced but after some industrialization had occurred, there was believed to be a shortage of landless laborers. The new wheat technology increased the initial demand for labor, because the new varieties required more labor-intensive methods for total output (not per unit of output); the additional irrigation permitted more intensive cropping, and the extension of multiple cropping required that more labor be available for harvesting when necessary. Cash wages for agricultural labor increased, and there is evidence that average real farm wages in the Punjab in 1967–69 were significantly above the pre-1966 average.[16] This increase in real wages took place even though the laborer's share fell from the traditional 1/20 to 1/30 of the wheat output. The landlord was unwilling to continue paying the traditional share. He originally sought to force it down to 1/40; only the threat of a strike by the laborers raised it to 1/30. But the great rise in total output permitted the laborer's absolute share to rise by about 25 percent. Since then, however, the Ludhiana landlords have begun mechanizing their operations as rapidly as possible to reduce their dependence on labor. Tractors, thresher-winnowers, etc., are being bought in large numbers; farmers are planning to introduce mechanical harvesting equipment that would reduce their reliance upon laborers for that bottleneck operation.

16. On real wages see R. W. Herdt and E. A. Baker, "Agricultural Wages, Production and High-Yielding Varieties," *Economic and Political Weekly* 7, no. 13 (March 25, 1972): A23–30, esp. A27–29.

The overall effect has been to increase the disparities between large farmers and other groups in the Punjab, even though almost all groups gained absolutely, if not relatively, from these economic changes. These same changes have had profound social consequences in substituting class relationships for the traditional patron-client relationships. This break has occurred largely on the initiative of the landlords.

No longer recognizing the obligation to maintain customary rates of crop-sharing, they have deprived tenants and agricultural laborers of proportional participation in "good times" and the rewards of productivity. In traditional terms, they have violated the common notions of equity. Indeed, when landlords arbitrarily raise rentals in their own favor . . . they reduce the scope of the relationship to a purely economic one, and the position of tenants to that of wage earners. The reduction in customary rates of crop share payment for harvesting has the same corrosive effect on extended ties with farm workers. . . . Moreover, large landowners are determined to convert all kind payments into cash. They are convinced that with the advent of labor-saving machines, which not only represent large capital outlays by the cultivator but also substantially reduce the manual labor exerted during farm operations, the traditional system of proportionate crop-share payments operates to exploit the innovative landowner. Some large landowners have already taken the final step toward complete dissociation from the traditional system by unilaterally redefining criteria of social status. No longer are surpluses used primarily to meet obligations within the village.[17]

Some farmers have actually moved to houses outside the village, and they have begun to imitate consumption standards of the upper middle class in nearby towns by acquiring refrigerators, telephones, and automobiles.

This pressure for commercialization of relationships on the part of landowners led to an economic response by laborers. For the first time they organized and threatened to quit work if the landowners did not offer them a larger share than the original 1/40. In exchange for yielding 1/30, however, the landowners deprived the

17. Francine Frankel, "The Politics of the Green Revolution" (paper delivered at workshop on "A Widened Perspective of Modernizing Agriculture," Cornell University, June 2–4, 1971), pp. 20–21. See also the recent book by Richard Critchfield, *The Golden Bowl Be Broken* (Bloomington: Indiana University Press, 1973), Ch. 3, for a discussion of the social changes arising from the new crop varieties in the Punjab.

laborers of some of their customary rights to fodder, and they refused to grant interest-free loans thereafter.

Ladejinsky's recent work on a national scale, summarized in the
previously cited article, found similar trends. Output has risen; industrial inputs are being used in far greater quantities. Gains to all
farmers have been large, although the position of tenants has deteriorated as land ownership becomes far more valuable. Total
labor requirements have been increasing as a result of the new
technology, so that labor has gained in terms both of days worked
and of real wages earned. Ladejinsky recognizes the continued existence of many problems in rural India; he rightly points out that
those problems of inequality and great poverty existed long before
the "Green Revolution" and cannot be blamed on the new technology. In fact, that technology offers the one hope of eventually dealing with those problems, and it would be foolhardy to renounce the
technology because those problems still exist. The greatest stress
must be placed in spreading the new technology to areas (especially dry regions) not currently benefiting from it, and to crops whose
benefits have been limited. In addition he argues that policy should
be directed toward equalizing access to inputs, and credits to buy
those inputs, to all farmers, and to preventing types of rural mechanization that might yield high private profits but would also create
greater unemployment.

Frankel and von Vorys point out a potential political impact of
these social changes in the Punjab. They argue that previously
politics was on communal grounds, but after 1967 a small radical
Communist group appealed to the *harijans* and other landless
castes on interest grounds. Several larger parties campaigned by
appealing to the interests of the larger landowners, who benefited
from the new seeds, by omitting the usual promises of land reform
and promising higher procurement prices and better roads. Violent
revolutionary groups also began to operate in the Punjab. In
1971 the new Congress party headed by Mrs. Gandhi campaigned
against the old parties on an anti-*status quo* platform to place
ceilings on urban income and property and carry out effective land
reform. Her new party, and the Communist party allied with it,
won sweeping victories in twelve of the Punjab's thirteen districts;

"for the first time in Punjab politics communal solidarity was breached by a class appeal." Frankel and von Vorys conclude that the "combination of growing disparities and the increasing commercialization of agriculture accelerates the erosion of traditional norms of agrarian relationships . . . the immediate political consequences are a decline in the moral claim of landed elites to positions of authority and the breakdown of vertical patterns of peasant mobilization. Over the longer term, large numbers of the landless become available for participation in new political commitments and groups based on egalitarian values and class struggle doctrines."[18] It appears in fact that these changes are occurring, if at all, at a slower rate than anticipated by Frankel and von Vorys. In the rural areas traditional dominant groups still exert great political power, and through their political power they control access to the scarce credit and inputs required to take advantage of the new technology. Massive inequalities in the distribution of landownership continue to exist, and the position of tenants may have worsened.

In addition to any short-term social and political changes from the revolution in wheat technology, several long-term trends may be of profound future consequence. Perhaps most important is the one noted by Ladejinsky when he remarks "that many a 'peasant' is turning into an enterprising 'farmer,' conscious of his heightened role politically, economically and socially. And this holds not only for big farmers but for the smaller ones as well with some irrigated land and some resources to go with it."[19] Two other such trends in the Punjab are the increase in the spread of education in general, as those benefiting from higher incomes send their children to school; and, possibly even more significant, the increases in education for women. New social institutions, such as banks and cooperatives, have also proliferated in the area. These provide farmers with opportunities to work in closer association, and thus to gain experience in forms of social behavior and entrepreneurship that transcend the family.

18. Frankel and von Vorys, "The Political Challenge," pp. 22–26; quotations from pp. 25, 26.
19. Ladejinsky, "How Green," p. A–135.

The different experience of Bihar and Uttar Pradesh with the new wheat varieties has already been mentioned. The farms are far smaller than in Ludhiana or the entire Punjab. This is considered by Frankel to be the major reason why the use of the new wheat varieties in those states is less than in the Punjab. It is also likely that in those states the gains from the introduction of those varieties are even more concentrated.

As pointed out earlier, the increase in rice output was far more limited. Total rice output in 1970/71 increased by only 3 million tons over the 1964/65 figure, in contrast to a target of 13 million tons. In 1971 only 16 percent of the major monsoon crop area was sown to the new varieties, and this proportion was falling; over 50 percent of the dry season crop area was so sown.

The reasons for this limited success with rice were partly technical, arising from the character of rice production. The original new rice varieties were nowhere near as suitable for India as the new wheat varieties; subsequently several new varieties, adapted to specific regions, were introduced, but they are still in the testing stage in many areas. In addition, the rice-growing areas in general are not as well irrigated as the northern wheat areas. The resulting absence of water control means that possible gains from the new varieties in the monsoon season are small, while in the dry season, when the sun is most favorable for these varieties, the lack of irrigation makes their use uneconomic. Average total cash expenditures required for inputs for the new rice varieties are much higher than for wheat,[20] while the increases in output are far more doubtful. This combination of factors meant that several of the supposedly high-yielding rice varieties yielded only a small increment in output during the monson season, in relation to a substantial increase in the costs of the inputs required for their optimal use. The resulting profit on the use of these varieties was therefore less than on local varieties, so it would clearly not pay a peasant to use them during that season.[21]

There are significant differences in the social character of rice

20. Lockwood, Mukherjee, and Shand, "The High-Yielding Varieties," p. 68.
21. G. M. Desai, "Some Observations on Economics of Cultivating High-Yielding Varieties of Rice in India," in IRRI, "Viewpoints," mimeographed (Los Banos: IRRI, 1971).

farming and wheat farming that may contribute to the difference in responses to the new varieties. The average holding in the rice-growing areas is two or three acres, and the concentration of holdings is far greater than for the Punjab wheat area. This would help explain the fact that in many rice areas "the incidence of adoption was predominantly amongst large farmers and . . . the increase in the proportion of farmers adopting HYV seed over time amongst the larger farmers was considerably faster than among the smaller farmers."[22] In the case of wheat in the Punjab, while larger farmers may have taken the lead in trying the new varieties, almost all farmers used them after several years. In the Punjab, and especially in Ludhiana, even the average farm is relatively large in the Indian context; the owner is therefore a reasonably good credit risk. This is not true for the average rice farm. The larger and wealthier farmers can best make the investment in tube wells to improve water control and they can afford the higher expenditures for inputs. They often have sufficient resources of their own, or they have preferential access to credit institutions. Those resources are much less available to small farmers, especially if they are tenants. Institutional credit sources are still a relatively minor source of rural credit in India, and where they do function they are reluctant to lend to small farmers or tenants. Landowners do not serve either as credit intermediaries from institutions to small farmers, or as direct sources of credit to small farmers at concessional terms, to the same extent as in the Philippines. Thus there are in India comparatively few sources of low-cost credit for small farmers; this helps explain the far more limited use of new rice seeds in India than in the Philippines. But while small farmers are less able to get the credit to adopt the new varieties, if they do get credit and successively adopt the new varieties, they apparently devote a greater proportion of their holdings to them. This may be simply because their farms are smaller; Schulter and Mellor suggest a contributory factor may arise from the ability of the small farmer to better supply and control the additional labor required for the new rice varieties. However, Frankel's general conclusion concerning the distribution of gains from the new rice varieties is that only the

22. Lockwood, Mukherjee, and Shand, "The High-Yielding Varieties," p. 91.

small minority of large farmers with over 10 acres gained absolutely and relatively; the small rice farmers at best maintained their previous position: where they were part tenants they lost absolutely, as their landlords either raised rents or resumed production themselves. "Probably as many as 75 percent to 80 percent [of the farmers] in the rice belt have experienced a relative decline in their economic positions. Some proportion, representing unprotected tenants cultivating under oral lease, have suffered an absolute deterioration in living standards."[23]

The new rice varieties do call for increased agricultural labor. They are most profitable where double-cropping is possible; this results in a great increase in the demand for labor between harvesting the first crop and sowing the second, and in doubling labor inputs in general. As a result, in Kerala and Madras, the two rice-growing states with the highest proportions (17 and 14 percent respectively) of their foodgrain acreage in the new varieties, real wages of farm labor rose significantly in 1967–69 over the 1954–66 average; in other rice-growing states such real wages declined.[24] This need to pay higher wages in the rice-growing areas exacerbated relationships between the larger landowner and the laborers, as larger landowners brought in migrants and began to mechanize to keep wages down. However, the smaller landowners and tenant farmers who were not able to introduce the new seeds, but had to pay higher wages to hired labor, were especially hard hit. The bitterness arising from the relations of these farmers with their laborers contributed to some of the violent incidents that have occurred in South India. In some areas there has been increasing polarization of laborers and landowners. This polarization is even more bitter because it is on caste lines, with the laborers often *harijans* and the landowners member of high castes.[25]

23. Frankel, *India's Green Revolution*, p. 193; M. Schulter and John W. Mellor, "New Seed Varieties and the Small Farm," *Economic and Political Weekly* 7, no. 13 (March 25, 1972): A32–33, A34–35. The comparison between the Philippines and India was brought out in conversation with Randolph Barker, Los Banos, March, 1972.

24. Herdt and Baker, "Agricultural Wages," pp. A27–30.

25. Frankel, *India's Green Revolution*, Ch. 4; conversation with David Hopper, Manila, 1969.

But while recognizing the occurrence of social changes in specific rice-growing areas, it is important to realize that there has *not* been a Green Revolution in rice and that those changes and conflicts are only slightly related to the adoption of new technologies. (This emphasizes the point made earlier by Ladejinsky in writing about wheat.) In some areas of South India land reform has long been an issue; the Communist party has been strong in Andhra and Kerala, as well as in West Bengal and the northeast, for many years. The differential gains and losses from new technology exacerbate relationships among large and small farmers, and between owners and laborers, that may have been deteriorating for some time. This long-run deterioration, together with the experience that has occurred where new technology has been adopted, supports the need for a deliberate policy to insure that the gains of a future Green Revolution in rice are spread to a large section of the population.[26]

Although gains in wheat production have been great and certainly represent a national improvement in well-being, the relatively poor 1972 crop season (because of the inadequate monsoon in large sections of India) points up the need for continued efforts to raise farm output. There is some evidence that wheat yields per acre are no longer increasing, and may in fact be decreasing—there are problems with use of lower qualities of seed inputs and less than optimal quantities and mixes of fertilizers; in addition, diseases to which the new varieties are susceptible may be becoming more important. In 1969 one of India's foremost planners, Pitamber Pant, bluntly stated the case for still greater efforts to raise food output.

After the harrowing experience of the previous couple of years, India needed to concentrate on increasing [agricultural] production. We need price stability for four or five years; we need to meet the demand for consumer goods. That means agricultural growth. We need to reduce our dependence on foreign aid. That also means sustained agricultural growth. The essential criterion for land reform is its possible contribution to production. . . . India appears poised for a breakthrough to an

26. A very good picture of the recent changes brought about in a rice-growing village in Mysore without a Green Revolution is in Scarlett Epstein, *South India: Yesterday, Today, and Tomorrow* (New York: Holmes and Meier, 1973), esp. Ch. 7.

agricultural growth rate of about 5 percent per year over the next ten to fifteen years. Achieving it would solve a number of problems. Others could be taken up when conditions are favorable. Everything cannot be attempted at once.[27]

Since that was written, some inconclusive evidence has appeared indicating that the type of tenancy system in the rice-growing areas, as compared with that in wheat-growing areas, may inhibit the adoption of new rice varieties. If further exploration supports this conclusion, one could make a strong case for reform on the grounds of production.[28] On the supply side also, the experience with rice production has shown that unless small farmers have access to credit, they are unable to adopt the new technology. Furthermore, to the extent that there are economies of scale in such projects as tube wells, the government can encourage cooperation or consolidation of holdings among small farmers so that they are able to introduce such projects. Steps to improve the position of small farmers in these respects would increase output, both by widening the use of new technology and by encouraging the more intensive cultivation of new varieties that smaller farmers tend to practice.

In addition, on the demand side, the continuation of the Green Revolution beyond its initial success in wheat will require steps to improve distribution of income, or the demand for the foodgrains may not be sufficient to take up the potential supply. This possibility was first raised by Lefeber and Datta-Chaudhuri as a theoretical issue.[29] Dharm Narain has pointed out, however, that this is more than a theoretical possibility in India. The past growth of wheat output was sustained by a demand arising from the replacement of wheat imports and the building up of large buffer stocks. (Those buffer stocks were substantially diminished during the recent drought.) But for long-term growth it will have to depend on continued increases in domestic demand. Even if one assumes an

27. E. A. G. Robinson and Michael Kidron, eds., *Economic Development in South Asia* (London: Macmillan, 1970), pp. 149–150; see also Ladejinsky, "How Green," for a discussion of these problems.
28. Dharm Narain, "Rice, Policies and Problems," p. 9.
29. See Ch. 2 above.

expenditure elasticity of demand for wheat of about 1.0[30] (which is probably too high an estimate), the domestic demand will only moderately exceed the projected 5 percent growth rate of output. If elasticity is less, the domestic demand may not be sufficient to take up the possible supply. One step to relieve this would be to redistribute incomes in favor of the lower income groups in Indian society, whose demand elasticity for food grains is higher. The case for such action is much stronger on a total food crop basis when rice is included in the supply picture, since the expenditure elasticity of demand for rice is estimated at only about 0.5. "Should a vigorous process of expansion overtake the production of rice in the coming years, then, given the limited possibilities of the export outlet, the growth rate of its output could hit against the barrier set—at a lower level than that for wheat—by the growth rate for the demand for rice." In summary Narain estimates that if "no effort is made to improve the income distribution, the demand for foodgrains would grow over the next decade at an annual rate of 3.5 percent per annum."[31] This is well below the 5 percent planned annual growth rate of food output, and below the hoped-for potentialities of the new technologies, once they are generally practiced. It would result in either stockpiles at present fixed prices (unless the stockpiles built up in good years are exhausted by a year or more of disastrous crops), or a collapse of food prices that would harm all farmers.

A desirable policy on the supply side, aimed at reducing this potential problem of ever increasing stockpiles, would involve encouraging diversification of production to other crops (including cash crops) and livestock, for which demand elasticities are higher. But the high profits to be made in wheat, caused in part by the price support policy, have encouraged shifts in acreage formerly under cotton, groundnuts, and pulses to wheat. Thus, while the per

30. This means, for example, that a 1 percent increase in total personal expenditures is associated with a 1 percent increase in demand for wheat; an elasticity of 0.5 would indicate that a 1 percent increase in personal expenditures would be accompanied by a 0.5 percent increase in the demand for wheat.

31. Dharm Narain, "Growth and Imbalances in Indian Agriculture," *Economic and Political Weekly* 7, no. 13 (March 25, 1972): A2–6; quotes from pp. A3, A6.

acre productivity of those cash crops has not declined, their output has[32]—and this has meant that prices of those products have risen to manufacturers using them as raw materials, and to final consumers. The price support program for wheat had a strong initial justification as a stimulus to the new technology, and the government had no difficulty in procuring wheat at the price fixed during 1971/72 and before the 1972/1973 drought, when prices rose sharply. There was strong criticism of the procurement price as reflecting the political power of the large northern farmers who gained the most from it; there was objection to the large stockpiles and demands for reduction in the support price. But most of these criticisms became academic in the face of the 1972/73 drought. Prices rose sharply, so the procurement price became relatively low rather than high, and had to be raised to purchase any wheat. The large existing stockpiles made it possible for the government to combat the threat of a famine with its own resources, without requiring food aid or large expenditures for food imports. Thus while a high support price would appear to be a waste of resources in the short run, in India the ever present threat of a disastrous monsoon makes it desirable in the long run for the government to build up stockpiles sufficient to meet basic food needs in the event of such occurrences. However, in setting the support price for any one crop, consideration should be given to the effect of these prices on outputs of other crops, including commercial crops whose output has fallen in recent years. Such a decline in output hinders the growth of industry using the affected crops.

In addition to the build-up of stockpiles, government policy should strive to reduce the dangerous effects of a poor monsoon. It is therefore equally necessary to extend the tube wells and irrigation systems to drought-stricken areas of the country where they would alleviate the problem, so that farm output in those regions would not be sharply reduced in a bad year. This would also require an associated policy to broaden the availability of credit to farmers for installing tubewells. If these steps were taken, the normal stockpiling to carry over the economy in bad years might be reduced.

32. Ibid.

INDUSTRIAL PERFORMANCE AND POLICY

Rapid industrial growth has been a major economic policy goal since independence, given the pressure of population upon the land in agriculture and the need for alternative employment opportunities. Its urgency has not diminished; in fact, recent agricultural growth has pointed up the necessity for parallel growth in the industrial sector. The conclusions of Hayami and Ruttan, which stressed the close relationship between growth in the two sectors, are supported by the fact that previous industrial growth in the Punjab contributed significantly to the success of the Green Revolution there. The relatively large industrial employment resulted in the larger size of land holdings in the Punjab, and in higher farm as well as urban incomes; the same industries in turn supplied Punjabi farmers with inputs required for the new technology. The increased output of food grains should make possible the employment of additional workers outside agriculture, either in processing the farm products, or in producing manufactured inputs and consumer goods for the farmers whose incomes have improved, or for constructing nationally needed infrastructure projects, or in meeting greater urban demands for manufactured goods arising because of relative or absolute declines in food prices. With constant or falling food prices the possible profits for entrepreneurs should also increase, since the workers' pressure for wage increases would diminish; for the government, revenues should increase out of higher producer incomes. In addition, savings of foreign exchange by lower imports of foodstuffs would reduce the force of what has been a key constraint to industrial growth. All these factors should stimulate both private and public nonagricultural sectors to greater economic activity. Expansion of the industrial sector is also important in contributing to a continuously expanding urban demand for the technically possible farm output. Lower incomes and demand elasticities in rural areas can result in a demand barrier to higher foodgrain output there; the growth of industry and related urban activities would raise the potential demand for both foodstuffs and other farm products, thus bypassing any potential rural demand constraint. It has been estimated that to absorb the 5 percent projected increase in foodgrain output in India, the growth of output from the organized industry, trade, and services sector should be on the order of 12–14 percent per year.[33]

In fact, India's recent rate of growth of industrial output has been far less than this—it is lower than in earlier periods, lower than planned for the future, and (perhaps most important) it has been declining in recent years. The Fourth Plan projected a growth rate of 8–10 percent during the five years beginning with 1968/69. Following the industrial depression associated with two disastrous crop years, industrial production rose to 6.6 percent in 1968/69 and to 6.9 percent in 1969/70. But during 1970/71 this growth rate fell to 3.5 percent, and it may have declined even further in the following year. The weak performance of this sector is a major worry for the government.[34]

Why this low industrial growth, in spite of the stimulus to be expected from the sharp increase in wheat output over the same period? First, gains in farm output have been limited both in area and type of crop; only a small proportion of the total rural population has gained—especially the wheat farmers in Punjab, Haryana, and part of Uttar Pradesh, and some larger rice farmers in Andhra and Madras. Production of such inputs as fertilizer, diesel and electric motors, and tractors has increased to meet farmers' demands, although this increase has been less than planned, partly because of the limited spread of the technology. The wheat-milling and flour industries have expanded markedly to process the additional wheat output. Wealthier farmers are also buying such urban consumer goods as radio sets, batteries, electric lamps, motorcycles, and scooters; production of those goods has risen substantially. But here, too, the limited spread of the gains from the new technology, when accompanied by the initially skewed rural income distribution, has meant that most farmers have not been able to afford such amenities.

Many of these latter products can be produced by small-scale

33. Louis Lefeber and Mrinal Datta-Chaudhuri, *Regional Development Experiences and Prospects in South and Southeast Asia* (The Hague: Mouton, 1971), pp. 69–70.

34. Government of India Planning Commission, *The Fourth Plan: Mid-Term Appraisal* (Delhi: Government of India, 1971), I, 9–12; II, 152–154.

industries; these have been growing very rapidly. Although the output data for small-scale industries are very uncertain, the rate of increase in their output from 1968 to 1970 was estimated at around 10 percent per year. Much of this growth has occurred in response to demand in the wheat-growing areas where these industries already existed; a substantial part of the growth may have been financed by the savings of larger farmers in the Punjab and Haryana. This growth has also been stimulated by government policies lifting controls on the expansion of smaller industries, and by a vigorous program to expand credit to smaller entrepreneurs.

Apart from the direct stimulus from within the wheat-growing sector, there has been little stimulus to industry, since food and farm prices have not fallen with the increased output. Government policy has aimed at keeping food prices stable for the farmer and urban consumer. The index number of wholesale prices of food grains, which reflects the price the farmer receives, showed little change from 1968 to 1971; the working-class food index has likewise shown little change, although both showed fluctuations around that trend. During the same 1968–71 period the index of prices of manufactured goods rose by over 10 percent. This relative shift in favor of prices of industrial products (as compared to those of agricultural products) over three years was only a minor correction to the longer-term shift toward higher farm prices since 1965. Furthermore, prices of raw agricultural commodities other than food grains, such as edible and groundnut oils, raw cotton, and groundnuts, have all been rising rapidly since 1968; these increases in raw material costs may have outweighed any downward effects of the constant food prices upon wages. Thus there were no stimulating cost declines as a result of the increased grain output. With the government's stable price policy for food grains, these are unlikely to occur in any dramatic short-term fashion, although in the long run policy should aim toward a gradually declining real trend line, if relative costs of grains are in fact to decline to an extent that would stimulate industry.[35]

Apart from a price policy which prevents stimulating industry

35. Government of India, *Economic Survey, 1970–71* (New Delhi: Government of India, 1971), Tables 5.1–5.4, pp. 122–131.

via lower costs, government taxation policy has made it unlikely that the government sector itself will directly share in the gains from increased output. During the poor years 1965–67, many state governments gave up their direct taxing power over farmers, while the central government never did tax them directly. The political power of the farm groups that have benefited from the new technologies has meant that the taxes have not been replaced during the present abundance. Thus the government itself has not gained from the increased output, and the well-to-do farmers are taxed far less in relative terms than high-income groups in the urban sector. The effect of the former has contributed to the lack of government resources for development; the effect of the latter has discouraged industrial investment by well-to-do farmers, and it has encouraged well-to-do urban groups to invest in agriculture rather than in industry.

The lag in government revenues has also contributed to the lag in public sector capital formation since the mid-1960's. Gross capital formation financed out of the central government's budgetary resources had not reached the 1965/66 rupee figure in 1969–70, and was only budgeted to exceed this in 1970/71. Plan outlays by central and state governments in 1969/70 were at about the same rupee level as in 1966/67, although a one-third increase was forecast for 1970/71. The average wholesale price index for all commodities rose by almost 40 percent from 1965/66 (and by 20 percent from 1966/67) to 1970/71; this has meant a large real decline in public investment. It is therefore not surprising that the share of public investment in total investment also fell significantly. In the past public investment not only contributed directly to total investment but also served as a major stimulus to private investment. While the relationship between the decline in real public investment and the decline in private investment is uncertain, the decline of the former certainly would be expected to discourage the latter. The result in any case has been that the proportion of gross capital formation to gross national product declined by almost one-third, from close to 18 percent in 1965/66 to about 12 percent in 1970/71.[36]

36. Government of India, *Fourth Plan: Midterm Appraisal; Commerce Research Bureau,* "Recent Trends in Capital Formation in India, 1965/1966 to 1970/1971,"

Thus the government by its price and tax policies has more or less deliberately blocked two of the channels through which the effects of greater food output could have stimulated more general economic growth in India. The failure of real public investment to recover to the levels reached years earlier has had a similar consequence.

But in addition various government policies have discouraged large-scale private investment; this contributes to lagging industrial growth. The government simplified various long-standing licensing and foreign exchange controls, and delays from these causes have been reduced. However, at about the same time, it introduced a new set of controls to curb monopolistic trends. These have had a particular impact upon the largest firms, which are the only ones able to implement major industrial projects. The controls have delayed the implementation of a number of otherwise economically desirable large-scale industrial projects for many years. Again, while the direct relationship is uncertain, this must have slowed the growth of that part of small-scale industry which supplies inputs to large-scale industry. This anti-monopoly policy reflects a genuine worry about concentration of economic power, but it arises also out of several other long-standing elements in the society: the traditional populist distrust of businessmen and their practices, carried over from the dislike of the village trader and moneylender and also reflecting caste attitudes; the socialistic bias and distrust of business on the part of intellectuals and government officials; some belief among important political figures that the existence of such controls force businessmen to contribute to their political campaigns; and the feeling among at least some businessmen (possibly the less efficient) that such controls and contributions provide them with protection against competitors. In fact, the effect of such controls, with consequent delays, is that only the largest firms can afford to make an application, follow it up, and tie up capital while waiting for a decision. Thus these very controls may contribute to, rather than reduce, monopolistic elements in the economy. The stimulating effect of an imaginative,

mimeographed (Bombay: January, 1971). A slash between two years, as in 1965/66, indicates the Indian fiscal year, which extends from April 1, 1965, to March 31, 1966.

and on the whole successful, program to stimulate small-scale industry is vitiated by the discouraging effect of the hampering controls on large-scale industry.

Currently Indian policymakers are seeking to break through this impasse. One possibility for such a breakthrough may arise from the ongoing discussion of joint-sector operations. As a result of recent legislation the government has become a large stockholder in many private industrial firms to which it had made loans. This may provide a rationale for relaxing controls on such firms, on the grounds that a significant portion of their profits revert to the government.[37] If the joint-sector concept is used to fasten onto the private firms tighter government controls and management rules of the type that have been generally unsuccessful in the government-owned industrial enterprises, the consequences could be even more unfortunate for the operations of private industry in India.

There is an urgent need for both more total employment and greater industrial employment in India. One opportunity arising from the Green Revolution, limited though it has been in India, is the creation of a food surplus which can be used for labor-intensive employment works in the rural sector. Those public works may in turn make possible a still wider spread of the new agricultural technology which is partly confined by the absence of irrigation and water control. In addition, continued creation of industrial jobs is necessary if the increasing general unemployment and the number of educated unemployed are to be reduced. "[The] process of commercialisation is itself likely to convert latent unemployment within household enterprises into open unemployment among those seeking wage unemployment. . . . Even now, data on open unemployment would suggest that it is more severe in urban than rural areas; in large cities than in smaller towns; in States with high rather

37. See several unsigned pieces in *Opinion Magazine* (Bombay), December, 1971; see also "Joint Sector Becomes Respectable," *Economic and Political Weekly* 7, no. 14 (April 1, 1972): 692–693. Howard Erdman, *Politics and Economic Development in India* (Delhi: D. K. Publishing House, 1973), discusses the operations of a joint sector firm in Gujarat. Sir Arthur Lewis, *Socialism and Economic Growth* (London: London School of Economics Pamphlet, 1971), discusses the relationship between public or private management to socialism in a very realistic fashion.

than low per capita income; and in commercialised areas with considerable wage employment rather than in relatively less commercialised areas with little wage employment."[38]

Mrs. Gandhi's government came to power with a promise to reduce poverty and provide greater employment. Her initial victory reflected a change in traditional voting patterns in some states and a response to the poverty issue; that victory was confirmed by an even greater election sweep following the defeat of Pakistan in 1971. For the first time in many years India appeared to have a strong national political leadership committed to policies of economic growth and the reduction of economic inequality.

But the results have not been favorable, and the economy has moved slowly of late. Part of the reasons may be related to short-term factors.[39] The energies devoted to dealing with the problems of Pakistan and Bangladesh were shifted from dealing with internal problems. The poor 1972/73 crops were due to a monsoon failure. The reductions in aid were not entirely at India's desire. But the inability to raise the level of public investment to construct irrigation works and tube wells in anticipation of the drought, or to take steps for the consolidation of farm holdings and extension of institutional rural credit programs to encourage wider use of the new farm technology, reflects long-standing realities of power in Indian politics that have not changed even since Mrs. Gandhi assumed power. Those realities are that power lies in a coalition of the large and middle-size farmers in rural areas, and an urban elite consisting of bureaucrats, businessmen, factory trade-union members, and intellectuals. The rural elements in the coalition normally gain by high price supports and low taxes, and the urban elements gain by stable food prices. Resources are therefore used to maintain this arrangement. However, droughts and poor crops upset this balance; they adversely affect farmers on a random basis, and food prices rise in the city. Crop failures from 1965 to 1967

38. Government of India Planning Commission, *Report of the Committee of Experts on Unemployment Estimates* (New Delhi: Government of India, 1970), p. 203.

39. Since I have not been in India since early 1972 and have not seen much material on India, I cannot analyze the reasons for this economic lag in anything but a superficial manner.

forced a change in farm policy to raise output; the most recent drought may force a shift in patterns of investment and in use of political energies toward policies that will once again encourage a wider group of farmers to increase output. Meanwhile, ideological considerations led to temporary nationalization of the wheat trade, which sought to deal with the problem of higher food prices in the cities, but did not improve the underlying farm production basis, and upset the distribution system for foodstuffs.[40]

In the industrial field the peasants' distrust of businessmen, plus the ideological attitudes of urban groups, prevent the adoption of policies to stimulate private industrial expansion by larger firms. The government's own industrial expansion efforts are hampered both by its inability to raise resources and even more by the ineffectiveness and inefficiencies of its system of industrial controls and the functioning of its own industrial enterprises.

It is essential to recognize that economic development in a country as large and diverse as India is unlikely to be very rapid under the best of circumstances. But if the present government, after five years of power, fails to even approach the fulfillment of the hopes raised in its election campaign, there is bound to be an erosion of popular confidence. If this continues, it could lead to another period of diffusion of power and weakness after the next election, or a search for alternatives that may lead to other forms of government, under either Mrs. Gandhi or some successor.

40. The nationalization of the wheat trade was ended in March, 1974. See *New York Times,* March 31, 1974, sec. 1, p. 9.

PART III CONCLUSION

CHAPTER 7   A COMPARISON AMONG COUNTRIES

The present world . . . is witnessing . . . the end . . . of societies based primarily on agriculture and craftsmanship in which towns were rarely more than centres for the organisation and servicing of these activities, or of religion and government. . . . Of course . . . [these] societies differed greatly in complexity, in extent of power, in achievement and in sophistication. And yet there are basic similarities, whether we compare T'ang China with the France of Louis XIV or Peru of the Incas. In general the same social institutions are common to them all. . . . And between the literate societies there are many resonances in ideology. . . . There are many common factors in literature . . . if seemingly less in [other] arts, but even here common expression of a common situation can be discerned.

        —J. H. Plumb, "The Function of History"

Part One presented a hypothetical peasant society and sought to draw implications as to how such a society might carry out economic policies for development. The test of these hypotheses against actual experience in four countries does show that these four countries have social structures which are markedly similar to the model; there are also some important variations among the countries, which are partly responsible for their different political character and their responses to economic demands. In all of the countries, however, the following characteristics of peasant society exist to a degree that significantly influences their social, political, and economic behavior.

(1) The family is the basic unit of organization and is the center of confidence and trust. There are variations as to the extent of the family, but there are increasing degrees of distrust toward non-family members, which vary directly with distance from the family and from the village.

(2)Hierarchical relationships among families, expressed in various forms of patron-client relations with varying degrees of formality, permeate all these societies. In the economic area these are closely related to the requirements of food grain production and are closely tied to landownership; they are also related to the political and religious structure of the village.

(3) Patron-client relationships serve to protect individual families against minor disasters through a redistributive ethic that insures a subsistence flow of goods from patron to client if there is any output at all in the village; in exchange the client provides labor and (perhaps more important) a variety of social, political, and religious services to the patron.

(4) Among peasants farming is regarded as the "good life," which implies a sense of relatively open and equal relationships among all the landowning farmers in the villages. Trading is generally considered an inferior occupation, and such trading characteristics as stinginess and calculation in dealing with others are despised. As a result, trading activities in all four countries are carried on by relatively low-status outsiders or special groups.

(5) As a corollary of these attitudes toward farming, trade, and outsiders there is a repugnance on the part of peasants to such economic behavior as holding surplus cash or investing savings outside farming and other rural activities. If not spent for land or related activities, any surplus is expected to be distributed among kinsmen and neighbors, or for religious purposes, at appropriate ceremonies.

(6) Urban centers of government, religion, and trade have long existed in all these countries and have been supported by a flow of revenue from the village to the city. People associated with government and cities are traditionally looked up to by the peasants; this reflects their higher status and education. Government employment is both a goal for those outside government and an obligation to be offered to the educated. Business employment is in general considered inferior; the role of the businessman is in many respects that of a client of the government.

(7) Related to this respect toward government is a belief that the government is the main initiator of activities beyond the vil-

lage, and that the peasant or commoner can only respond. However, there is the equally strong belief that government officials do not know what the problems of the peasant or commoner are, and that they cannot be trusted; they must therefore be propitiated, if they cannot be avoided.

(8) Within the government and the political parties, as within the village, patron-client relationships are the basis for employment and promotion, and they create factional chains of leaders and supporters. Efficiency of performance is only one of a variety of elements determining status within the bureaucracy; this contributes to the poor performance of many government-operated industries in all these countries.

(9) Political success, with its resulting power, is proof of virtue. Failure means not only an inability to support one's followers, but also a loss of virtue; therefore, failure is a reason for shift in allegiance by supporters not bound by family ties. Ideologies, or differences on issues, play little role in party structure, bureaucratic behavior, or voter support in this system. The political system tends to be organized along vertical patron-client relationships, rather than along horizontal groupings based on class or issue coalitions.

(10) Throughout the system there is stress upon avoiding open disagreement or conflict; the reaching of a consensus which recognizes the status of the decision-maker is the normal mode of decision-making. Time is not considered a constraint in reaching a compromise which all can accept.

While these characteristics exist to some degree in all four countries, their strength varies, based on the individual country's history, including its independent and/or colonial past, its religion, and its economic endowments. With differences in the peasant society, one would also anticipate differences in the functioning of the countries' political systems and government bureaucracies, and ultimately differences in their agricultural and industrial development policies and achievements. The remainder of this chapter tries to point out some of the differences and their consequences.

One immediately noticeable social difference involves the different strengths of the family. The role of the family is probably strongest in the Philippines and in India. In the Philippines the strength of the nuclear family arises in part from the absence of a Great Tradition, with a consequent lack of strong native states and urban centers prior to the Spanish conquest. Both the Spanish experience of a highly centralized but inefficient government that was weak outside of Manila, and the United States experience stressing a laissez-faire approach, placed still greater reliance upon the family. In India, the extended family is the basis of the caste system at the local level; this system is the most formalized and rigid of the hierarchical systems examined. In the Philippines great efforts are devoted to widening family claims, either by marriage or by symbolic arrangements, as a means of formalizing patron-client relationships. In India the caste system makes possible a family's even wider extension to include other families, possibly remotely related, in a close indirect relationship, both in the village and beyond it to a larger geographical area. In the two other countries the limits of family influence and loyalty are narrower. In Indonesia, particularly Java, the great increases in population since the mid-nineteenth century and the mobility of that population have broken down ties beyond the nuclear family, so that within the village the neighborhood performs some of the social functions formerly performed by the family. This in turn implies that as people move to other villages and neighborhoods, their relationships with others also become looser. In Thailand what Piker calls the "kindred" family serves as a basis for traditional loyalties and patron-client relationships. Beyond such kindreds, relationships with others are on a strict quid pro quo basis with services exchanged for other precisely measured services. This Thai system assumes an abundance of land that in turn made possible mobility and a far greater degree of individual behavior than found in other countries. This individuality is also supported by the Buddhist religion, with its stress on individual merit. In more recent years scarcity of land and the growth of differences among peasants based on quantity of land owned, including the existence of landless farmers, has led to a breakdown of even this limited kindred relationship in certain regions. In such areas there has arisen a far more tenuous and short-lived system of hierarchical relationships—one which accentuates both greater individual responsibilities and a greater desire for some sort of a dependency relationship.

The differing roles of the family in these countries also result in differing types of patron-client relationships. In the Philippines the family forms the bases of those relationships; there is an unusually high degree of family ties among landlords and tenants. This unquestionably influences the character of the obligations among various groups in society, and it may help to explain the relatively great role of landlords in relation to tenants, including the willingness of Filipino landlords to lend money directly or to guarantee loans to their tenants. It also provides a basis for political relationships and groupings from a village to a national level, and for economic relations extending to natural and symbolic members of the family. In India caste relationships perform a somewhat similar role, but the very rigidity of the relationships among castes precludes the type of rural relationship found in the Philippines. However, the caste system has encouraged the formation of caste groupings for both political and economic reasons. In politics castes serve as voting groups and pressure groups; castes also provide pools of skills and capital that enable entrepreneurs to transcend family limits in the size of their enterprises. In both Indonesia and Thailand such groupings beyond the small family are weak or nonexistent, playing only minor roles in economic relationships; politically, while strong patron-client relationships exist within political parties and the bureaucracy, family influence plays a smaller role in the patron-client system. Rather, the patron-client system operates more around individual relationships within a framework of regional or religious loyalties.

Varying pressures of population in relation to land have influenced the differing development of patron-client relationships in the different countries. Indonesia (especially Java) and India are the most crowded, with average holdings smaller than those in the Philippines and Thailand. In both those countries, and in the Philippines, because of the historical development of its landownership patterns, there is much inequality among peasants, measured by size of holding and extent of tenancy and landlessness. In Thailand,

on the contrary, there has been easy mobility and more equal landholdings, although the degree of equality is becoming less in the
Central Plains region around Bangkok. The day of the "cheap"
frontier has ended in all these countries. It is significant that an-
thropologists are beginning to speak of the rise of a rural proletariat
and class system, as distinguished from the older patron-client
system. In India and Indonesia religious differentiations, in India
between clean castes and Harijans and in Indonesia between
santri and *abangan*, which divide peasants along lines somewhat
parallel to the emerging class lines, exacerbate economic issues between the landed and the landless and contribute to political unrest.
It is significant that, although land reform legislation has been
passed in all these countries other than Thailand, implementation
lags far behind.

Comparing another aspect of social structure, in the Philippines,
with its absence of a Great Tradition extolling the position of the
king and state, there is less reverence for the government than in
the other countries. Under Spanish rule a government role was
largely denied to Filipinos, and under American rule the government's role was limited by philosophy. The government is therefore
regarded more as a tool than as an object of veneration. This may
be one reason why leading Filipinos have regarded government as
an instrument to be used for family advantage, and as only one
channel to power, longer than in the other countries, where the king
and state have long been held in a combination of religious and political respect. The "clouds of glory" trailing such beliefs also ad-
hered to colonial governments and officials. These attitudes, even
though weaker, are influential today in independent Indonesia and
India. In always independent Thailand, the bureaucratic group
that overthrew the king in 1932 retained his person as a symbol and
derives some of its power from the traditional respect for the king
and government. Today in all those countries these attitudes toward government have contributed to the great expectations of government, to the sizable increases in government employment since
1950, to concentration of power and population in the capital cities.

The different histories of the countries also help explain the different characteristics of the governments and political systems.

India is a working democracy, formally based on a modified English model, but in practice also reflecting its own indigenous traditions; it is reasonably effective as such. Until September, 1972, the Philippines too was a working democracy modeled on an American pattern, but modified to take into account Filipino practices and traditions. This was replaced by martial law; whether there will be a return to an American pattern, a Spanish pattern, or some unique Filipino pattern is unpredictable. Indonesia has both an effective local government, partly reflecting its colonial heritage, and a history of popular participation in the independence struggle and in politics to which dictatorial governments since 1960 have had to pay lip service. In Thailand, without a colonial past, the political public is far smaller and power is concentrated in an urbanized bureaucracy, although there is lip service to greater future democracy. One effect of the apparently successful student unrest of October, 1973, may be a sudden and unprecedented expansion of this political public to include a greater proportion of at least Bangkok's population. But the past small size of the political public has had significant consequences for differences in the responsiveness of the governments to major interest groups, such as the landowners. In the first three countries the larger peasants and landowners who serve as patrons in the patron-client systems are village political leaders, and they exercise a great deal of political influence through control of their clients (the Indians have a useful term, "vote banks," to describe this); in Thailand any influence which larger landowners may have is far less direct. This factor helps to explain the greater ability of the Thai government to tax rice farmers for the benefit of urban inhabitants and the bureaucracy, while in the other three countries taxes on the larger landlords in the rural sector have become almost negligible since independence.

In all the countries trade is looked down upon by large sections of the population. However, this attitude is probably least significant in the Philippines. There has been intermarriage between Chinese with Filipino families for many centuries; in the nineteenth century both Spaniards and various other European immigrants came to the Philippines to engage in trade, intermarrying both among themselves and with leading Filipino families. These families today are some of the leading business groups in the country. The American colonial experience, and the education of many Filipinos in the United States, also contributed to the relatively high status of business. However, in the rural areas trade is still a low-status activity and businessmen are distrusted; retail trade and moneylending are carried on largely by Chinese, and significant anti-Chinese feeling exists. On Java, partly as a result of colonial policy, there is an absence of Indonesian businessmen, and trade is largely controlled by Chinese. This is less so in the Outer Islands; but anti-Chinese feelings are strong in the entire country, probably stronger than in the other countries. In Thailand trade has been traditionally left to the Chinese; there has been extensive intermarriage at all levels of society so that today the Chinese are largely Thai citizens and accepted as such. Although a residue of anti-Chinese attitudes remains, relations with the ethnic Chinese in the country are far friendlier than in the previously mentioned two countries, and in the economic sphere an effective relationship has been worked out between Thai political leaders and Chinese entrepreneurs. In India there always was an effective, recognized trading caste; thus, unlike in the Southeast Asian countries, there was never any action by the ruling power to introduce Chinese, nor did Chinese businessmen have any advantage in carrying on trade. However, the relatively low status of the traders in India, together with the distrust of trading activity by both peasants and high-caste officials, contributes to a suspicion of indigenous businessmen and their practices that is somewhat similar to the negative attitude toward the Chinese in the other countries.

There is no evidence that peasants in any of these countries are unwilling to take advantage of economic opportunities, including new technologies, that will increase their incomes if the potential gains are sufficient to cover any greater costs associated with those technologies, and certain enough to offset the possible risk such technological change may have on their own food supplies as well as any opprobrium from disregarding traditional limitations on behavior. The force of economic motives is stronger today than in the past, precisely because long-standing patron-client relationships have been weakened over centuries by the pressures of commercialization, urbanization, and Westernization; at the same time, potential economic gains from changes in output or technology may be greater. The economic history of Thailand since 1850 has been a history of farmers responding to commercial forces both by expanding acreage to a profitable crop and by choosing among crops; in the Philippines and India farmers have responded eagerly to various new seed varieties where the use of these either promises massive gains or proves economic; in Indonesia history shows a strong positive response to new crops and new varieties.

But with this similarity, and in part because of it, there have been differences in response to the recent new technology. While there has been much talk of a Green Revolution, in the countries studied this term could only be used with respect to the acceptance of new rice varieties in the Philippines and new wheat varieties in northern India. In the past few years even in the Philippines it appears that the increases in output have been less than the potential, and that the effects of poor weather and disease have reduced the rate of output increase substantially; in India the spread of the new technology to rice and various cash crops has been slight. While relating these differences to social structure or history is difficult at best, and impossible with any precision, it is worth attempting.

First, the successes of rice in the Philippines and of wheat in North India were closely related to the availability of controlled water supplies in both areas. New technology was initially taken up by large farmers, but over the next two years it spread to small farmers. A key element in this spread was the availability of finance—in the Philippines there is a fairly widespread private rural banking system which is controlled by larger landowners, as well as the usual non-institutional credit sources. This system supplied credit directly to landowners against their own land, and to tenants either through the landowners or with landlord's guarantee. In northern India there is also an effective rural credit system, and the average size holding for cultivation is comparatively large, so that the Punjabi farmer was quite a good credit risk. Credit was available to even the small Punjabi farmer once the success of the new technology had been proven on the larger farms. In both areas fertilizer was available in adequate supply at a price low enough to make its use worthwhile to the peasant; in both countries there was a price support program for the products (it was more effective in India); in both countries the initial research was supplied from international sources, and there were effective ways for disseminating the new varieties.

However, the weakness of this underpinning in both countries may jeopardize the continued success of the new varieties. In the Philippines the threat of land reform may have encouraged landowners to supply finance in the past; at the same time, the failure to implement land reform on a larger area may well have discouraged tenants from using new varieties and may encourage landowners to limit finance in the future. It is too early to evaluate the effect of the extension of land reform since martial law. A further constraint may arise on the demand side: rural incomes are highly skewed, and there is apparently a low income elasticity of demand for rice in the rural sector. Both of these factors probably contributed to rural demand's failure to take off the greater output, and the need for stockpiling; when government resources were unable to support such stockpiling, prices fell. The future of the new rice varieties also depends on the existence of domestic research facilities capable of developing disease-resistant varieties, and on an extension service capable of spreading such new varieties; there is some question with respect to both these capabilities in the Philippines. But the past success with the new technology is believed to have contributed to a change in attitude among the farmers by showing them that they can gain by adopting a more scientific approach to rice farming. Where land reform has been adopted, the fact that gains belong to the peasant may have also contributed to such an attitude. If the recent poor crop years, which once again show the risks of adopting new technology, do not vitiate these attitudes, then long-term prospects are probably favorable.

In India with respect to wheat there may be significant demand problems in the near future—problems which have been concealed by the desirable reduction of PL 480 imports, the buildup of stockpiles at high support prices, and their use to combat drought. The rice farms in India are on average far smaller than those in the

Philippines and also smaller than those in the Punjab wheat area. While large rice farmers may have the internal resources to adopt new varieties, the small ones certainly do not; the weakness of the rural credit system restricts low-cost credit to large farmers. Even where the new rice varieties appear to have been economic, they in fact have been adopted by only a small proportion of the farmers. When this consideration is combined with the absence of controlled water supplies in many of the rice-growing regions, and numerous problems of technology, all of which reduce the potential gains and increase the risk, the slow spread of the new rice varieties is understandable. With the highly skewed distribution of holdings and probably of incomes in the rice-growing areas, and the low income elasticity of demand for rice, problems of demand may also set rather low limits within which India will be able to take advantage of the eventual output potential of the new rice technology. Political power in India is so held that it discourages action to deal with these problems in normal years, although an emergency may force change.

In India the rigidity of the caste system with respect to the position of the Harijans in the rural areas is likely to result in serious social and political problems as traditional relationships weaken. The Harijans are usually landless laborers; their low economic status is supported by low social and religious status. These factors combine to make it very difficult for them to rise within the caste system. The combination of economic and social differences worsens the problems between the clean peasant castes and the often unclean landless castes. This has contributed to periodic violence between the two groups in regions where the unclean castes see hindrances to improving their position within the present system and the dominant clean castes see themselves threatened by any such efforts.

Because of the absence of even the weak underpinning of infrastructure that exists in the Philippines and India, as well as past policies, the new varieties have not been widely used in either Thailand or Indonesia. In Thailand this is partly due to past policies which taxed the price of rice exports and kept the price of fertilizers high to protect a small domestic fertilizer plant. In part, too, it reflects the absence (until recently) of new varieties suitable to Thailand's peculiar growing circumstances. However, several new varieties have recently been developed and are being used for their low-cost disease prevention rather than higher-cost output-increasing qualities. In addition, the institutional rural credit system in Thailand is very weak, although because of the farmer's independence the need for a strong one is probably greater than in India or the Philippines.

In Indonesia the weaknesses in the research and extension system and in the marketing of both inputs and outputs, the deterioration of the water supply system after 1960, and the absence of industry have all combined to limit the adoption of new technology. Many of these inadequacies stem from inefficiencies in government operation and from the conscious destruction of a Chinese-controlled marketing system, both of which reflect long-standing trends and attitudes within the government and the society. Only since the change in government in 1967 have some of these problems been attacked; this may encourage more widespread use of new varieties in the future. The new program to expand credit to the rural areas and to allow farmers to make their own judgments on inputs is one of the most hopeful policy changes. However, the gains of this new program may be confined to the large farmer unless it is associated with an employment program that would provide the smaller peasant with additional cash and enable him to repay all he borrows, rather than forcing him to use some of any credit he receives for consumption purposes. This is especially important given the skewed distribution of land holdings in Java. Certainly, too, unless the qualities of such infrastructure as the irrigation system, the agricultural research program, and the extension service are upgraded, continued gains in output are doubtful.

In all the countries the weakness of the industrial structure is a major hurdle, not only to future agricultural growth but also to absorbing the increasing numbers of landless in nonfarm employment and the increasing numbers of the educated in jobs outside already swollen governments. Given popular attitudes toward government, it is not difficult to understand government's major role in whatever industrial development has occurred. In all cases it has set the framework of policy within which industry has operated; in all countries except the Philippines it, as entrepreneur, has established many industrial enterprises; in all countries it has been a major supplier of credit; and by controls or licenses it has determined who may or may not enter production. The reasons for these activities vary: the government's traditional position at the center of the society; the belief, in several of the countries, in socialism and in the desirability of government controlling the "commanding heights"; the efforts to prevent control of industry by foreign elements, especially Chinese and colonial enterprises; a national crisis, such as war or shortage of foreign exchange, felt to call for government action; the private sector's lack of ability to raise resources for large-scale enterprises; and finally as a way of raising non-budgetary revenue to carry on activities some government leaders or departments may feel desirable for either national or more limited purposes.

It is unusual for government-owned manufacturing activity to be efficiently operated when measured by economic results, and to show socially desirable rates of return. But in setting up and operating such enterprises maximum profitability has only rarely been a single or even the prime objective. Because of the patronal character of the government, other objectives, such as to increase employment, or to reduce prices, or to divert resources to a particular group, have been at least as important. In any case, decision-making procedures in such enterprises often repeat the procedures of government and are oriented toward status and consensus, rather than toward production and profits.

In relations with the private sector all too often the governments have regarded the private industrialist as a client. Controls are seen as ways of enforcing this clientage, and of thereby exchanging a private contribution to the governing group for a required permit. When controls have been used in this fashion, they have contributed to the building up of inefficient firms, which in turn require special protection and assistance. In fact, an alliance has at times developed between political figures and less efficient firms, at the expense of the more efficient ones, in which the political figure is supported and the inefficient firms are enabled to survive.

In the Philippines, partly because of American background, there are few if any government-owned firms, and such a system functioned through controls and access to credit. In Indonesia there were various efforts to establish government firms, and the government nationalized many foreign-owned firms; only now is the government attempting to distinguish among those it owns or operates, between those that are profitable and those not, and to require its firms to introduce effective management methods. In Thailand various departments set up a variety of enterprises on their own; only after 1957 did the government give up direct entrepreneurship and confine its role in industry to one of policy-making and approval. Various Thai political leaders are involved closely with private industrial or commercial firms, but in a personal capacity. In India the private sector is under very close control, while public firms are often capital intensive and low yielding in their returns on investment.

The private sectors in these countries differ in size and function with varying degrees of efficiency. In Indonesia there is a major absence of indigenous entrepreneurs; most of those that do exist are of Chinese origin. They are heavily controlled, but the government has not yet adopted a successful policy to develop non-Chinese entrepreneurs and firms. In Thailand there are few indigenous Thai entrepreneurs, and most industrial firms are owned by ethnic Chinese of Thai nationality. With the degree of assimilation of the Chinese, the close relationship between Thai political leaders and Chinese industrialists, and increasing entry of Thai into industry, this present absence of indigenous Thai entrepreneurs does not raise the serious political problems that it raises in Indonesia, and it is likely to be a short-term phenomenon unless government policy toward the Chinese changes.

The Philippines and India both have indigenous entrepreneurs. However, in the Philippines the stress upon family ownership and control makes it difficult for many firms to expand to take advantage of economies of scale either from their own resources or from the private capital market. This has forced a reliance upon government credit, and has contributed to the close tie between political leaders and parties and industrial leaders. In India private industrialists are able to draw upon sources of capital and managerial skill that transcend the family, and they thus have been able to build large enterprises. However, the record of past business behavior in some respects, combined with a distrust of businessmen in part because of their caste or community background and their style of functioning, and in part on ideological grounds, led to a degree of control of large-scale industrial activity that has tied it very closely to politics and inhibited the largest entrepreneurs. This in fact has contributed to results in recent years opposite to those desired: output has lagged, while distribution of control over industry has been concentrated rather than widened. This is unfortunate, since it also weakens the benefits derived from an especially imaginative program to encourage small-scale industrial firms.

There is a close relationship between business and government in all these countries. It may be stronger than economists think desirable, but, given the past traditions and power of government and the lower status of business, it is likely to continue. One consequence has been to support an already existing pressure for import substitution policies, which may be necessary in starting new industries but can be socially costly if applied to the wrong industries or continued indefinitely and with very high protection. In all countries concerned, examples of the latter are easily found.[1]

Apart from the direct economic costs of such close connection, there are various social costs reflected in charges of corruption, diminishing confidence in the government, and the concentration of economic and political power and its gains in few hands. Such costs can become especially serious if they are associated with increasing unemployment and popular fear of economic dominance by such groups as the Chinese or foreigners, or if this distrust is concentrated in a particular social group, such as the young. In any case, those not benefiting object, and even many of those that do gain complain of the high cost and delay.

In addition, in each country there is a nucleus of technocrats.

1. For the Philippines see John H. Power and Gerardo P. Sicat, *The Philippines* (London: Oxford University Press, 1971); for India see Jagdish Bhagwati and Padma Desai, *India: Planning for Industrialization* (London: Oxford University Press, 1970). Both of these country studies are in the same series and are published by Oxford University Press for the OECD, which sponsored the studies.

The new generation involved is trained in Western ways and imbued with efficiency goals; the existing system of government often fails to win their support. In India Kochanek noted that in 1967 "each section of the business elite longs for . . . a strong central government and they would like the leadership to be recruited on the basis of merit for the purpose of getting a job done, rather than on the basis of criteria intended to satisfy the conflicting forces of caste, language, community and religious pressures."[2] The same words could be and have been heard in the Philippines, Indonesia, and Thailand—they reflect a disillusionment with politics that can be dangerous to the existing governments, not only by creating support for more dictatorial rule in which the technocrat administrator can function less politically,[3] but also by discouraging technocratic involvement with the government except at the patron-client level. Where there is technocratic participation in government, there is a frequent split between the so-called technocrats or administrators and the politicians, who appeal to more traditional communal and national issues.

Another new and significant group which is somewhat related to the technocrats is the college student group. In every country this group by its actions and demands has played a major role in either directly overthrowing governments, or in serving as a center of the discontent that led to martial law. This group is modern enough to be unhappy with the old ways of the political system, and at the same time large enough to worry about the jobs available to it. It is also idealistic, embodying the hopes of large parts of the total population, and thus is able to command public sympathy if not support. Above all, it is a group that wishes to be heard, and those governments that are unduly repressive of that desire will be opposed by it.

While the four governments have been relatively ineffective in their direct industrial production activities, they have traditions

2. S. A. Kochanek, *Business and Politics in India* (Berkeley and Los Angeles: University of California Press, 1974), p. 34.

3. Many of the technocrats and leading entrepreneurs in the Philippines have supported President Marcos's introduction of martial law precisely because it offers a chance for greater efficiency and fewer political pressures than the democratic system he overthrew.

of effective operations in other fields. Departments of a technical nature, such as public works, irrigation, and transportation, are often staffed with well-trained engineers and have a tradition of effective performance and high-quality work. All of the countries have expanded their educational activities with varying degrees of success; nearly all have or have had good agricultural research institutes and are either expanding these activities or, as in the case of Indonesia, seeking to recover from the ravages of inflation. All have had some success in banking, and all have industrial promotion programs. While these activities are strongly subject to political pressures, and while there is a tendency for division of responsibility and lack of coordination reflecting the factional character of the bureaucracies, there is long experience in these fields with a tradition of effective performance. The work itself is accepted as technical and can be judged on that basis. Furthermore, since such work can be handled departmentally and speed of decision-making is not vital, normal government procedures can be used and traditional practices are tolerable. Because of the nonprofit or general character of such activities, they are unlikely to be attractive to private entrepreneurs—nor do private entrepreneurs have any particular comparative advantage in performing them. This would imply that the countries concerned would gain quicker benefits at lower cost by using their scarce administrative and financial resources to improve the already existing departments and agencies engaged in these functions, which yield a high social return if no private return and are so essential for development. These must be expanded and improved and would be a far better field for government action than direct industrial production, in which traditional government attitudes and procedures can be and have been very wasteful.

In addition to these effects in the agricultural and industrial sectors, the carryover of the structure and attitudes of peasant society to the modern national state results in certain macroeconomic biases. In all the countries government employment is considered to be a privilege and reward for the educated; in turn, the government is considered to have varying degrees of obligation to provide education and employment for the educated, as the employer not only of first but also of last resort. This attitude has contributed strongly to mushrooming government employment in the three recently independent countries. There has been a smaller increase in Thailand since the war, because of its long independence, its (until recently) limited higher education programs, and its long-term traditions of employing the educated. But even in Thailand, with rapidly increasing numbers of educated in relation to the government's limited financial resources and the slower rate of increase of government vacancies, there has arisen a demand for additional nongovernment employment that requires further labor-intensive industrialization.

This pressure for employment, together with regional and party pressures for the distribution of the rewards of government, in turn leads to steady pressure upon the budget. In the Philippines this led to the presidential and senatorial election booms, each followed by a period of "austerity" before the next election. In Indonesia the need to satisfy all supporting groups contributed to a steady inflationary pressure under Sukarno's Guided Democracy, although other major shocks set off the accelerated inflationary periods. Worsening inflation contributed to the collapse of President Sukarno's government and his replacement by President Suharto, under whom the inflation was largely ended. In India and Thailand, while such inflationary pressures exist and prices have been rising slowly over the long run, there are also strong counterpressures of long-standing conservative financial attitudes. In India these have been supported by patterns of austerity and by continued rule of one party; in Thailand the generally favorable foreign exchange situation and the absence of mass political parties contribute to a relatively stable financial and price situation.

An economic factor that could have political and social consequences is the different trends in income distribution among these countries in recent years. All data on this matter are doubtful, and the observed results may reflect weaknesses of the data rather than portraying the actual situation; furthermore, there are no data for Indonesia. But apparently in the Philippines and India concentration of income has been increasing over the period observed; in Thailand the degree of income concentration has been decreasing in the urban areas, but not in the rural areas. It is difficult to explain why this has happened in Thailand; perhaps there used to be a wide gap between earnings of government officials and businessmen at the top of the income ladder, and workers at the lower end. With economic development in Bangkok salaries of government officials have lagged, wages of manual workers have risen, and more educated people are employed in industry or business outside the government at higher or at least comparable salaries. The effect would be to diminish the degree of income inequality among those employed in cities (largely Bangkok). At the same time the gap between urban and rural incomes in Thailand has been widening. But little is known about the entire matter of income distribution over time in these countries; improved data and further research are needed, because the subject is so significant for the economic and political futures of these countries. Increasing concentration of incomes, and either absolute income losses to some groups or relative declines in income position of politically sensitive groups, can give rise to significant economic problems of expanding demand for the increasing output arising from agricultural and industrial growth, as well as political unrest in all of the countries. In Thailand the increasing number of urban jobs and the trend toward greater equality in that sector is encouraging, but it is most important for rural incomes to continue to rise.

Two major economic and social differences among these four countries will unquestionably influence their economic and political futures. First, the Philippines and Thailand start at significantly higher levels of economic well-being than Indonesia and India. The comparative per capita income figures, while of dubious value, indicate that incomes in the two former countries are 50 or 100 percent above those in the two latter countries. In addition, while figures show that income levels are approximately equal at about $100 per head in Indonesia and India, observation within the country supports a belief that per capita well-being in Indonesia is significantly higher than in India, where the margin above subsistence is probably least. This comparison would support a belief that the populations in the Philippines and Thailand are better able to set aside resources for future development without reducing current consumption than in Indonesia and India; it would also support a belief that they are better able to absorb short-term economic stresses than the latter two. Indonesia is probably in a better position than India, a conclusion which might be supported by Indonesia's ability to absorb the protracted drawing down of capital and probable reduction in per capita economic well-being that took place during President Sukarno's long rule. Two consecutive poor harvests were a severe strain on India's economy; it is questionable whether a more extended strain of this type can be absorbed without serious political problems.

The second significant difference among the countries involves the far smaller populations of the Philippines and Thailand compared to Indonesia and India. There is also far greater homogeneity of population with respect to religion and/or language, as well as fewer regional geographic and economic differences. It is politically easier to adopt and implement a national economic policy in the former countries than in the latter, and the regional effects of those policies may also be less.

In each country the traditional social structure, whose characteristics have been described under the term "peasant society," is under strong pressure. In agriculture, where these characteristics have their roots, they are breaking down; in industry, to which they have often been transferred, they stand in the way of efficient production at lowest cost, of flexibility in response, and of maximum yield on investment and growth; in government and politics, to which these village attitudes have been transferred most strongly, they discourage efficiency and encourage patterns of nepotism and corruption (as seen by outsiders) in making choices among staff and actions. The costs appear heavy. However, social benefits should not be disregarded since they are significant, especially in a rapidly changing environment. The benefits are in the form of security of work and status, a minimum living based on some accepted principle of equity or "fair shares," and some political and social stability. One economist, writing more generally, has used the term "proud and serene" to describe the traditional Thai, and various observers of the Thai scene clearly regret the effect of societal changes on the quality of Thai life.[4] In India Mahatma Gandhi was clearly worried by the effects of the spread of large-scale industry on the quality of Indian life, and he argued for the alternative of a handicraft economy centered around the village. The danger of violent breakdown in the structures of such peasant societies arises if the costs imposed by these structures on the process of economic development are too great either to allow the process to yield the general benefits which are expected, or to spread the benefits that are achieved beyond a small group. If at the same time the process of development breaks down the former social structure and destroys the minimal security it provides by leaving the peasant landless and unemployed, and substitutes nothing in its place, serious dissatisfaction and unrest on the part of the peasants is inevitable. The final chapter will address itself to the policy issues raised both by these conclusions and in the introductory chapters. How can the costs which social structure imposes on economic development be reduced, and how can the gains of economic development be spread to all the population?

4. On Thailand see Thomas H. Silcock, *Proud and Serene* (Canberra: Australian National University Press, 1968); and E. van Roy J. V. Cornehls, "Economic Development in Mexico and Thailand, Part II," *Journal of Economic Issues* 3, no. 4 (December, 1969).

CHAPTER 8   SOME IMPLICATIONS FOR POLICY

*Western policies toward Asia that take no account of agrarian relationships,
and that interpret Asian societies solely in terms taken from a dubious view
of Western liberal experience are, I submit, symptoms of political incom-
petence or deliberate deception, or both.*
> —Barrington Moore, Jr., *Reflections
> on the Causes of Human Misery*

*The long-run consequences of developmental policy may result in promoting
the well-being of greater numbers; but the developmental process, unless it
is self-consciously utilized, can greatly accentuate existing disparities, create
new ones, and in a spiralling fashion stage the setting for the articulation
of relative deprivation.*
> —Satish K. Arora, "India's Rural Politicians"

*It has been the genius of Mao to have converted the terminology and certain
of the principles of Marx into Chinese terms that evoke a response in China, a
response as much of reassuring familiarity as of innovation. Hence the aston-
ishing acceptability of Mao thought throughout China and the energies it
has aroused in the Chinese people.*
> —W. A. C. H. Dobson, "China's
> Twentieth-Century Ascendancy"

In all these countries the need for economic development is greater
than it has been. The continued population growth, currently at
rates as high as at any time in the past; the current growth in their
labor forces from past population growth, combined with the even
more rapid increases in the number of educated people; the end of
their low-cost frontiers in land; and the need for sharp increases in
agricultural productivity call for the pursuit of conscious economic
development policies by their respective governments. Such policies are necessary both to achieve rates of economic growth that
will be politically acceptable to the people and to insure that the
benefits of such growth are spread among the rapidly growing

populations. The latter will call for deliberate efforts to increase employment significantly as development proceeds in order to absorb new entrants into the labor market, and to spread the gains in income widely. In fact, these two efforts are interrelated— without a spreading of income gains, there are likely to be far fewer jobs, since an excessive concentration of income encourages a more capital-intensive type of development. Furthermore, if income concentration becomes extreme, there will be serious potential demand constraints to the increasing production of those basic foodstuffs and consumer goods which have low income elasticities of demand, and thus to lower employment in both the agricultural and industrial sectors.

In the past additional jobs and food at current standards of living could be provided for the peasants on empty lands, and for the educated by the government. As the empty lands became occupied, the social structure of peasant society enabled the growing population to be absorbed by sharing poverty on the land; some of the uneducated surplus farm population migrated to marginal jobs in the cities but maintained a family connection to the land, while the educated were absorbed by marginal government jobs. But the increasing population could no longer be absorbed on the land at constant levels of productivity; these workers were only absorbed by decreasing per capita productivity and increasing poverty. In fact, this process of "agricultural involution" was so regressive that it hampered the adoption of methods leading to more efficient use of land and retarded industrial development. This was accompanied by growing landlessness on the one hand and concentration of landownership on the other. In the cities it became increasingly difficult to absorb migrants from the rural areas without far more rapid and labor-intensive industrialization.

In any case, the rate of growth of the labor force is so great in all these countries that agriculture must continue to be the main source of employment in the foreseeable future. The government, with its limited resources, is unable to employ more than a small segment of the educated, while the great increase in educated employment that has occurred has contributed to a decline in efficiency in many government operations. This in turn makes even more urgent the need for additional employment opportunities in industry and industrially related services.

These pressures are creating demands that governments either must meet or face mounting political dissatisfaction. However, while these pressures are mounting, the potentialities for meeting them successfully exist. Advances in agricultural technology create possibilities for substantial increases in yields, and for greater diversification of output for many agricultural products—food and cash—in all countries. In the industrial field the growing internal demand for manufactured products as development proceeds and incomes rise, the apparent possibilities of transferring industrial experience and technology from other countries, and the rapidly changing pattern of comparative advantage in international trade in manufactured products create continued opportunities for industrial growth.

The effect of what remains of "peasant society" attitudes and social structure has at best a neutral, and probably a negative effect on the achievement of these agricultural and industrial potentialities. In the field of agriculture "peasant society" does not in itself appear to unduly discourage peasants from adopting new crops or technology. It does add to the costs of adopting new technology where that technology would disturb existing social relationships; the expected benefits from adoption must be greater than otherwise.[1] However, the existence of a client relationship may at least initially insure a low-cost labor supply to a patron if his use of technology requires such a labor supply; it can also serve as an instrument for making credit available to the client. But the increasing concentration of landholding and accompanying parcelization of lands and landlessness that occur in peasant society as land becomes scarcer discourage smaller peasants from using those types of new technology that require large financial resources and intensive care of land. Increasing tenancy and landlessness mean that many farmers either will not have the resources to adopt new technology or will not have the incentive to take intensive care of the land. Obviously the extent of this trend varies, but all the

---

1. Edward van Roy has pointed out to me in conversation that this leads to a kink in the demand curve for such technology.

countries need an institutional credit program that will provide small farmers with resources to use the new technology; otherwise, unless the traditional sources provide such resources at low cost, small farmers will be unable to buy the new inputs. Even if small farmers do get such credit, unless underemployed members of their families are also provided with cash from additional employment, the family will be unable to use the credit for production instead of consumption. In countries where operating plots have been minutely parceled, action, either among farmers to voluntarily cooperate or by the state to consolidate holdings for operational purposes, may be necessary before the farmers on such holdings could take advantage of any economies of scale. Land reform legislation or changes in tenancy systems may also be required before tenant farmers would be willing to devote the necessary care to their land. But any land reform must be associated with positive action to set up institutions which would provide the financial resources that the landowner formerly supplied. Land reform might also accelerate the dividing of land into very small plots, which would call for consolidation steps parallel with any reforms. Without these supplementary actions, land reform could be harmful rather than helpful to production, and the effect upon production must be one of the main criteria upon which to judge the economic desirability of the reforms.

The ability to take full advantage of the new agricultural technology will depend on increasing employment and improving distribution of incomes in rural areas, and on developing greater demand outside the rural areas. For the former goal the government must take positive steps to insure that the new technology maximizes, rather than reduces employment. The new technology introduced so far apparently demands significantly more labor per unit of land, but less labor per unit of output. Currently various policies in the different countries may even encourage more capital-intensive technologies by reducing prices of agricultural machinery relative to other prices. All such policies on agricultural equipment should be carefully reviewed to insure that use of equipment is only encouraged as a supplement to labor; for example, by increasing the speed of harvesting to permit double-cropping, rather than a substitute. In addition, the government should undertake such rural public works programs as a local irrigation works and construction of roads and storage facilities, both necessary for the most effective use of the new technology and in order to provide employment. Such employment would provide farmers with needed cash, as described earlier, and distribute the gains of the technology more widely.[2]

One of the most important tasks which the government can undertake and in which government policy must play the major role is the creation or expansion of the institutional and physical infrastructures on which the continued advance in farm technology depends. This calls for a level of technological competence and efficiency that traditional patron-client methods of bureaucratic functioning do not encourage. In all of the countries the level of agricultural research for many crops does not now permit the continuous development and adaptation to local conditions of new varieties of food or cash crops and livestock, of new technologies including those usable in rain-fed rather than irrigated land areas, and of new possibilities for diversification. In addition, agricultural extension service is frequently weak in terms of the quality of extension personnel and the coordination of extension services with research, so that extension workers are often unaware of advances and problems in farm technology. This weakness has not been too serious, since the need for such services could be filled by merchants; but in the future, given the complexity and the breadth of the new technology, there is need for a large technically qualified extension staff. To build up such services will call for an education program directed specifically toward the training of more qualified agricultural technicians and extension workers, as well as toward providing farmers with tools to make appropriate judgments and use of the new technologies.

2. There have been numerous papers and books on this need. See among others Louis Lefeber and Mrinal Datta-Chaudhuri, *Regional Development Experiences and Prospects in South and Southeast Asia* (The Hague: Mouton, 1971); John P. Lewis, "Wanted in India: A Relevant Radicalism," mimeographed (Princeton: Princeton University Center for International Studies, 1969); V. M. Dandekar and N. Rath, "Poverty in India," mimeographed (New Delhi: Ford Foundation, 1970); B. S. Minhas, "Rural Poverty, Land Redistribution and Development Strategy," *Indian Economic Review* 5, 1 (April, 1970): 97–128.

To make maximum use of the existing advances in technology will call for modifications and extensions of existing irrigation systems, the construction of new ones, and the digging of wells to insure required water control. Improvements in transportation, storage, and other facilities will be necessary to market the greater outputs. All such programs, as well as those indicated in the previous paragraph, will demand additional financial resources, some of which must be raised from the increasing farm incomes. Most of the countries do not have tax systems that can effectively capture some of the rural sector's gains in income from the new technology; this is recognized as an important problem, and ways of improving the tax systems in this respect are being explored. Direct taxation is only one of the possibilities, of course; another method involves the adoption of a price policy for inputs that will result in higher profits for the nonagricultural sector. In fact, price policy has sometimes acted in the opposite fashion. While a price support policy may be desirable to prevent undue fluctuations in prices, and a high support price may be initially necessary to encourage farmers to adopt the new technology, the initial relatively high price should not be continued indefinitely. Apart from its income gains for a limited portion of the population, it may increase stockpiles of the product whose price is so supported and thereby drain budgetary resources, as well as diverting production from other crops. In India one writer argues convincingly that, as a result of the high support price for wheat, "the success on the wheat production front, instead of becoming a factor for stimulating the economy, and providing surpluses for development, has thus actually become a burden and resulted in a redistribution of income in favour of wheat farmers."[3]

One of the clearest conclusions of various studies on the interrelation between the growth of the agricultural and industrial sectors, as well as a clear result from the previous country chapters, is the

3. *Economic and Political Weekly* 7, no. 17 (April 22, 1972): 826. This was written before the 1973 drought, when wheat stockpiles were reduced sharply to provide food for those peasants in the farm areas hit by the drought, and to moderate price rises in the cities. But as pointed out in the chapter on India, the use of high price support programs is a costly way of achieving those results, at the expense of long-term investment programs.

importance of industrial development for agricultural growth. Industrial development is also necessary to achieve high rates of income growth and to increase employment opportunities for surplus agricultural labor and the increasing numbers of educated.

The structure and attitudes of peasant society have had mainly negative effects on the development of industry. They have discouraged entrepreneurial attitudes by the bulk of the population and led to the creation of what Riggs has perceptively called pariah entrepreneurial groups of foreigners or local minorities. These entrepreneurs are limited and controlled in their industrial activities, at the same time that other higher-status groups are unable or unwilling to carry out those functions as effectively. In economic terms there should be no objection to allowing various minority groups to play a free industrial role, subject to the limits applicable to all citizens, but this appears to be politically impossible in the short run. Thailand has dealt with this problem with some success by establishing enterprises of mixed entrepreneurship in which the minority Chinese or other groups perform their entrepreneurial functions under the protection of the political leaders, but at some cost in corruption. In India the discussion of the joint sector may result in a somewhat similar outcome of firms run by private Indian businessmen but with the government sharing in the profits and in various aspects of the management as a stockholder. (This could also have unfortunate effects, depending on the extent and character of the government's direct intervention.)

As a result of their social traditions, the demand for rapid industrialization, and the absence of indigenous entrepreneurs, the governments inevitably play an active and initiating role in promoting industry. *Laissez-faire* is not possible, regardless of ideology. The government may play this leading role in a variety of ways: as a strategic policy-maker, by which it sets general limits on the pace and direction of industrial development and on the activities of the country's entrepreneurs; as a creator of institutions and infrastructure which may be necessary as underpinning for entrepreneurial behavior; as a direct controller and licensor of entrepreneurial activity; and as an entrepreneur itself.

These various government activities will be discussed in reverse order. In a society structured along patron-client hierarchical lines, with both the speed and pattern of decision-making already noted in such a society, and with its criteria for personal advancement often determined by patron-client relationships, the government itself is run along the lines of the peasant family or village. It is difficult for the governments of those countries to efficiently and profitably operate firms whose operations call for rapid action, either of an innovative nature or in response to external forces, whether in terms of price or technology or quality. While there are exceptions to such a generalization, often resulting from the use of technocrats to head those firms or activities, they have proved the rule. The type of industrial activities best carried out by such governments are those which are routinized, or where profit is not the major goal, or in which a monopoly may exist; examples occur in such fields as transportation, public utilities, postal service, banking, and insurance. In manufacturing *per se* repeated examples have been cited to show that the government's entrepreneurial function is often subordinated to its patron function. It would be preferable, therefore, in such a society not to use scarce administrative and management talents to directly run a manufacturing enterprise, although some exceptions may be necessary if private finance or management is unavailable. Where such exceptions are necessary, it would be preferable to bring in a technocrat to run the firm, to require reports to the government not so detailed that operations are constantly hampered, and to use techniques of management and accounting that permit the manager to quickly identify profit-making and cost-raising or -reducing areas, and to act rapidly with respect to both. These are unlikely to be normal governmental methods in peasant societies. Furthermore, there may be a strong argument for the sale of such firms to private groups at an early stage.

With respect to the use of specific direct controls, experience in both developed and developing countries relying significantly upon market economic forces shows the difficulties of operating these under normal conditions. In time of war or great emergencies such controls are necessary, and they have been highly effective under the spur of patriotism and general recognition of their need. But they become far more questionable in normal peacetime. In the developing countries the use of such specific controls is made even more difficult by the patron-client character of the political system; businessmen, who have low prestige anyway, frequently serve as clients of the government, receiving licenses and permits in exchange for financial support in politics. This incestuous relationship creates an oligarchy of political leaders and industrialists who jointly control the political and the industrial systems. This is contrary to the all too often expressed rationale for the controls on grounds of greater equality, or fairer access to scarce resources, or break up of monopoly. In turn, the growth of robber baron capitalism, with gains largely and obviously confined to a few families supported by the government, has been a major force behind student and more general unrest in many Asian countries. The problems arising from such growth are real in all the countries; direct controls contribute not to their solution, but to their worsening.

One main area of institution-building for all the governments is the deliberate development of local entrepreneurs. India has set up an effective and widespread network of institutions to provide financial aid to small-scale industry, often in conjunction with programs of technical assistance and specific technical or management education. Industrial estates have also been used to achieve economies of scale for small firms. Similar programs are at least desirable in the other countries, and are essential in Indonesia.

In no country is subcontracting used widely as a way of encouraging small-scale enterprises to grow up with large ones. Encouragement of subcontracting calls for deliberate government policies which might take some of the following directions: requiring the government's own industrial and public utility enterprises to subcontract the production of at least some of their inputs; making some subcontracting a condition for large-scale local and foreign investors; in exchange introducing protective measures in the early stages of such a program by guaranteeing the purchasing firms against loss due to quality failures and loss of credit advances, and protecting small firms against being swallowed up by the larger ones. In addition, licensing of foreign private investment can be used as a tool to train local businessmen by requiring foreign firms, as a condition of entry, to employ and train a steadily rising proportion of local staff up to an agreed-on maximum at all levels; the performance of these firms in this respect should be continuously reviewed.

Extension of small-scale enterprise is essential to develop the local entrepreneurs usually lacking. Such enterprises are also more labor intensive than larger ones, and thus contribute to increasing employment. An expanding group of entrepreneurs competing against each other can create wider access to both economic and political power, spreading the gains of economic development. But such smaller firms must be allowed to grow; their growth must not be cut off by financial difficulties or controls of other kinds. All too often controls penalize newer establishments, perpetuating the very inequalities against which they were supposedly introduced.

This in turn brings up another role that the government can play, either independently or with private firms. In no country is there an effective capital market which serves as a channel for long-term investment capital. The government, either by setting up long-term capital institutions or by supporting others who do so, can take the risk of providing long-term industrial financing. By legislation to protect investors against fraud or misuse of inside knowledge, it can provide a framework within which a capital market might arise.

Perhaps most important, the government by its general education policies and programs, and by its tariff, quota, foreign exchange, and taxation policies, determines both that the skilled manpower for industry will be available, and that the initial rate of return will encourage businessmen to enter industry.

The former may require an expansion of existing education programs and their conversion to more immediately useful technical needs, rather than training of small numbers of men of good families for government service and politics, as in the past. With respect to foreign trade policies, there has been excessive use of tools to protect enterprises which contribute little to economic growth but make possible substantial profits to political leaders and favored domestic or foreign business groups. While initial protection may be necessary to encourage any industry at all, continued high levels of protection by tariffs, quotas, prohibitions, and grossly overvalued exchange rates have proved self-defeating by building up clearly uneconomic establishments and encouraging monopolies. In fact, permitting the importation of goods that are produced by only one or a few firms can reduce the effects of a production monopoly within a country.

In order to increase employment in industry policies must seek, on economic grounds, to maximize rather than minimize industrial employment. Economists have long talked of the abundance of labor and the scarcity of capital in countries such as those we have looked at; yet in fact the types of technology and the labor-capital proportions are similar to those found in developed countries with reverse factor endowments. Encouragement of small-scale industry and subcontracting will have beneficial effects toward an appropriate level of technology for the country as a whole. The government should consider and if possible adopt a policy of wage subsidization in factories to bring labor costs to the entrepreneur down toward the social (rather than the private) cost of labor. Domestic entrepreneurs should be rewarded for developing and using labor-intensive technologies. Foreign firms should be encouraged to develop and use new, labor-intensive technologies rather than the same technologies used at home; this might be a condition of investment, and success in such efforts could be a reason for special reward. The education system should be geared to turning out workers who can be employed in industry; the government, by its trade and foreign exchange policies and its labor welfare programs, should discourage the use of capital-intensive labor-saving machinery. Access to both domestic and foreign credits, especially by suppliers, should be examined in terms of its employment-creating effects before it is allocated.

Such policies would contribute to establishing a vigorous industrial sector that can act on its own initiative in terms of developing new products and exports, as well as responding to external challenges. This is a key requirement of rapid national economic growth in the countries concerned; it is also a condition for the growth of their agricultural sectors, in which most of their populations will continue to be employed for at least the next generation. This growth will inevitably undermine much of the structure, attitudes, and behavioral styles of the peasant society. But this society and economy is being undermined anyway; the policies advocated would, if successful, replace an economy of shared and increasing poverty, if matters proceed without conscious goals, by an economy capable of creating more jobs at higher and increasing levels of income. These goals would be achieved by a set of policies that, in Albert Hirschman's words, "sharpen the perception of available avenues toward change by defending the right to a non-projected future in which the inventiveness of history and a 'passion for the possible' are admitted as vital factors."[4]

But the peasant society also contains values of equality which provide a basis of fair sharing for all. Therefore, in addition to policies to increase growth and to maximize its spread, the governments should adopt and administer a tax program that would prevent the more glaring inequities associated with an extreme concentration of incomes and gains from economic development. This should be associated with a social welfare program that does not simply copy the social welfare schemes of more developed countries, which frequently make labor unduly expensive and create a high-income large-scale factory worker group in the developing countries. Rather, any program must provide an acceptable low-cost level of housing, health service, and food for all levels of the population. Related is the need to prevent excessive concentration of economic development in one or two areas in the country. The government, by its incentives and a regional investment program, can and should encourage would-be industrialists to expand away from the great cities and toward other smaller cities in various sections of the country.

Barrington Moore has examined the historical relationships between economic change and peasant society in a group of specific countries, some of which had major peasant revolutions. He concludes that peasant rebellions broke out in those countries where the rural leadership, either on its own estates or through its control of government, was unable to carry out an economic transformation

4. Albert Hirschman, *A Bias for Hope* (New Haven: Yale University Press, 1971), p. 37.

to higher levels of output; at the same time, the breakdown of old relationships and the creation of new bureaucratic structures imposed ever greater burdens on the peasantry.[5]

In the four countries examined here significant economic growth has occurred since 1950, and further growth can be expected. But in these countries, with their growing populations and labor forces, the pressures on the peasant social system and the requirements for economic development are growing. No country has yet reached a period of self-sustaining growth; while there is a potential for more rapid agricultural growth, it is still undeveloped. All the countries need to step up the pace of industrial growth significantly. Furthermore, in all these countries centralized bureaucracies have become more important. At the same time, enough remains of the traditional system of relationships on the land to provide some basis for political stability, at least in the near future. Among the great masses of the rural population, traditional relationships are still strong. These have supported the traditional types of parties based on cliques or factions cemented by patron-client relationships and elements of communal and group loyalties, or rulers who by achieving power have cloaked themselves in the respect given to rulers in peasant societies. Landowning groups have become major forces in politics in all countries except Thailand, where power is concentrated in leaders of the bureaucracy. It has also meant that where and when elections occur they are rarely fought over issues; debates over policies are subordinated to efforts to swing vote banks. In cities, which contain a small minority of the total population but probably the largest proportion of the educated population (either employed or not), issues are more important precisely because traditional relations have broken down most. Furthermore, in the cities problems of government, claims on government, and inefficiencies of government are more strongly felt. It is therefore not coincidental that opposition parties frequently have won elections in Manila, Bangkok, Calcutta, Bombay, and Delhi, that governments have been toppled

5. See Barrington Moore, Jr., *Social Origins of Dictatorship and Democracy* (Boston: Beacon Press, 1967), esp. Ch. 9, "The Peasants and Revolution."

by coups and popular violence in Jakarta and Bangkok, and that a coup has occurred in Manila.

In some countries the traditional patron groups are now in control. Golay argued before the 1972 coup that the Philippines was controlled by a land-based oligarchy which has moved into industry, and that this group had successfully used its power to maintain control. However, new groups were becoming powerful in industry and politics, and these served as counterforces. The effect of the coup on relationships among these groups is still unknown. While President Marcos comes from the traditional oligarchy, he has to some extent broken with it by assuming personal power. He has also made very effective use of new technocratic groups within the country, and he is apparently implementing a land reform program. But it is still too early to foresee long-term consequences. In Thailand, where power is not held by a land-based oligarchy, the small ruling group had until recently been quite pragmatic in adopting policies to satisfy both the general well-being and independence of the Thai people and its own survival and well-being. The effect of the student-inspired overthrow of the military dictatorship upon this ruling group is still uncertain, but clearly the political public has been widened. In India at the state level power has been concentrated in groups supported by or representing dominant landowning elements, interested in their own well-being and survival; at the national level the leadership has often been more broadly oriented, with social goals expressed in terms of general well-being but policy constrained by the powers of the state groups. There has been the least cohesion among various political and social groups in Indonesia, and as a result greater conflict on religious, economic, and social issues. Following the severe unrest associated with President Sukarno's fall, power became concentrated largely in the hands of the military. The present government rightly stressed the solution of short-term economic problems as a major first goal; long-term questions of industrial growth, distribution of the benefits of development and foreign investment, and land ownership have received only minor attention. Within the next five years such long-term issues will almost certainly require greater attention.

Will the governments introduce policies along the lines described earlier? It is hard to say. Steps to encourage small-scale industry or to reform education systems are more likely to be adopted than measures of tax reform or greater income equality. The latter will directly and adversely effect the incomes of the ruling groups within a country; the former do not directly harm vested groups and could therefore be acceptable if a workable program is presented. But some of the ends of tax reform and income equality may be approached indirectly, if not directly. All the governments have carried out major reforms over the past twenty-five years, and they are clearly interested in their own survival. If reform has been a condition of survival, governments have shown a willingness to act. If the public senses a willingness to deal with the problems and some improvement in them, the governments can survive. But where economic conditions steadily worsen—as in Indonesia in 1966—the government may be overthrown; one rationale for President Marcos's coup in the Philippines was that the democratic government was unable and unwilling to deal with economic and social problems.

Influential groups are urging reforms. Technocratic influence is quite strong in certain areas of policy. In India the sweeping national and state victories of Mrs. Gandhi's New Congress party in 1971 and 1972 were due to promises for reform; the strength of her party in the rural area was at least partly due to the promise of reform at a time when old relationships are breaking down. In Indonesia the new government has made great changes and has carried out effective economic policies; in Thailand there has been a long tradition of flexibility and responsiveness to social needs; the Philippines has undergone a coup, and the president has taken some legal actions to introduce reforms supposedly impossible before the coup.

But in every country the demand for reforms is mounting. Development must be increased in agriculture and industry, where recent growth rates have been lagging and potentials have been unutilized; the gains of development also must be spread more widely. In India these needs contributed to Mrs. Gandhi's victory, but now her government must show achievements (in the economic field, especially to increase food output and control inflation). In the Philippines the initial glories of President Marcos's term, centering on the success with the Green Revolution and culminating in his re-election, were clouded before his coup by poor crops, high prices, and charges of personal corruption; his party lost the 1971 elections, unrest reached new levels, and he took over the government as dictator. The 1971 military coup in Thailand was a traditional means of dealing with newer problems arising from the introduction of some democracy in a changing economic and political picture. It failed, because it reduced responsiveness in a rapidly changing scene with greatly increasing numbers of educated people, and it was overthrown in October, 1973, by a student uprising. In Indonesia President Suharto and the army have so far been successful in dealing with the short-run economic problems and in confirming political power, but the long-range economic problems and the need for developing a mass political base have not been faced or dealt with so successfully. As economic policies attract foreign investors and encourage local investment, the problem of distributing the gains of this investment beyond a small group of soldiers, Indonesians of Chinese origin, and foreigners becomes important. The outcry against neo-colonialism contributed to President Sukarno's assumption of power; the outcry against corruption under his rule contributed to his overthrow. Both fears still remain, and they can hamper the future of the present government. There is no way of telling whether the demands for land reform—which were encouraged by the Communists—are still strong, even if not openly expressed. It is unlikely that the sentiments have disappeared, even if they are now latent. There is some question as to whether the leaders, who derive strength from important elements of traditional peasant society and whose governments function in accordance with that society, will be able to adopt policies and create structures modeled on institutions alien to that society, while retaining at least some of the peasant society's values and broader goals.

Chinese communism presents an ideology that breaks with the traditional system in many respects. New groups are thrown up in the system and new values are followed; decisions are no longer made in terms of preserving the social status and political and economic powers of the older groups. Under this system there has been economic growth, but it is doubtful whether the long-term growth rates exceed the past achievements of any country studied here except Indonesia. However, from the relatively little that is known of its operation, Chinese communism is a system in which certain traditional Chinese social goals are fulfilled by traditional Chinese institutions. The desirability of the commune is part of a Confucian ideal; insurance of a minimum subsistence to the common people has always been regarded as a prime function of government, and the Communist government has achieved this goal for its supporters. Obvious poverty is less extreme and equality is apparently greater than in some of the other countries examined. This seems to be a result of a deliberate policy and some sacrifice of economic growth. The appeal of Chinese communism to the peasantry in China, and its potential appeal elsewhere, lies precisely in its provision, in accordance with traditional goals, of some equity and minimum shares to farmers and mass urban populations threatened by the collapse of old social relations, known positions of status, and economic security.[6]

The origins of the Mexican Revolution of 1910 lay partly in the excesses of political dictatorship, robber baron capitalism, and foreign control of key sectors of the economy. However, among the peasants who supported Zapata, the major factor behind that support was the destruction under the Diaz regime of traditional rights in land, of traditional sharing of output, and of long-standing social relationships in favor of widespread commercialization of agriculture. This commercialization took the form of the spread of sugar estate landholding and the concentration of land in a few hands.[7]

In both China and Mexico pre-revolutionary governments were apparently unable or unwilling to deal with these issues. I am not arguing on this ground as to the imminence of revolution in any of these four Asian countries. I am arguing, however, that the bases of traditional political rule in all these countries are being eroded by pressures arising from both the need for economic development

6. On this see W. A. C. H. Dobson, "China's Twentieth-Century Ascendancy," *New York Times*, June 30, 1973, p. 33.

7. On the Mexican peasant revolution see John Womack, Jr., *Zapata and the Mexican Revolution* (New York: Knopf, 1969).

and the results of that development. In all these countries there is a good deal of historical evidence (and a more recent record) of effective administration, of being able to respond to problems and to take advantage of opportunities. In several countries reform administrations have achieved power within the past five years. Nevertheless, the undermining pressures are becoming stronger. To obtain desired economic growth, the governments will have to devise new policies which will lead to still further breakdown of traditional economic practices and social relationships in agriculture, industry, and administration. This will be difficult in itself, but at the same time those same governments must introduce and carry out policies which meet certain traditional requirements by providing minimal levels of living and employment to the population. The latter policies may be more difficult, since they will often run counter to the short-term interests of traditional economic and political power-holders who have broken with those traditions for gain, and of new power-holders who have been freed to increase their profits and outputs. But recent experience shows the political limitations of robber baron development.[8] As traditional political relationships break down, one must hope that new political parties or groups appealing to the masses of the population on grounds of policy rather than patronage will arise; and that on the basis of support for solutions to policy issues they will be able to win support for the policies needed to increase growth rates and spread the gains. The recent Thai student-led uprising may be a movement in this direction. Another possibility, of course, is the use of military or other power by traditional power-holders to retain power and either prevent reforms or introduce marginal reforms politically palatable to themselves. But without significant change one cannot underestimate the possibility of revolution occurring in one or more of these Asian countries. These may be of a Chinese type, or of a Mexican type, or led by the military or by students with the appeal that the present governments have failed to reconcile the goals of

8. This term was used by Gustav Papanek to describe certain aspects of Pakistan's development. The political problems created by this type of development contributed significantly to the overthrow of the Ayub Khan government and Pakistan's subsequent political problems. See Gustav Papanek, *Pakistan's Development* (Cambridge: Harvard University Press, 1967).

economic growth and more jobs with the traditional norm of some
shares to all in the distribution of the greater output. New forms of
government may be required to reach this objective.[9]

9. One of the major themes of Frances Fitzgerald's *Fire in the Lake* (Boston:
Atlantic-Little, Brown, 1972) is the relationship of the ways of thought and social
structure of Vietnamese peasant society to the conflict in Vietnam. She is especially
revealing in pointing out how Ho Chi Minh successfully adapted principles of
Marxism to the social structure and attitudes of North Vietnam's changing peasant
society, and how that adaptation contributed to the political successes of his party
and government. She also argues that the failure of the Diem government in South
Vietnam was specifically related to the inability of that government to adapt traditional Confucianism to the changing character of South Vietnam's peasant society.

INDEX

NEW YORK UNIVERSITY

CENTER FOR INTERNATIONAL STUDIES

Studies in Peaceful Change

Why Federations Fail: An Inquiry into the Requisites for Successful Federalism, by Thomas M. Franck, Gisbert H. Flanz, Herbert J. Spiro, and Frank N. Trager. New York: New York University Press, 1968.

A Free Trade Association, ed. Thomas M. Franck and Edward Weisband. New York: New York University Press, 1968.

Comparative Constitutional Process, by Thomas M. Franck. New York: Praeger; London: Sweet and Maxwell, 1968.

The Structure of Impartiality, by Thomas M. Franck. New York: Macmillan, 1968.

Agents of Change: A Close Look at the Peace Corps, by David Hapgood and Meridan Bennett. Boston: Little, Brown, 1968.

Law, Reason and Justice: Essays in Legal Philosophy, by Graham B. Hughes. New York: New York University Press, 1969.

Czechoslovakia: Intervention and Impact, ed. I. William Zartman. New York: New York University Press, 1970.

Sierra Leone: An Experiment in Democracy in an African Nation, by Gershon Collier. New York: New York University Press, 1970.

Microstates and Micronesia: Problems of America's Pacific Islands and Other Minute Territories, by Stanley A. de Smith. New York: New York University Press, 1970.

International Business Negotiations: A Study in India, by Ashok Kapoor. New York: New York University Press, 1970.

Foreign Capital for Economic Development: A Korean Case Study, by Seung Hee Kim. New York: Praeger, 1970.

The Politics of Trade Negotiations between Africa and the European Economic Community: The Weak Confront the Strong, by I. William Zartman. Princeton, N.J.: Princeton University Press, 1971.

Word Politics: Verbal Strategy among the Superpowers, by Thomas M. Franck and Edward Weisband. New York: Oxford University Press, 1971.

The United States and International Markets: Commercial Policy Options in an Age of Controls, ed. Robert G. Hawkins and Ingo Walter. Lexington, Mass.: D. C. Heath, 1972.

Developing Democracy, by William A. Douglas. Washington, D.C.: Heldref Publications, 1972.

Turkish Foreign Policy 1943–1945: Small State Diplomacy and Great Power Politics, by Edward Weisband. Princeton, N.J.: Princeton University Press, 1973.

U.S. East-West Trade Policy: Economic Warfare Versus Economic Welfare, by Thomas A. Wolf. Lexington, Mass.: D. C. Heath, 1973.

Classical Liberalism, the Monroe Doctrine, and the Ideology of American Foreign Policy, by Edward Weisband. Beverly Hills: Sage Publications, 1973.

International Law in the Western Hemisphere, ed. Nigel S. Rodley. The Hague: Martinus Nijhoff, 1973.

Secrecy and Foreign Policy, ed. Thomas M. Franck and Edward Weisband. New York: Oxford University Press, 1974.